"Bearing Thorough Witness"
About God's Kingdom

This book is the property of

_____

Photo Credits: Page 4, Section 4: Courtesy Canada Wide;
page 44 bottom and index: *Neue Berliner Illustrierte;* page 84 bottom and index: Courtesy Canada Wide

Publishers
WATCHTOWER BIBLE AND TRACT SOCIETY OF NEW YORK, INC.
Brooklyn, New York, U.S.A.
2009 Printing

This publication is not for sale. It is provided as part of a worldwide Bible educational
work supported by voluntary donations.

Unless otherwise indicated, Scripture quotations are from the modern-language
New World Translation of the Holy Scriptures—With References.

"Bearing Thorough Witness" About God's Kingdom English (*bt*-E)
Made in the United States of America

Dear Kingdom Proclaimer:

Imagine that you are one of the apostles standing on the Mount of Olives. Jesus appears before you. Just as he is about to ascend to heaven, he says: "You will receive power when the holy spirit arrives upon you, and you will be witnesses of me both in Jerusalem and in all Judea and Samaria and to the most distant part of the earth." (Acts 1:8) How would you react?

Perhaps you would feel overwhelmed by the enormity of the task. You may wonder, 'How can we—a small band of disciples—possibly bear witness to "the most distant part of the earth"?' You may recall the warning Jesus gave on the night before his death: "A slave is not greater than his master. If they have persecuted me, they will persecute you also; if they have observed my word, they will observe yours also. But they will do all these things against you on account of my name, because they do not know him that sent me." (John 15:20, 21) Reflecting on those words, you might ask yourself, 'How can I bear thorough witness in the face of such opposition and persecution?'

Today, we face similar questions. Our commission as Jehovah's Witnesses likewise requires that we bear thorough witness to "the most distant part of the earth," to "people of all the nations." (Matt. 28:19, 20) How can this work be accomplished, especially in view of the foretold opposition?

Acts of Apostles gives us a thrilling account of how the apostles and their fellow Christians in the first century C.E. were able, with Jehovah's help, to fulfill their assignment. The publication that you are now reading is designed to help you examine that record and feel the excitement of the fast-moving events recorded therein. You will be amazed at the number of parallels that exist between God's servants of the first century and his people today. You will see that these parallels involve not only the work we do but also the way we are organized to do that work. Reflecting on these similarities will no doubt fortify your belief that Jehovah God is continuing to direct the earthly part of his organization.

It is our hope and prayer that examining the book of Acts will strengthen your confidence that Jehovah will help you and that the power of his holy spirit will sustain you. May you thereby be encouraged to continue "bearing thorough witness" about God's Kingdom and helping others get on the path to salvation.—Acts 28:23; 1 Tim. 4:16.

Your brothers,
Governing Body
of Jehovah's Witnesses

"Bearing Thorough Witness"
About God's Kingdom

CONTENTS

CHAPTER 1

"Go . . . and Make Disciples"

Overview of Acts of Apostles and how it relates to our day

REBECCA, a young Witness of Jehovah in Ghana, regards her school as her own preaching territory. She always has Bible-based literature in her schoolbag. During break time, she looks for opportunities to give a witness to fellow students. Rebecca has started Bible studies with several of her classmates.

² On the island of Madagascar, just off the east coast of Africa, two pioneers regularly walk some 15 miles in the tropical heat to get to a remote village. There they conduct a number of Bible studies with interested ones.

³ To reach people living along the Paraguay and Paraná rivers, Witnesses in Paraguay together with volunteers from 15 other countries worked to build a riverboat. The 45-ton boat can accommodate up to 12 people. From this floating home, zealous Kingdom preachers have spread the good news into areas that were otherwise inaccessible.

⁴ In the Far North, Witnesses in Alaska take advantage of a unique opportunity to preach during the summer tourist season. When warmer weather brings cruise ships loaded with visitors of many different nationalities, local Witnesses station themselves on the dock with an attractive display of Bible literature in a wide variety of languages. In that same region, an airplane proved invaluable in reaching isolated villages, thus allowing the good news to be spread to Aleut, Athabascan, Tsimshian, and Klinket communities.

⁵ Larry, in Texas, U.S.A., has a special territory—the nursing home in which he resides. Although confined to a wheelchair as a result of an accident, Larry keeps busy. He shares with others the Kingdom message, including his Bible-based hope that under Kingdom rule he will one day walk again.—Isa. 35:5, 6.

⁶ To attend an assembly in upper Myanmar, a group of Witnesses made a three-day journey by ferryboat from Mandalay. Eager to preach the good news, they took along Bible literature, which they offered to fellow passengers. Each time the ferry stopped at a town or a village, the energetic preachers got off and quickly went through the settle-

---

1-6. Relate an experience showing that Jehovah's Witnesses preach under a wide variety of circumstances.

ment, offering literature. In the meantime, new passengers boarded the ferry, becoming "fresh territory" for the returning Kingdom publishers.

[7] As these few examples show, zealous worshippers of Jehovah around the world are "bearing thorough witness concerning the kingdom of God." (Acts 28:23) They call from house to house, approach people on the street, and speak to them over the phone. Whether riding on a bus, walking in a park, or taking a break at their place of secular work, they eagerly look for every opportunity to give a witness about God's Kingdom. The specific methods may vary, but the goal is the same—preach the good news wherever people can be found.—Matt. 10:11.

[8] Are you, dear reader, among the throngs of Kingdom proclaimers who are now active in more than 235 lands? If so, you play a part in the thrilling expansion of the Kingdom-preaching work! What has been accomplished in the worldwide field is nothing short of miraculous. In spite of formidable obstacles and challenges—even governmental bans and outright persecution—Jehovah's Witnesses are giving a thorough witness about God's Kingdom to people of all nations.

[9] An intriguing question to consider is, Why has no obstacle, not even satanic opposition, been able to stop the forward movement of the Kingdom-preaching work? To answer that question, we need to look back to the first century C.E. After all, we modern-day Witnesses of Jehovah are continuing the work that started back then.

A Far-Reaching Commission

[10] The Founder of the Christian congregation, Jesus Christ, devoted himself to the preaching of the good news of God's Kingdom; it was his lifework. He once explained: "I must declare the good news of the kingdom of God, because for this I was sent forth." (Luke 4:43) Jesus knew that he was initiating a work that he could not complete all by himself. Shortly before his death, he foretold that the Kingdom message would be preached "in all the nations." (Mark 13:10) How, though, would this be done, and by whom?

[11] Following his death and resurrection, Jesus appeared to his

---

7. In what ways do worshippers of Jehovah bear witness about God's Kingdom, and what is their goal?

8, 9. (a) Why is the expansion of the Kingdom-preaching work nothing short of miraculous? (b) What intriguing question is raised, and what do we need to do to find the answer?

10. To what did Jesus devote himself, and what did he know about this work?

11. What weighty commission did Jesus give his disciples, and what support would they have in carrying it out?

disciples and gave them this weighty commission: "Go therefore and make disciples of people of all the nations, baptizing them in the name of the Father and of the Son and of the holy spirit, teaching them to observe all the things I have commanded you. And, look! I am with you all the days until the conclusion of the system of things." (Matt. 28:19, 20) The words "I am with you" indicated that the disciples would have his backing in the preaching and disciple-making work. They would need such support, for Jesus had foretold that they would be "objects of hatred by all the nations." (Matt. 24:9) The disciples could count on something else for support. Just before ascending to heaven, Jesus told them that they would be empowered by holy spirit to be his witnesses "to the most distant part of the earth."—Acts 1:8.

[12] Now some important questions arise: Did Jesus' apostles and the other first-century disciples take their commission seriously? Did this relatively small band of Christian men and women bear thorough witness about the Kingdom of God even in the face of vicious persecution? Did they really have heavenly backing and the support of Jehovah's holy spirit in their disciple-making work? These and related questions are answered in the Bible book of Acts. It is vital that we know the answers. Why? Jesus promised that the work he commissioned would continue "until the conclusion of the system of things." So this commission applies to all true Christians, including those of us living in this time of the end. We therefore have a keen interest in the historical record contained in the book of Acts.

Overview of the Book of Acts

[13] Who wrote the book of Acts? The book itself never names its writer, but the opening words make it clear that the writer of Acts was also the writer of the Gospel of Luke. (Luke 1:1-4; Acts 1:1, 2) Thus, from early times, Luke, a "beloved physician" and a careful historian, has been held to be the writer of Acts. (Col. 4:14) The book covers a period of about 28 years, from Jesus' ascension in 33 C.E. to the apostle Paul's imprisonment in Rome about 61 C.E. The fact that Luke changes from "they" to "we" in his narrative suggests that he was present at many of the events that he describes. (Acts 16:8-10; 20:5; 27:1) A meticulous researcher, Luke no doubt obtained information firsthand from Paul, Barnabas, Philip, and others mentioned in the record.

[14] What does the book of Acts contain? Earlier, in his Gospel, Luke wrote about the things that Jesus said and did. In the book of Acts,

---

12. What important questions arise, and why is it vital that we know the answers?

13, 14. (a) Who wrote the book of Acts, and how did the writer obtain his information? (b) What does the book of Acts contain?

however, Luke reports what Jesus' followers said and did. Acts, then, is about people who accomplished an extraordinary work, although many of them were viewed by outsiders as "unlettered and ordinary." (Acts 4:13) In brief, the inspired record tells us how the Christian congregation was founded and how it grew. Acts shows how the first-century Christians preached—their methods and their attitude. (Acts 4:31; 5:42) It highlights the role of holy spirit in spreading the good news. (Acts 8:29, 39, 40; 13:1-3; 16:6; 18:24, 25) Acts picks up the Bible's theme, which involves God's Kingdom under Christ, and shows the triumphant spread of the Kingdom message in the face of fierce opposition.—Acts 8:12; 19:8; 28:30, 31.

¹⁵ Indeed, it is thrilling and faith-strengthening to examine the Bible book of Acts! If we reflect on the bold and zealous example of Christ's early followers, our hearts will be touched. We will be moved to imitate the faith of our first-century counterparts. We will thus be better equipped to fulfill our commission to "go . . . and make disciples." The publication that you are now reading is designed to help you make a careful study of the book of Acts.

A Bible Study Aid to Assist Us

¹⁶ What is the overall purpose of this publication? The threefold objective of this book is (1) to strengthen our conviction that Jehovah by means of his holy spirit is backing the Kingdom-preaching and disciple-making work, (2) to stimulate our zeal for the ministry by examining the example of first-century followers of Christ, and (3) to deepen our respect for Jehovah's organization and for those taking the lead in the preaching work and in overseeing the congregations.

¹⁷ How is this publication organized? You will notice that it is divided into eight sections, each covering a portion of the book of Acts. The aim of the chapters that follow is, not to provide a verse-by-verse discussion of Acts, but to draw lessons from the events recounted in that Bible book and help us to see how we can make personal application of points learned. At the beginning of each chapter, a focus line explains the thrust of that chapter and a Scripture citation indicates the portion of Acts that will be discussed.

¹⁸ There are other features of this publication that will prove helpful in personal Bible study. Beautiful artwork portraying exciting events

15. In what ways will we benefit from examining the book of Acts?
16. What is the threefold objective of this publication?
17, 18. How is this publication organized, and what features will prove helpful in personal Bible study?

in the book of Acts will help you to visualize what was happening as you reflect on the Bible account. Many chapters include boxes that supply helpful supplementary material. Certain boxes provide a profile of a Bible character whose faith is worthy of imitation. Some offer more details about places, events, customs, or other characters mentioned in Acts. Wide margins allow you to make notes as you study.

Work your assigned territory with a sense of urgency

[19] This publication can help you to make an honest self-examination. No matter how long you have been serving as a Kingdom publisher, it is good to pause from time to time and analyze your priorities in life and your view of the Christian ministry. (2 Cor. 13:5) Ask yourself: 'Am I maintaining a sense of urgency in my ministry? (1 Cor. 7:29-31) Am I preaching the good news with conviction and zeal? (1 Thess. 1:5, 6) Am I having as full a share as possible in the preaching and disciple-making work?' —Col. 3:23.

[20] Let us keep ever in mind that we have been commissioned to do an important work—to preach and make disciples. With each day that passes, the urgency of that commission becomes greater. The end of this system of things is rapidly approaching. Never before have so many lives been at stake. We do not know how many more rightly disposed ones may yet respond to our message. (Acts 13:48) But it is our responsibility to help such ones before it is too late.—1 Tim. 4:16.

[21] It is vital, then, that we imitate the example of zealous Kingdom preachers of the first century. May your careful study of this publication move you to preach with ever greater zeal and boldness. And may you be strengthened in your determination to continue "bearing thorough witness concerning the kingdom of God."—Acts 28:23.

---

19. What self-examination should we make from time to time?

20, 21. Why is our commission so urgent, and what should be our determination?

"Go . . . and make disciples of people of all the nations."
—Matthew 28:19

IMPORTANT DATES IN THE SPREAD OF CHRISTIANITY DURING THE FIRST CENTURY C.E.

33
Jesus resurrected

Jesus commissions his followers to make disciples

Outpouring of holy spirit at Pentecost

Christian congregation founded

c. 33-34
Stephen martyred

Ethiopian eunuch baptized

c. 34
Saul of Tarsus converted

c. 34-36
Saul preaches in Damascus

c. 36
Paul first visits Jerusalem as follower of Christ

Paul visits Peter in Jerusalem (Gal. 1:18)

36
Cornelius converted

First Gentiles become Christians

c. 41
Matthew's Gospel written

Paul's vision of "the third heaven" (2 Cor. 12:2)

c. 44
Agabus prophesies famine

James (son of Zebedee) martyred

Peter imprisoned, miraculously released

44
Herod Agrippa I dies

c. 46
Foretold famine strikes

Paul brings relief ministration to Jerusalem

c. 47-48
Paul's first missionary tour

c. 49
Circumcision issue at Antioch

Conference in Jerusalem

Paul resists Peter (Gal. 2:11-14)

c. 49-52
Paul's second missionary tour

Barnabas and Mark preach in Cyprus

c. 49-50
Claudius expels Jews from Rome

c. 50
Luke joins Paul at Troas

Paul's vision of Macedonian man

Paul visits Philippi

Philippian congregation founded

Thessalonian congregation founded

Paul visits Athens

c. 50-52
Paul visits Corinth

1 Thessalonians written

Galatians written

c. 51
2 Thessalonians written

c. 52-56
Paul's third missionary tour

c. 52-55
Paul visits Ephesus

c. 55
1 Corinthians written

Titus sent to Corinth

2 Corinthians written

c. 56
Romans written

Paul resurrects Eutychus in Troas

Paul and Luke stay with Philip in Caesarea

Paul arrested in Jerusalem

c. 56-58
Paul in custody in Caesarea

Luke's Gospel written

c. 58
Festus succeeds Felix

58
Herod Agrippa II hears Paul

c. 59-61
Paul's first imprisonment in Rome

c. 60-61
Colossians written

Ephesians written

Philemon written

Philippians written

c. 60-65
Mark's Gospel written

c. 61
Acts written

Hebrews written

c. 61-64
1 Timothy written

Titus left in Crete (Titus 1:5)

Titus written

b. 62
James written

c. 62-64
1 Peter written

c. 64
2 Peter written

c. 65
Paul's second imprisonment in Rome

2 Timothy written

Titus leaves for Dalmatia (2 Tim. 4:10)

Paul executed

"YOU HAVE FILLED JERUSALEM WITH YOUR TEACHING"
ACTS 5:28

From the moment the holy spirit was poured out upon them at Pentecost 33 C.E., Jesus' disciples got busy in the work of bearing witness about God's Kingdom. In this section, we will consider the exciting record of the birth of the Christian congregation, the intensified witness given in Jerusalem, and the apostles' bold stand in the face of mounting opposition.

CHAPTER 2

"You Will Be Witnesses of Me"

How Jesus prepared his apostles to spearhead the preaching work

Based on Acts 1:1-26

THEY do not want it to end. To the apostles, the past weeks have been thrilling! The resurrection of Jesus lifted them from the depths of despair to the heights of joy. For 40 days now, Jesus has appeared repeatedly, further teaching and encouraging his followers. This day, however, he is appearing for the last time.

² Standing together on the Mount of Olives, the apostles hang on Jesus' every word. When he finishes—all too soon, it seems—he lifts his hands and blesses them. Then, he begins to rise from the earth! His followers gaze after him as he ascends into the sky. Finally, a cloud hides him from their view. He is gone, but they keep staring into the heavens. —Luke 24:50; Acts 1:9, 10.

³ This scene marks a turning point in the life of Jesus' apostles.

1-3. How does Jesus part from his apostles, and what questions arise?

What will they do now that their Master, Jesus Christ, has ascended to heaven? Rest assured, their Master has prepared them to take up the work he began. How did he equip them for this important assignment, and how did they respond? And how are Christians today affected? The first chapter of Acts contains the encouraging answers.

"Many Positive Proofs" (Acts 1:1-5)

[4] Luke begins his account by addressing Theophilus, the same man to whom he earlier wrote his Gospel.* Making it clear that this record is a continuation of the first, Luke begins by summarizing the events recorded at the end of his Gospel, using different wording and providing some fresh detail.

[5] What will keep the faith of Jesus' followers strong? At Acts 1:3, we read: "By many positive proofs [Jesus] showed himself alive." In the Bible, only "the beloved physician" Luke used the word rendered "positive proofs." (Col. 4:14) It was a term used in technical medical writings, and it signifies evidence that is demonstrative, conclusive, reliable. Jesus furnished such evidence. He appeared to his followers many times, sometimes to one or two, sometimes to all the apostles, and on one occasion to more than 500 believers. (1 Cor. 15:3-6) Positive proofs indeed!

[6] The faith of true Christians today is likewise based on "many positive proofs." Is there evidence that Jesus lived on earth, died for our sins, and was raised up? Absolutely! Reliable eyewitness accounts in God's inspired Word provide all the convincing evidence we need. Studying these accounts prayerfully can greatly strengthen our faith. Remember, solid evidence can make the difference between genuine faith and mere credulity. Real faith is essential to gaining everlasting life.—John 3:16.

[7] Jesus was also "telling the things about the kingdom of God." For example, he explained prophecies that showed that the Messiah would have to suffer and die. (Luke 24:13-32, 46, 47) When Jesus clarified his role as the Messiah, he stressed the theme of God's Kingdom, for

---

* In his Gospel, Luke addresses this man as "most excellent Theophilus," suggesting to some that Theophilus might have been a prominent person who was not yet a believer. Here in Acts, however, Luke addresses him simply with the words, "O Theophilus." Some scholars suggest that Theophilus became a believer after reading Luke's Gospel; hence, they say, Luke leaves out the honorific address and writes to the man as a spiritual brother.

---

4. How does Luke open his account recorded in the book of Acts?

5, 6. (a) What will help Jesus' followers to keep their faith strong? (b) How is the faith of Christians today based on "many positive proofs"?

7. Jesus set what example for his followers in teaching and preaching?

he was King-Designate. The Kingdom was always the theme of Jesus' preaching, and his followers today stick to the same theme as they preach.—Matt. 24:14; Luke 4:43.

"To the Most Distant Part of the Earth" (Acts 1:6-12)

[8] When the apostles gathered on the Mount of Olives, they had their last meeting with Jesus on earth. Eagerly, they asked: "Lord, are you restoring the kingdom to Israel at this time?" (Acts 1:6) In this one question, the apostles revealed two faulty ideas that they were entertaining. First, they assumed that God's Kingdom would be restored to fleshly Israel. Second, they expected the promised Kingdom to begin its rule right away, "at this time." How did Jesus help them to adjust their thinking?

[9] Jesus likely knew that the first notion would be corrected soon enough. In fact, his followers were about to witness the birth of a new nation, spiritual Israel, just ten days later! God's dealings with fleshly Israel were almost at an end. As to the second idea, Jesus kindly reminded them: "It does not belong to you to get knowledge of the times or seasons which the Father has placed in his own jurisdiction." (Acts 1:7) Jehovah is the Great Timekeeper. Before Jesus died, he himself said that even the Son did not then know the "day and hour" when the end would come but "only the Father." (Matt. 24:36) To this day, if Christians become unduly concerned about the timing of the end of this system of things, they are, in effect, worrying about what does not belong to them.

[10] Still, we should be careful not to look down on Jesus' apostles, who were men of great faith. They humbly accepted correction. What is more, although their question sprang from faulty thinking, it also revealed a good attitude. Jesus had repeatedly urged his followers: "Keep on the watch." (Matt. 24:42; 25:13; 26:41) They were spiritually alert, eagerly watching for evidence that Jehovah was about to act. That is the attitude we need to cultivate today. In fact, these climactic "last days" make it ever more urgent that we do so.—2 Tim. 3:1-5.

[11] Jesus reminded the apostles of what should be their main concern. He said: "You will receive power when the holy spirit arrives upon you, and you will be witnesses of me both in Jerusalem and in all Judea and Samaria and to the most distant part of the earth." (Acts 1:8) In Jerusalem, where people had put Jesus to death, the news of his

---

8, 9. (a) What two faulty ideas were Jesus' apostles entertaining? (b) How did Jesus adjust the apostles' thinking, providing what lesson for Christians today?

10. What attitude of the apostles should we cultivate, and why?

11, 12. (a) Jesus gave his followers what commission? (b) Why was it fitting for Jesus to mention the holy spirit in connection with the commission to preach?

resurrection would be proclaimed first. From there, the message would radiate outward into all of Judea, then to Samaria, then far beyond.

¹² Fittingly, Jesus mentioned the preaching commission only after renewing his promise to send the holy spirit to help them. This is one of more than 40 times that the expression "holy spirit" occurs in the book of Acts. Again and again, this vivid Bible book makes it clear that we cannot accomplish Jehovah's will without the aid of holy spirit. How important it is, then, that we pray for that spirit regularly! (Luke 11:13) We need it now more than ever.

¹³ The meaning of what constitutes "the most distant part of the earth" has changed since those days. As noted in the preceding chapter, however, Jehovah's Witnesses have wholeheartedly accepted this assignment to witness, knowing that God wants all sorts of people to hear the good news of his Kingdom. (1 Tim. 2:3, 4) Are you immersed in this lifesaving work? You will not be able to find a more fulfilling, satisfying work anywhere! Jehovah will give you the power you need to do it. The book of Acts will tell you much about the right methods to use and the attitude to develop in order to be effective.

¹⁴ As mentioned at the outset of this chapter, Jesus rose from the earth and disappeared from view. Yet, the 11 apostles kept standing there, looking into the sky. Finally, two angels appeared and offered this gentle rebuke: "Men of Galilee, why do you stand looking into the sky? This Jesus who was received up from you into the sky will come thus in the same manner as you have beheld him going into the sky." (Acts 1:11) Did the angels mean that Jesus would return in the same body, as some religionists teach? No, they did not. How do we know?

¹⁵ The angels said that Jesus would return, not in the same form, but "in the same manner."* In what manner did he depart? He was out of sight when the angels spoke. Only those few men, the apostles, perceived that Jesus had left the vicinity of the earth and was on his way to his Father in heaven. The manner of Christ's return was to be similar. So it has been. Today, only those with spiritual discernment realize that Jesus is present in kingly power. (Luke 17:20) We need to discern the evidence of his presence and convey it to others so that they too may see the urgency of our times.

---

* Here the Bible uses the Greek word *tro'pos*, denoting "manner," and not *mor·phe'*, meaning "form."

---

13. How extensive is the preaching assignment given to God's people today, and why should we embrace it eagerly?

14, 15. (a) What did the angels say about Christ's return, and what did they mean? (See also footnote.) (b) How did Christ's return prove to be "in the same manner" as his departure?

"Designate Which One . . . You Have Chosen" (Acts 1:13-26)

¹⁶ It is little wonder that the apostles "returned to Jerusalem with great joy." (Luke 24:52) How, though, would they respond to Christ's guidance and instruction? In verses 13 and 14 of Acts chapter 1, we find them gathered in an "upper chamber," and we learn some interesting details about such gatherings. Houses in Palestine at that time often had an upstairs chamber, accessible by an outside stairway. Might this "upper chamber" have been atop the house mentioned at Acts 12:12, which belonged to the mother of Mark? At any rate, it was likely a simple, functional place for Christ's followers to gather. But who gathered, and what did they do?

¹⁷ Notice that the gathering was not limited to the apostles, nor just to men. "Some women" were there, including Jesus' mother, Mary. This is the last direct mention of her in the Bible. It is fitting to think of her in that setting, not seeking prominence, but humbly gathering to worship with her spiritual brothers and sisters. It must have been a comfort to her that her four other sons, who had not been believers during Jesus' lifetime, were now with her. (Matt. 13:55; John 7:5) Since their half brother's death and resurrection, they were changed men.—1 Cor. 15:7.

¹⁸ Note, too, why these disciples gathered: "With one accord all these were persisting in prayer." (Acts 1:14) Gathering together has always been essential to Christian worship. We gather to encourage one another, to receive instruction and counsel and, above all, to join in worship of our heavenly Father, Jehovah. Our prayers and songs of praise at such times are very pleasing to him and vital for us. May we never forsake these sacred and upbuilding gatherings!—Heb. 10:24, 25.

¹⁹ Those followers of Christ now faced an important organizational need, and the apostle Peter took the lead in addressing it. (Verses 15-26) Is it not comforting to note how far Peter had come in the weeks since he had three times denied his Lord? (Mark 14:72) We are all prone to sin, and we need reminders that Jehovah is "good and ready to forgive" those who sincerely repent.—Ps. 86:5.

²⁰ Peter perceived that Judas, the apostle who had betrayed Jesus, should be replaced. But by whom? Peter said that the new apostle should be one who had followed Jesus throughout His minis-

16-18. (a) From Acts 1:13, 14, what do we learn about Christian gatherings for worship? (b) What can we learn from the example set by Jesus' mother, Mary? (c) Why are Christian meetings vital today?

19-21. (a) What do we learn from the active role that Peter played in the congregation? (b) Why did Judas need to be replaced, and what can we learn from the way the matter was handled?

We remain submissive and obedient to the lead of appointed overseers

try and had witnessed His resurrection. (Acts 1:21, 22) That was in harmony with Jesus' own promise: *"You who have followed me* will also yourselves sit upon twelve thrones, judging the twelve tribes of Israel." (Matt. 19:28) Jehovah evidently purposed to have 12 apostles who followed Jesus during his earthly ministry form the future "twelve foundation stones" of New Jerusalem. (Rev. 21:2, 14) God thus allowed Peter to see that the prophecy, "his office of oversight let someone else take," applied to Judas. —Ps. 109:8.

²¹ How was the selection made? By casting lots, a common practice in Bible times. (Prov. 16:33) However, this is the last time that the Bible shows lots being used in this way. Evidently, the later outpouring of holy spirit rendered that method obsolete. Note, though, *why* lots were used. The apostles prayed: "You, O Jehovah, who know the hearts of all, designate which one of these two men you have chosen." (Acts 1:23, 24) They wanted the choice to be Jehovah's. Matthias, likely one of the 70 disciples whom Jesus had sent out to preach, was chosen. Thus, Matthias became one of "the twelve."*—Acts 6:2.

²² This incident reminds us of the importance of organization among God's people. To this day, responsible men are selected to serve as overseers in the congregation. The elders carefully consider the Scriptural qualifications required of such overseers, and they pray for the guidance of holy spirit. The congregation thus views such men as appointed by holy spirit. For our part, we remain submissive and obedient to their lead, promoting a cooperative spirit in the congregation.—Heb. 13:17.

²³ Now that those disciples had been strengthened by Jesus' resurrection appearances and fortified by organizational refinements, they were fully prepared for what lay ahead. The next chapter will discuss that momentous event.

---

* Paul was later appointed to be "an apostle to the nations," but he was never reckoned among the 12. (Rom. 11:13; 1 Cor. 15:4-8) He had not followed Jesus during His earthly ministry, so he did not qualify for that special privilege.

22, 23. Why should we be submissive and obedient to those taking the lead in the congregation today?

"We hear them speaking in our tongues about
the magnificent things of God."
—Acts 2:11

CHAPTER 3

"Filled With Holy Spirit"

The effects of the outpouring of holy spirit at Pentecost

Based on Acts 2:1-47

THE streets of Jerusalem are bustling with excitement.* Smoke ascends from the temple altar as the Levites sing the Hallel (Psalms 113 to 118), likely in antiphonal, or call-and-response, style. Visitors crowd the streets. They have come from such far-flung places as Elam, Mesopotamia, Cappadocia, Pontus, Egypt, and Rome.# What is the occasion? Pentecost, also called "the day of the first ripe fruits." (Num. 28:26) This annual festival marks the end of the barley harvest and the beginning of the wheat harvest. It is a joyous day.

2 At about nine o'clock on this mild spring morning in 33 C.E., something happens that will be marveled at for centuries to come. Suddenly, there occurs from heaven "a noise just like that of a rushing stiff breeze," or "like the roaring of a mighty windstorm." (Acts 2:2; *International Standard Version*) The loud sound fills the house where about 120 disciples of Jesus are gathered. Next, something amazing takes place. Tongues as if of fire become visible, and one sits upon each of the disciples.△ Then, the disciples become "filled with holy spirit" and begin speaking in foreign languages! When the disciples leave the house, those visitors they encounter on the streets of Jerusalem are astonished, for the disciples are able to speak to them! Indeed, each one hears them "speaking in his own language."—Acts 2:1-6.

3 This stirring account describes a milestone in true worship—the founding of the nation of spiritual Israel, the anointed Christian congregation. (Gal. 6:16) But there is more. When Peter addressed the

---

* See the box "Jerusalem—The Center of Judaism," on page 23.

See the boxes "Rome—Capital of an Empire," on page 24; "Jews in Mesopotamia and Egypt," on page 25; and "Christianity in Pontus," on page 26.

△ The "tongues" were, not of literal fire, but "*as if* of fire," evidently indicating that the observable manifestation upon each disciple had the appearance and radiance of fire.

---

1. Describe the atmosphere of the Festival of Pentecost.

2. What amazing events occur at Pentecost 33 C.E.?

3. (a) Why can Pentecost 33 C.E. be called a milestone in the history of true worship? (b) How did Peter's speech tie in with the use of "the keys of the kingdom"?

crowd that day, he used the first of three "keys of the kingdom," each of which would open up special privileges to a different group of people. (Matt. 16:18, 19) This first key made it possible for Jews and Jewish proselytes to accept the good news and to be anointed with God's holy spirit.* They would thus become part of spiritual Israel, and as such, they would have the hope of ruling as kings and priests in the Messianic Kingdom. (Rev. 5:9, 10) In time, that privilege would be extended to Samaritans and then to Gentiles. What can Christians today learn from the momentous events of Pentecost 33 C.E.?

"All Together at the Same Place" (Acts 2:1-4)

⁴ The Christian congregation began with about 120 disciples who were "all together at the same place"—an upper room—and who were anointed with holy spirit. (Acts 2:1) By the end of that day, baptized members of that congregation numbered into the thousands. And that was just the beginning of the growth of an organization that continues to expand today! Yes, a community of God-fearing men and women—the modern-day Christian congregation—is the means by which the "good news of the kingdom" is being "preached in all the inhabited earth for a witness to all the nations" before the end of this system of things. —Matt. 24:14.

⁵ The Christian congregation would also be a source of spiritual

* See the box "Who Were the Proselytes?" on page 27.

4. How is the modern-day Christian congregation an extension of the congregation that was formed in 33 C.E.?

5. What blessing would come from associating with the Christian congregation, both in the first century and today?

strength to its members, both those of the anointed and, later on, those of the "other sheep." (John 10:16) Paul showed his appreciation for the mutual support that members of the congregation provide when he wrote to the Christians in Rome: "I am longing to see you, that I may impart some spiritual gift to you in order for you to be made firm; or, rather, that there may be an interchange of encouragement among you, by each one through the other's faith, both yours and mine."—Rom. 1:11, 12.

⁶ Today, the Christian congregation has the same objectives that it had in the first century. Jesus gave his disciples a challenging yet thrilling work to perform. He told them: "Make disciples of people of all the nations, baptizing them in the name of the Father and of the Son and of the holy spirit, teaching them to observe all the things I have commanded you."—Matt. 28:19, 20.

⁷ The Christian congregation of Jehovah's Witnesses is the agency through which that work is accomplished today. Of course, it is a challenge to reach people of different languages. Yet, Jehovah's Witnesses have produced Bible literature in more than 400 languages. If you are actively associated with the Christian congregation and are sharing in the Kingdom-preaching and disciple-making work, you have reason to rejoice. You are counted among the comparatively few on earth today who have the privilege of bearing thorough witness to Jehovah's name!

⁸ To help you endure with joy during these critical times, Jehovah God has provided a worldwide association of brothers. Paul wrote to the Hebrew Christians: "Let us consider one another to incite to love and fine works, not forsaking the gathering of ourselves together,

---

**JERUSALEM
—THE CENTER OF JUDAISM**

Much of the action of the first chapters of Acts takes place in Jerusalem. This city stands among the hills of Judea's central mountain range, about 34 miles east of the Mediterranean Sea. In 1070 B.C.E., King David conquered the hilltop fortress of Mount Zion, located here, and the city that grew up around it became the capital of the ancient nation of Israel.

Close by Mount Zion stands Mount Moriah, where, according to ancient Jewish tradition, Abraham attempted to sacrifice Isaac, some 1,900 years before the events described in Acts. Mount Moriah became part of the city when Solomon built the first temple of Jehovah atop it. This edifice came to be the focal point of Jewish public life and worship.

It was to Jehovah's temple that all devout Jews regularly gathered from all over the inhabited earth to sacrifice, worship, and observe seasonal festivals. They did so in obedience to God's command: "Three times in the year every male of yours should appear before Jehovah your God in the place that he will choose." (Deut. 16:16) Jerusalem was also the seat of the Great Sanhedrin, the Jewish high court and national administrative council.

6, 7. How is the Christian congregation today fulfilling Jesus' commission to preach to all nations?

8. In what way are congregation members individually blessed?

During the period of time covered by the book of Acts, Rome was the largest and politically the most important city in the then-known world. It was the capital of an empire that at its peak dominated lands stretching from Britain to North Africa and from the Atlantic Ocean to the Persian Gulf.

Rome was a melting pot of cultures, races, languages, and superstitions. A network of well-maintained roads brought travelers and merchandise from every corner of the empire. At the nearby port of Ostia, ships that plied busy trade routes unloaded foodstuffs and luxury goods destined for the city.

By the first century C.E., well over a million people lived in Rome. Perhaps half of the population were slaves—condemned criminals, children sold or abandoned by their parents, and prisoners captured during campaigns by the Roman legions. Among those brought to Rome as slaves were Jews from Jerusalem, following the conquest of that city by Roman General Pompey in 63 B.C.E.

Most of the free population were paupers, who lived in crowded multistory housing and depended on government subsidies. The emperors, however, adorned their capital with some of the most magnificent public buildings ever seen. Among them were theaters and great stadiums that offered such spectacles as stage performances, gladiatorial contests, and chariot racing—all free for the entertainment of the masses.

as some have the custom, but encouraging one another, and all the more so as you behold the day drawing near." (Heb. 10:24, 25) The Christian congregation is a provision from Jehovah so that you can encourage others and also be encouraged yourself. Stay close to your spiritual brothers and sisters. Never forsake gathering together at Christian meetings!

"Each One Heard . . . in His Own Language" (Acts 2:5-13)

9 Imagine the excitement that must have surged through the mixed company of Jews and proselytes at Pentecost 33 C.E. Most of those present likely spoke a common language, perhaps Greek or Hebrew. But now "each one heard [the disciples] speaking in his own language." (Acts 2:6) Surely those listeners must have been touched to hear the good news in their mother tongue. Of course, Christians today are not gifted with a miraculous ability to speak foreign tongues. Many, however, have made themselves available to spread the Kingdom message to people of all national groups. How? Some have learned a new language so that they can serve with a nearby foreign-language congregation or even move to a foreign land. Often, they have found that their listeners are quite impressed by their efforts.

10 Consider Christine, who took a Gujarati course along with seven other Witnesses. When she encountered a Gujarati-speaking workmate, she greeted the young woman in her native tongue. The woman was impressed and wanted to know why Christine was making the effort to learn Gujarati. Christine was able to give a fine witness. The young woman remarked to Christine: "No other religion would encourage its

---

9, 10. How have some made themselves available to reach out to those who speak a different language?

members to learn such a difficult language. You must really have something important to say."

[11] Of course, not all of us can learn another language. Nevertheless, we can be prepared to preach the Kingdom message to people of other language groups. How? One way is by using the publication *Good News for People of All Nations.* This booklet contains a brief message in many different languages. Consider one experience in which this publication was put to good use. A Witness family visited three national parks shortly after the booklet was released. There they met people from India, the Netherlands, Pakistan, and the Philippines. The husband noted: "Though all these people spoke some English, they were impressed when we showed them the message in their own language, since they were thousands of miles from home. The worldwide nature of our work as well as our unity became clear to them."

"Peter Stood Up" (Acts 2:14-37)

[12] "Peter stood up" to speak to the multinational crowd. (Acts 2:14) He explained to all who would listen that the miraculous ability to speak in different languages had been granted by God in fulfillment of the prophecy uttered by Joel: "I shall pour out my spirit on every sort of flesh." (Joel 2:28) Prior to his ascension to heaven, Jesus told his disciples: "I will request the Father and he will give you another helper," which Jesus identified as "the spirit."—John 14: 16, 17.

[13] Peter's concluding words to the crowd were firm: "Let all the house of

---

11. How can the booklet *Good News for People of All Nations* be put to good use?

12. (a) How had the prophet Joel alluded to the miraculous event that took place at Pentecost 33 C.E.? (b) Why had a first-century fulfillment of Joel's prophecy been expected?

13, 14. How did Peter strive to reach the hearts of his listeners, and how can we imitate his approach?

JEWS IN MESOPOTAMIA AND EGYPT

The History of the Jewish People in the Age of Jesus Christ (175 B.C.–A.D. 135) states: "In *Mesopotamia, Media* and *Babylonia* lived the descendants of members of the kingdom of the ten tribes [of Israel], and of the kingdom of Judah, once deported there by the Assyrians and the Babylonians." According to Ezra 2:64, only 42,360 Israelite men, along with their wives and children, returned to Jerusalem from their Babylonian exile. This took place in 537 B.C.E. Flavius Josephus remarks that in the first century C.E., the Jews who "dwelt about Babylonia" numbered into the tens of thousands. In the third to the fifth centuries C.E., these communities produced the work known as the Babylonian Talmud.

Documentary evidence exists of a Jewish presence in Egypt at least as early as the sixth century B.C.E. During that period, Jeremiah directed a message to Jews living in various localities of Egypt, including Memphis. (Jer. 44:1, ftn.) It is likely that large numbers immigrated to Egypt during the Hellenistic period. Josephus says that Jews were among the first settlers of Alexandria. In time, an entire section of this city was allotted to them. In the first century C.E., Jewish writer Philo asserted that a million of his fellow countrymen lived throughout Egypt, from "the side of Libya to the boundaries of Ethiopia."

Israel know for a certainty that God made him both Lord and Christ, this Jesus whom you impaled." (Acts 2:36) Of course, most of Peter's listeners were not personally present when Jesus was put to death on the torture stake. Yet, as a nation they bore community responsibility for this act. Note, though, that Peter addressed his fellow Jews respectfully and appealed to their hearts. Peter's goal was to move his listeners to repentance, not to condemn them. Did the crowd listening take offense at Peter's words? By no means. Instead, the people were "stabbed to the heart." They asked: "What shall we do?" Peter's positive approach likely played a role in his reaching the hearts of many, so that they were moved to repent.—Acts 2:37.

[14] We can imitate Peter's manner of appealing to hearts. When witnessing to others, we need not take issue with every unscriptural view that the householder may express. Rather, we would do well to build on points on which we can agree. If we establish common ground with our listener, we can then tactfully reason from God's Word. Often, when Bible truths are presented in such a positive fashion, righthearted ones are more likely to respond favorably.

"Let Each One of You Be Baptized" (Acts 2:38-47)

[15] On the thrilling day of Pentecost 33 C.E., Peter said to responsive Jews and proselytes: "Repent, and let each one of you be baptized." (Acts 2:38) As a result, about 3,000 were baptized, likely in pools in or near Jerusalem.* Was this an impulsive act? Does this account serve as a precedent for Bible students and for children of Christian parents to rush into

---

* By comparison, on August 7, 1993, at an international convention of Jehovah's Witnesses in Kiev, Ukraine, 7,402 persons were baptized in six pools. The entire baptism took two hours and fifteen minutes to complete.

---

15. (a) What statement did Peter make, and what was the response? (b) Why could thousands who heard the good news at Pentecost qualify to be baptized on the same day?

CHRISTIANITY IN PONTUS

Among those who heard Peter's speech at Pentecost 33 C.E. were Jews from Pontus, a district of northern Asia Minor. (Acts 2:9) Evidently, some of them took the good news back to their homeland, for those to whom Peter addressed his first letter included believers who were "scattered about" in such places as Pontus.* (1 Pet. 1:1) His writing reveals that these Christians had been "grieved by various trials" because of their faith. (1 Pet. 1:6) Likely, this included opposition and persecution.

Further tests faced by Christians in Pontus are alluded to in correspondence between Pliny the Younger, governor of the Roman province of Bithynia and Pontus, and Emperor Trajan. Writing from Pontus in about 112 C.E., Pliny reported that the "contagion" of Christianity threatened everyone, regardless of gender, age, or rank. Pliny gave those accused of being Christians opportunity to deny it, and those who would not, he executed. Any who cursed Christ or recited a prayer to the gods or to Trajan's statue were released. Pliny acknowledged that these were things that "those who are really Christians cannot be made to do."

---

* The phrase rendered "scattered about" comes from a Greek word that means "of the Diaspora." The term has Jewish overtones, indicating that many of the first converts were from Jewish communities.

baptism before they are ready? Not at all. Remember, those Jews and Jewish proselytes who were baptized on the day of Pentecost 33 C.E. were keen students of God's Word, and they were part of a nation that had been dedicated to Jehovah. Moreover, they were already demonstrating their zeal—in some cases, by traveling great distances to be present at this annual festival. After accepting the vital truths concerning Jesus Christ's role in the outworking of God's purpose, they were ready to continue serving God—but now as baptized followers of *Christ*.

[16] Jehovah's blessing was certainly on that group. The account relates: "All those who became believers were together in having all things in common, and they went selling their possessions and properties and distributing the proceeds to all, just as anyone would have the need."* (Acts 2:44, 45) Surely all true Christians want to imitate that loving, self-sacrificing spirit.

[17] Christian dedication and baptism involve several necessary Scriptural steps. A person must take in knowledge of God's Word. (John 17:3) He needs to exercise faith and must repent over his past course, demonstrating true sorrow over it. (Acts 3:19) Then he must convert, or turn around, and start engaging in right works that are in harmony with God's will. (Rom. 12:2; Eph. 4:23, 24) These steps are followed by his making a dedication to God in prayer and then getting baptized.—Matt. 16:24; 1 Pet. 3:21.

[18] Are you a dedicated, baptized disciple of Jesus Christ? If so, be grateful for the privilege that has been extended to you. Like the first-century disciples who were filled with holy spirit, you can be used in a powerful way to bear thorough witness and do the will of Jehovah!

WHO WERE THE PROSELYTES?

"Both Jews and proselytes" heard Peter's preaching at Pentecost 33 C.E.—Acts 2:10.

Among the qualified men appointed to care for the "necessary business" of the daily distribution of food was Nicolaus, who is identified as "a proselyte of Antioch." (Acts 6:3-5) Proselytes were Gentiles, that is, non-Jews, who had converted to Judaism. They were considered Jews in all respects, since they accepted the God and the Law of Israel, rejected all other gods, underwent circumcision (if male), and joined themselves to the nation of Israel.

After the Jews were released from exile in Babylon in 537 B.C.E., many settled far from the land of Israel but continued to practice Judaism. By this means, people throughout the ancient Near East and beyond became acquainted with the Jewish religion. Ancient writers, such as Horace and Seneca, testify that multitudes in different lands who were attracted to the Jews and their beliefs joined their communities and became proselytes.

---

* This temporary arrangement filled the need that arose because visitors remained in Jerusalem to take in further spiritual enlightenment. This was a voluntary sharing and is not to be confused with some form of communism.—Acts 5:1-4.

---

16. How did first-century Christians show a self-sacrificing spirit?

17. What steps are necessary for a person to qualify for baptism?

18. What privilege is open to baptized disciples of Christ?

CHAPTER 4

"Men Unlettered and Ordinary"

The apostles take bold action, and Jehovah blesses them

Based on Acts 3:1–5:11

THE afternoon sun slants onto the milling crowd. Devout Jews and disciples of Christ are filing into the temple compound. Soon it will be "the hour of prayer."* (Acts 2:46; 3:1) Among the throng, Peter and John edge toward the temple gate called Beautiful, which has an impressive set of doors overlaid in glowing Corinthian bronze. Above the clamor of conversation and the sound of shuffling feet, a middle-aged beggar, crippled from birth, calls for alms.—Acts 3:2; 4:22.

² As Peter and John draw close, the beggar recites his well-worn plea for money. The apostles stop, catching the hopeful man's attention. "Silver and gold I do not possess," Peter states, "but what I do have is what I give you: In the name of Jesus Christ the Nazarene, walk!" Picture the astonishment of the crowd as Peter takes the crippled man by the hand and—for the first time in his life—the man stands upright! (Acts 3:6, 7) Can you just see the man gazing down at his healed limbs and taking his first tentative steps? No wonder he begins leaping about and loudly praising God!

³ The ecstatic crowd runs to Peter and John at Solomon's colonnade. Here, at the very place where Jesus once stood and taught, Peter informs them of the real significance of what just happened. (John 10:23) He offers to the crowd and the formerly crippled man a gift worth more than silver or gold. This gift involves much more than restored health. It is the opportunity to repent, to have their sins blotted out, and to become followers of Jehovah's appointed "Chief Agent of life," Jesus Christ.—Acts 3:15.

⁴ What a remarkable day! One person was healed physically and could now walk. Thousands more were given the opportunity to be

---

* Prayers were offered at the temple in conjunction with the morning and evening sacrifices. The evening sacrifice was held at "the ninth hour," or about three in the afternoon.

1, 2. What miracle did Peter and John perform near the temple gate?

3. What surpassing gift could the formerly crippled man and the crowd receive?

4. (a) The miraculous healing set the stage for what confrontation? (b) What two questions will we answer?

healed spiritually so that they could walk worthily of God. (Col. 1:9, 10) In addition, the events of that day set the stage for a confrontation between loyal followers of Christ and people in power who would try to prevent them from fulfilling Jesus' command to preach the Kingdom message. (Acts 1:8) What can we learn from the methods used and the manner displayed by Peter and John—"men unlettered and ordinary"—as they witnessed to the crowd?* (Acts 4:13) And how can we imitate the way they and the other disciples dealt with opposition?

Not "by Personal Power" (Acts 3:11-26)

⁵ Peter and John stood before the crowd, knowing that some there may have recently clamored for Jesus to be impaled. (Mark 15:8-15; Acts 3:13-15) Think of the courage Peter displayed as he boldly declared that the crippled man was healed in Jesus' name. Peter did not water down the truth. He forthrightly condemned the crowd's complicity in the death of Christ. But Peter harbored no animosity toward these people, for they had "acted in ignorance." (Acts 3:17) He appealed to them as his brothers and focused on the positive aspects of the Kingdom message. If they repented and put faith in Christ, "seasons of refreshing" would come to them from Jehovah. (Acts 3:19) We likewise need to be bold and forthright when declaring God's coming judgment. At the same time, we should never be brash, harsh, or judgmental. Instead, we view those to whom we preach as our potential brothers, and like Peter, we focus especially on the positive aspects of the Kingdom message.

⁶ The apostles were modest men. They did not take credit for the miraculous deed they had performed. Peter said to the crowd: "Why are you gazing at us as though by personal power or godly devotion we have made him walk?" (Acts 3:12) Peter and the other apostles knew that any good they accomplished in their ministry was due to God's power, not their own. As a result, they modestly directed all praise for their achievements to Jehovah and Jesus.

⁷ We need to show similar modesty as we engage in the Kingdom-preaching work. Granted, God's spirit does not empower modern-day Christians to perform miraculous healings. Even so, we can help people to develop faith in God and Christ and to receive the same gift Peter offered—the opportunity to have their sins forgiven and to be refreshed

---

* See the boxes "Peter—From Fisherman to Dynamic Apostle," on page 30, and "John —The Disciple Whom Jesus Loved," on page 33.

---

5. What do we learn from the way Peter addressed the crowd?

6. How did Peter and John display humility and modesty?

7, 8. (a) What gift can we offer to people? (b) How is the promise of a "restoration of all things" being fulfilled today?

Peter is identified by five names in the Scriptures. He is known as Symeon in Hebrew and its Greek equivalent, Simon, and as Peter and its Semitic equivalent, Cephas. The apostle is also identified as Simon Peter, a combination of two names.—Matt. 10:2; John 1:42; Acts 15:14.

Peter was married and shared his home with his mother-in-law and brother. (Mark 1:29-31) He was a fisherman from Bethsaida, a town on the north side of the Sea of Galilee. (John 1:44) He later lived nearby in Capernaum. (Luke 4:31, 38) It was in Peter's boat that Jesus sat when addressing a multitude that gathered on the shore of the Sea of Galilee. Immediately afterward, at Jesus' direction, Peter hauled in a miraculous catch of fish. Peter fell to his knees in fear, but Jesus said to him: "Stop being afraid. From now on you will be catching men alive." (Luke 5:1-11) Peter fished with his brother Andrew, as well as with James and John. All four abandoned their fishing business when they accepted Jesus' invitation to become his followers. (Matt. 4:18-22; Mark 1:16-18) About a year later, Peter was among the 12 whom Jesus chose to be his "apostles," meaning "sent-forth ones."—Mark 3:13-16.

Jesus selected Peter, James, and John to accompany him on special occasions. They witnessed Jesus' transfiguration, saw him resurrect Jairus' daughter, and shared his grief in the garden of Gethsemane. (Matt. 17:1, 2; 26:36-46; Mark 5:22-24, 35-42; Luke 22:39-46) The same three, along with Andrew, questioned Jesus regarding the sign of his presence.—Mark 13:1-4.

Peter was forthright, dynamic, and sometimes impulsive. It seems that he often spoke up before his fellows did. The Gospels record his words more often than those of the other 11 apostles put together. Peter raised questions while the others remained silent. (Matt. 15:15; 18: 21; 19:27-29; Luke 12:41; John 13:36-38) He was the one who objected to Jesus' washing his feet and then, on being reproved, asked Jesus to wash also his hands and head!—John 13:5-10.

Strong feelings moved Peter to try to persuade Jesus that He would not have to suffer and be killed. Jesus firmly corrected him for that lapse in judgment. (Matt. 16:21-23) During Jesus' final night on earth, Peter declared that even though all the other apostles might abandon Jesus, he never would. When Jesus' enemies arrested Him, courage moved Peter to defend Jesus with the sword and later to follow him right into the courtyard of the high priest. Yet, not long afterward, Peter denied his Master three times and then wept bitterly when he realized what he had done.—Matt. 26:31-35, 51, 52, 69-75.

Shortly before Jesus' first post-resurrection appearance to his apostles in Galilee, Peter announced that he was going fishing, and other apostles joined him. On recognizing Jesus on the beach, Peter impulsively plunged into the water and swam ashore. At the breakfast of fish that Jesus cooked for his apostles, Jesus asked Peter if he loved him more than "these"—that is, the fish that were before them. Jesus was urging Peter to choose to follow him full-time rather than pursue a career, such as the fishing business.—John 21:1-22.

In about 62-64 C.E., Peter preached the good news in Babylon, in modern-day Iraq, where there was a large Jewish population. (1 Pet. 5:13) In Babylon, Peter composed the first and possibly the second of the two inspired letters bearing his name. Jesus entrusted Peter with "powers necessary for an apostleship to those who are circumcised." (Gal. 2:8, 9) With compassion and vigor, Peter fulfilled his commission.

by Jehovah. Each year, hundreds of thousands accept this offer and become baptized disciples of Christ.

[8] Indeed, we are living at the time of the "restoration of all things" referred to by Peter. In fulfillment of the word "God spoke through the mouth of his holy prophets of old time," the Kingdom was established in heaven in the year 1914. (Acts 3:21; Ps. 110:1-3; Dan. 4:16, 17) Shortly thereafter, Christ began overseeing a spiritual restoration work on earth. As a result, millions have been brought into a spiritual paradise, becoming subjects of God's Kingdom. They have stripped off the old, corrupted personality and "put on the new personality which was created according to God's will." (Eph. 4:22-24) As with the healing of the crippled beggar, this astounding work has been accomplished, not by human efforts, but by God's spirit. Like Peter, we must boldly and effectively use God's Word to teach others. Any success we may have in helping people to become disciples of Christ is achieved by God's power, not our own.

"We Cannot Stop Speaking" (Acts 4:1-22)

[9] Peter's speech and the leaping, shouting, formerly crippled man caused quite a commotion. In response, the captain of the temple—appointed to oversee the security of the temple area—and the chief priests rushed to investigate. These men likely were Sadducees, a rich and politically powerful sect that worked for peaceful relations with the Romans, rejected the oral law so loved by the Pharisees, and derided belief in the resurrection.* How irked they were to discover Peter and John in the temple, boldly teaching that Jesus had been resurrected!

[10] The angry opposers threw Peter and John in jail and dragged them before the Jewish high court the next day. From the viewpoint of the elitist rulers, Peter and John were "men unlettered and ordinary" who had no right to teach in the temple. They had not studied at any recognized religious school. Yet, their outspokenness and their conviction caused the court to wonder at them. Why were Peter and John so effective? One reason was that "they used to be with Jesus." (Acts 4:13) Their Master had taught with real authority, not like the scribes.—Matt. 7:28, 29.

[11] The court ordered the apostles to stop preaching. In that society, the court's orders carried much weight. Just weeks earlier, this same body declared Jesus "liable to death." (Matt. 26:59-66) Still, Peter and John were not intimidated. Standing in front of these rich, well-educated, influential men, Peter and John fearlessly but respectfully declared:

---

* See the box "The High Priest and the Chief Priests," on page 34.

9-11. (a) How did the Jewish leaders react to Peter and John's message? (b) What did the apostles resolve to do?

"Whether it is righteous in the sight of God to listen to you rather than to God, judge for yourselves. But as for us, we cannot stop speaking about the things we have seen and heard."—Acts 4:19, 20.

¹² Are you able to show similar courage? How do you feel when you have the opportunity to witness to the rich, the well-educated, or the influential in your community? What if family members, schoolmates, or workmates ridicule you for your beliefs? Are you intimidated? If so, you can overcome such feelings. While on earth, Jesus taught the apostles how to defend their beliefs with confidence and respect. (Matt. 10:11-18) After his resurrection, Jesus promised his disciples that he would continue to be with them "all the days until the conclusion of the system of things." (Matt. 28:20) Under Jesus' direction, the modern-day slave class teaches us how to defend our beliefs. (Matt. 24:45-47; 1 Pet. 3:15) This is done by instruction at congregation meetings, such as the Theocratic Ministry School, and through Bible-based publications, such as *Reasoning From the Scriptures*. Are you making good use of these provisions? If you do so, your courage and conviction will increase. And, like the apostles, you will let nothing stop you from speaking about the wonderful spiritual truths you have seen and heard.

Let nothing stop you from speaking about the wonderful spiritual truths you have learned

"They . . . Raised Their Voices to God" (Acts 4:23-31)

¹³ Immediately after being released from custody, Peter and John met with the rest of the congregation. Together, "they . . . raised their voices to God" and prayed for courage to keep preaching. (Acts 4:24) Peter knew only too well the folly of trusting in personal power when attempting to do God's will. Just weeks earlier, he had self-confidently told Jesus: "Although all the others are stumbled in connection with you, never will I be stumbled!" Yet, as Jesus foretold, Peter quickly succumbed to fear of man and denied his friend and teacher. However, Peter learned from his mistake.—Matt. 26:33, 34, 69-75.

12. What can help us to develop courage and conviction?

13, 14. If we face opposition, what should we do, and why?

The apostle John was a son of Zebedee and the brother of the apostle James. It seems that his mother's name was Salome, who was possibly the sister of Mary, the mother of Jesus. (Matt. 10:2; 27:55, 56; Mark 15:40; Luke 5:9, 10) So John may have been a relative of Jesus. John's family appears to have been materially prosperous. Zebedee's fishing business was large enough to have hired men. (Mark 1:20) Salome accompanied Jesus, ministered to him when he was in Galilee, and later brought spices to prepare Jesus' body for burial. (Mark 16:1; John 19:40) John probably had a house of his own.—John 19:26, 27.

John was likely the disciple of John the Baptizer who was standing with Andrew when John the Baptizer looked at Jesus and said: "See, the Lamb of God!" (John 1: 35, 36, 40) Following this introduction, John the son of Zebedee evidently accompanied Jesus to Cana and was an eyewitness to Jesus' first miracle. (John 2:1-11) The vividness and detail with which John describes Jesus' subsequent activity in Jerusalem, Samaria, and Galilee suggest that the Gospel writer may also have witnessed these events. The readiness with which John—like James, Peter, and Andrew—abandoned his fishing nets, boat, and livelihood when Jesus called him to be His follower testifies to his faith.—Matt. 4:18-22.

John does not appear as prominently as Peter does in the Gospel accounts. However, John too had a vigorous personality, as evidenced by the surname that Jesus gave to him and his brother James—Boanerges, meaning "Sons of Thunder." (Mark 3:17) Initially, John was ambitious for prominence, so much so that he and his brother got their mother to ask Jesus to give her sons privileged positions in his Kingdom. While this desire was selfish, it was also evidence of their faith in the reality of the Kingdom. The brothers' ambition gave Jesus occasion to admonish all his apostles regarding the need for humility.—Matt. 20:20-28.

John manifested his strong character when he tried to prevent a certain man who was not one of Jesus' followers from expelling demons in His name. On another occasion, John was ready to call down fire from heaven to destroy the inhabitants of a Samaritan village who were unresponsive when Jesus sent messengers to make some preparations for him. For these reactions, Jesus rebuked John. Evidently, as time went by, John developed the balance and mercy that he once seemed to lack. (Luke 9:49-56) Despite his shortcomings, however, John was "the disciple whom Jesus used to love." Thus, when He was about to die, Jesus entrusted his own mother, Mary, to John's care.—John 19:26, 27; 21:7, 20, 24.

John outlived the other apostles, just as Jesus had prophesied that he would. (John 21:20-22) John served Jehovah faithfully for some 70 years. Toward the end of his life, during the reign of the Roman Emperor Domitian, John was exiled to the island of Patmos "for speaking about God and bearing witness to Jesus." There, in about 96 C.E., John received the visions that he recorded in the book of Revelation. (Rev. 1:1, 2, 9) Tradition has it that after his release, John went to Ephesus, where he penned the Gospel that bears his name and the letters known as 1, 2, and 3 John, and that he died in Ephesus in about 100 C.E.

¹⁴ Determination alone will not sustain you as you fulfill your commission to be a witness of Christ. When opposers try to break your faith or attempt to stop you from preaching, follow the example of Peter and John. Pray to Jehovah for strength. Seek the support of the congregation. Tell the elders and other mature ones of the difficulties you face. The prayers of others can be a powerful sustaining force.—Eph. 6: 18; Jas. 5:16.

¹⁵ If you once succumbed to pressure and stopped preaching for a time, take heart. Remember, all the apostles stopped preaching for a while after Jesus' death but soon were active again. (Matt. 26:56; 28:10, 16-20) Rather than letting past mistakes weigh you down, can you draw on the experience and use the lessons you learned to strengthen others?

¹⁶ What should we pray for when those in authority oppress us? Notice, please, that the disciples did not ask that they be spared from facing trials. They well remembered Jesus' statement: "If they have persecuted me, they will persecute you also." (John 15:20) Instead, these loyal disciples asked Jehovah to "give attention to" the threats of the opposers. (Acts 4:29) The disciples clearly saw the big picture, recognizing that the persecution they faced was actually a fulfillment of prophecy. They knew that, as Jesus had taught them to pray, God's will would 'be done on earth,' no matter what mere human rulers may say.—Matt. 6:9, 10.

¹⁷ In order to do God's will, the disciples prayed to Jehovah: "Grant your slaves to keep speaking your word with all boldness." What was Jehovah's immediate response? "The place in which they were gathered together was shaken; and they were one and all filled with the holy spirit and were speaking the word of God with boldness." (Acts 4:29-31) Nothing can stop God's will from being accomplished. (Isa. 55:11) No matter how great

THE HIGH PRIEST AND THE CHIEF PRIESTS

The high priest represented his people before God. In the first century C.E., he was also head of the Sanhedrin. Surrounding him as leaders of the Jews were the chief priests. They included former high priests, such as Annas, and other adult males of the families—perhaps as few as four or five families—from which high priests were selected. "The mere fact of belonging to one of the privileged families," wrote scholar Emil Schürer, "must have conferred a particular distinction" among priests.

The Scriptures indicate that high priests served for their lifetime. (Num. 35:25) During the period covered by the book of Acts, however, Roman governors and kings who ruled by the grace of Rome appointed and deposed high priests at will. It does seem, though, that these pagan rulers chose their appointees from the line of priests descended from Aaron.

---

15. Why can those who once stopped preaching for a time take heart?

16, 17. What can we learn from the prayer offered by Christ's followers in Jerusalem?

the odds, no matter how powerful the opponent, if we raise our voice to God in prayer, we can be sure that He will grant us the strength to keep on speaking His word with boldness.

Accountable, "Not to Men, But to God" (Acts 4:32–5:11)

[18] The fledgling congregation in Jerusalem soon grew to more than 5,000 members strong.* Despite their diverse backgrounds, the disciples had "one heart and soul." They were united in the same mind and same line of thought. (Acts 4:32; 1 Cor. 1:10) The disciples did more than just pray to Jehovah to bless their efforts. They supported one another both spiritually and, when necessary, materially. (1 John 3:16-18) For example, the disciple Joseph, surnamed Barnabas by the apostles, sold land he owned and unselfishly donated the whole amount toward helping those from distant lands to stay in Jerusalem longer so that they could learn more about their new faith.

[19] A couple named Ananias and Sapphira also sold a possession and made a contribution. They made a pretense of giving the whole amount; however, they "secretly held back some of the price." (Acts 5:2) Jehovah struck this couple dead, not because the amount they gave was insufficient, but because their motive for giving was wicked and they were deceptive. They "played false, not to men, but to God." (Acts 5:4) Like the hypocrites whom Jesus condemned, Ananias and Sapphira were more concerned with seeking glory from men than the approval of God.—Matt. 6:1-3.

[20] With a generous spirit like that of faithful disciples in first-century Jerusalem, millions of present-day Witnesses support the worldwide preaching work by making voluntary donations. No one is forced to give either his time or his money to support this work. Indeed, Jehovah does not want us to serve him grudgingly or under compulsion. (2 Cor. 9:7) When we do give, Jehovah is interested, not in the amount, but in the motive for our giving. (Mark 12:41-44) Never would we want to be like Ananias and Sapphira, allowing our service to God to be prompted by self-interest or glory-seeking. Instead, like Peter, John, and Barnabas, may our service to Jehovah always be motivated by genuine love of God and of our fellow man.—Matt. 22:37-40.

---

* There may have been only about 6,000 Pharisees and a smaller number of Sadducees in Jerusalem in 33 C.E. This may indicate another reason why these two groups felt increasingly threatened by the teachings of Jesus.

---

18. What did members of the congregation in Jerusalem do for one another?

19. Why did Jehovah execute Ananias and Sapphira?

20. What lessons do we learn about giving to Jehovah?

"So they brought them and stood them
in the Sanhedrin hall."
—Acts 5:27

CHAPTER 5

"We Must Obey God as Ruler"

The apostles take a stand that sets a precedent for all true Christians

Based on Acts 5:12–6:7

THE judges of the Sanhedrin are simmering with rage! The apostles of Jesus are standing trial before this high court. The reason? Joseph Caiaphas, the high priest and president of the Sanhedrin, sternly addresses them: "We positively ordered you not to keep teaching upon the basis of this name." The angry president cannot bring himself even to utter the name of Jesus. "Yet," Caiaphas continues, "you have filled Jerusalem with your teaching, and you are determined to bring the blood of this man upon us." (Acts 5:28) The message is clear: Stop preaching —or else!

[2] How will the apostles respond? Their commission to preach came from Jesus, whose authority was divinely bestowed. (Matt. 28:18-20) Will the apostles cave in to fear of man and be silenced? Or will they have the courage to stand firm and continue preaching? The issue really boils down to this: Will they obey God or man? Without hesitation, the apostle Peter speaks for all the apostles. His words are unequivocal and bold.

[3] As true Christians, we are keenly interested in how the apostles responded to the threats of the Sanhedrin. The commission to preach applies to us as well. In carrying out this God-given assignment, we too may face opposition. (Matt. 10:22) Opposers may try to restrict or ban our work. What will we do? We can benefit by considering the stand taken by the apostles and the circumstances that led up to their trial before the Sanhedrin.*

"Jehovah's Angel Opened the Doors" (Acts 5:12-21a)

[4] Recall that when ordered to stop preaching the first time, Peter and John answered: "We cannot stop speaking about the things we have seen and heard." (Acts 4:20) After that encounter with the Sanhedrin,

---

* See the box "The Sanhedrin—High Court of the Jews," on page 39.

1-3. (a) Why have the apostles been brought before the Sanhedrin, and the issue boils down to what? (b) Why are we keenly interested in the apostles' stand?

4, 5. Why did Caiaphas and the Sadducees become "filled with jealousy"?

Peter and John, along with the rest of the apostles, continued preaching in the temple. The apostles performed great signs, such as healing the sick and expelling demons. They did so "in Solomon's colonnade," a covered portico on the east side of the temple, where many Jews would gather. Why, even Peter's shadow apparently effected cures! Many who were healed physically responded to words of spiritual healing. As a result, "believers in the Lord kept on being added, multitudes both of men and of women."—Acts 5:12-15.

⁵ Caiaphas and the Sadducees, the religious sect to which he belonged, became "filled with jealousy" and had the apostles thrown in jail. (Acts 5:17, 18) Why were the Sadducees outraged? The apostles were teaching that Jesus had been resurrected, yet the Sadducees did not believe in the resurrection. The apostles were saying that only by putting faith in Jesus can one be saved, but the Sadducees feared reprisal from Rome if the people looked to Jesus as their Leader. (John 11:48) No wonder the Sadducees were determined to silence the apostles!

⁶ Today, too, the principal instigators of persecution against Jehovah's servants are religious opposers. Such ones often try to use their influence with governmental authorities and the media to silence our preaching. Should we be surprised? No. Our message lays bare false religion. By accepting Bible truths, honesthearted people are set free from unscriptural beliefs and practices. (John 8:32) Is it any wonder, then, that our message often causes religious leaders to become filled with jealous hatred?

⁷ Sitting in jail awaiting trial, the apostles may have wondered whether they were about to suffer martyrdom at the hands of their enemies. (Matt. 24:9) But during the night, something most unexpected happened—"Jehovah's angel opened the doors of the prison."* (Acts 5:19) The angel then gave them specific direction: Take "a stand in the temple," and "keep on speaking." (Acts 5:20) That command no doubt assured the apostles that they had been doing the right thing. The angel's words may also have strengthened them to remain firm no matter what happened. With strong faith and courage, the apostles "entered into the temple at daybreak and began to teach."—Acts 5:21.

⁸ Each of us does well to ask, 'Would I have the faith and courage needed to continue preaching under similar circumstances?' We may draw strength from knowing that the vital work of "bearing thorough

---

* This is the first of some 20 specific references to angels in the book of Acts. Earlier, at Acts 1:10, angels are indirectly referred to as "men in white garments."

---

6. Who today are the principal instigators of persecution against Jehovah's servants, and why should this not surprise us?

7, 8. What effect did the angel's command no doubt have on the apostles, and we do well to ask ourselves what question?

witness concerning the kingdom of God" has angelic backing and direction.—Acts 28:23; Rev. 14:6, 7.

"We Must Obey God as Ruler Rather Than Men" (Acts 5:21b-33)

[9] Caiaphas and the other judges of the Sanhedrin were now ready to deal with the apostles. Unaware of what had happened at the jail, the court dispatched officers to fetch the prisoners. Imagine the officers' surprise when they discovered that the prisoners were missing, although the jail was found "locked with all security and the guards standing at the doors." (Acts 5:23) The captain of the temple soon learned that the apostles were back in the temple, bearing witness about Jesus Christ—the very work for which they had been thrown in jail! The captain and his officers quickly went to the temple to gather up the prisoners and escort them to the Sanhedrin.

[10] As described at the outset of this chapter, the furious religious leaders made it clear that the apostles were to stop preaching. The apostles' response? Serving as spokesman, Peter boldly replied: "We must obey God as ruler rather than men." (Acts 5:29) The apostles thereby set a precedent for true Christians throughout the ages. Human rulers forfeit their right to obedience in situations where they prohibit what God requires or require what God prohibits. So in our day, if "the superior authorities" ban our witnessing work, we cannot stop carrying out our God-given assignment to preach the good news. (Rom. 13:1) Rather, we will find discreet ways to continue bearing thorough witness about God's Kingdom.

[11] Not surprisingly, the apostles' bold response incited the exasperated judges to violent anger. They were determined "to do away with" the apostles. (Acts 5:33) Martyrdom now seemed certain for those bold and zealous witnesses. Ah, but help was about to come in a most unusual way!

9-11. How did the apostles respond to the Sanhedrin's demand that they stop preaching, and how did this set a precedent for true Christians?

THE SANHEDRIN —HIGH COURT OF THE JEWS

Although Judea was a province of the Roman Empire, Rome permitted the Jews to observe their own traditions and for the most part to govern themselves. Minor crimes and civil cases were handled by local courts, but questions that those courts could not decide were referred to the Great Sanhedrin in Jerusalem. This body functioned as the supreme court of the Jewish people and as a national administrative council. It also had the final word on the interpretation of Jewish law, and its authority was respected by Jews everywhere.

The Sanhedrin met in its decision chamber, which appears to have been located either in the temple precincts or in its immediate vicinity. The council was made up of 71 members—the high priest, who was the president; other priestly nobles, including Sadducees; lay aristocrats, and learned scribes. The decisions of the court were final.

"You Will Not Be Able to Overthrow Them" (Acts 5:34-42)

[12] Gamaliel, "a Law teacher esteemed by all the people," spoke up.* This jurist must have been highly respected by his colleagues, for he took charge, even giving "the command to put the [apostles] outside for a little while." (Acts 5:34) By citing past examples of uprisings that quickly fizzled after the leaders were dead, Gamaliel urged the court to be patient and tolerant in dealing with the apostles, whose Leader, Jesus, had only recently died. Gamaliel's reasoning was persuasive: "Do not meddle with these men, but let them alone; (because, if this scheme or this work is from men, it will be overthrown; but if it is from God, you will not be able to overthrow them;) otherwise, you may perhaps be found fighters actually against God." (Acts 5:38, 39) The judges heeded his advice. Still, they had the apostles flogged and ordered them "to stop speaking upon the basis of Jesus' name."—Acts 5:40.

[13] Now, as then, Jehovah may raise up prominent men like Gamaliel to intervene in behalf of His people. (Prov. 21:1) Jehovah can use his spirit to move powerful rulers, judges, or lawmakers to act in harmony with his will. (Neh. 2:4-8) But if he should permit us to "suffer for the sake of righteousness," we can be sure of two things. (1 Pet. 3:14) First, God can give us the strength to endure. (1 Cor. 10:13) Second, opposers "will not be able to overthrow" God's work.—Isa. 54:17.

[14] Did the flogging dampen the spirits of the apostles or weaken their resolve? By no means! They "went their way from before the Sanhedrin, rejoicing." (Acts 5:41) "Rejoicing"—why? Surely not because of the physical pain caused by the flogging. They rejoiced because they knew that they had been persecuted for keeping their integrity to Jehovah and for following in the footsteps of their Exemplar, Jesus.—Matt. 5:11, 12.

[15] Like our first-century brothers, we endure with joy when we suffer for the sake of the good news. (1 Pet. 4:12-14) No, we do not enjoy being subjected to threats, persecution, or imprisonment. But we find deep satisfaction in keeping our integrity. Consider, for example, Henryk Dornik, who endured years of harsh treatment under totalitarian regimes. He recalls that in August 1944, the authorities decided to send him and his brother to a concentration camp. The opposers said: "It is impossible to persuade them to do anything. Their martyrdom brings them joy." Brother Dornik explains: "Although I had no de-

---

* See the box "Gamaliel—Esteemed Among the Rabbis," on page 41.

12, 13. (a) What advice did Gamaliel give his colleagues, and what did they do? (b) How may Jehovah intervene in behalf of his people today, and of what can we be sure if we are permitted to "suffer for the sake of righteousness"?

14, 15. (a) How did the apostles respond to the flogging they received, and why? (b) Relate an experience showing that Jehovah's people endure with joy.

sire to be a martyr, suffering with courage and dignity for my loyalty to Jehovah did bring me joy."—Jas. 1:2-4.

¹⁶ The apostles wasted no time in resuming their witnessing work. Undaunted, they continued "every day in the temple and from house to house" the work of "declaring the good news about the Christ."* (Acts 5:42) These zealous preachers were determined to bear thorough witness. Notice that they took their message to the homes of people, as Jesus Christ had directed them. (Matt. 10: 7, 11-14) No doubt, that is how they had managed to fill Jerusalem with their teaching. Today, Jehovah's Witnesses are known for following that apostolic method of preaching. By calling at each house in our territory, we clearly demonstrate that we too want to be thorough, giving everyone an opportunity to hear the good news. Has Jehovah blessed our house-to-house ministry? Yes, he has! Millions have responded to the Kingdom message in this time of the end, and many first heard the good news when a Witness knocked on their door.

GAMALIEL —ESTEEMED AMONG THE RABBIS

The Gamaliel of Acts is generally identified as Gamaliel the Elder, the grandson of Hillel, who was founder of the more liberal of the two schools of Pharisaism. Gamaliel occupied a leading position in the Sanhedrin and was so highly esteemed among the rabbis that he was the first to be given the honorific title "Rabban." The Mishnah says: "When Rabban Gamaliel the Elder died, the glory of the Law ceased and purity and abstinence died." He is credited with various humane enactments. "Of particular importance," says the Encyclopaedia Judaica, "is his decision permitting a woman to remarry on the evidence of a single witness to the death of her husband." He is also said to have enacted laws protecting wives against unprincipled husbands and widows against unprincipled children and to have argued that poor Gentiles should have the same gleaning rights as poor Jews.

Qualified Men to Care for "Necessary Business" (Acts 6:1-6)

¹⁷ The young congregation now faced a subtle danger that threatened it from within. What was that? Many of the disciples being baptized were visitors to Jerusalem and wanted to learn more before returning home. Disciples living in Jerusalem willingly donated funds to meet the need for food and other supplies. (Acts 2:44-46; 4:34-37) At this time, a delicate situation arose. "In the daily distribution" of food, the Greek-speaking widows "were being overlooked." (Acts 6:1) The Hebrew-speaking widows, however, were *not* being overlooked. The problem, then, apparently involved discrimination. Few issues have the potential to be more divisive than this one.

---

* See the box "Preaching 'From House to House,'" on page 42.

---

16. How did the apostles show that they were determined to bear thorough witness, and how do we follow the apostolic method of preaching?

17-19. What divisive issue now arose, and what direction did the apostles give in order to resolve it?

¹⁸ The apostles, acting as the governing body of the expanding congregation, recognized that it would not be wise for them "to leave the word of God to distribute food." (Acts 6:2) To resolve matters, they directed the disciples to search for seven men "full of spirit and wisdom" whom the apostles could appoint over this "necessary business." (Acts 6:3) Qualified men were needed because the work likely involved not just serving food but also handling money, purchasing supplies, and keeping careful records. The men chosen all had Greek names, which perhaps made them more acceptable to the offended widows. After giving prayerful consideration to the recommendation, the apostles appointed the seven men to care for this "necessary business."*

¹⁹ Did caring for the distribution of food mean that the seven men appointed were now exempted from the responsibility to preach the good news? Definitely not! Among the men chosen was Stephen, who would prove himself to be a bold and powerful witness-bearer. (Acts 6:8-10) Philip too was one of the seven, and he is called "the evangelizer." (Acts 21:8) Evidently, then, the seven men continued to be zealous Kingdom preachers.

²⁰ Jehovah's people today follow the apostolic pattern. Men recom-

---

* These men may have met the general qualifications for elders, for handling this "necessary business" was a weighty matter. However, the Scriptures do not indicate precisely when men began to be appointed as elders or overseers in the Christian congregation.

---

20. How do God's people today follow the apostolic pattern?

PREACHING "FROM HOUSE TO HOUSE"

Despite the Sanhedrin's ban on their preaching activity, the disciples continued preaching and teaching "every day in the temple and *from house to house.*" (Acts 5:42) Exactly what does "from house to house" mean?

In the original Greek, the phrase *kat' oi'kon* literally means "according to house." Several translators state that the word *ka·ta'* is to be understood in a "distributive" sense, that is, the disciples' preaching was distributed from one house to another. A similar use of *ka·ta'* occurs at Luke 8:1, where Jesus is said to have preached "from city to city and from village to village."

The plural form, *kat' oi'kous,* is used at Acts 20:20. The apostle Paul told Christian overseers: "I did not hold back from . . . teaching you publicly and from house to house." That Paul here was not simply talking about teaching in the elders' homes, as some suggest, is indicated in the next verse: "But I thoroughly bore witness both to Jews and to Greeks about repentance toward God and faith in our Lord Jesus." (Acts 20:21) Fellow believers had already repented and put faith in Jesus. So the preaching and teaching from house to house clearly had to do with bearing witness to unbelievers.

mended for congregational responsibility must manifest godly wisdom and give evidence that the holy spirit is operating on them. Under the direction of the Governing Body, men who meet the Scriptural requirements are appointed to serve as elders or ministerial servants in the congregations.* (1 Tim. 3:1-9, 12, 13) Those who meet the qualifications can be said to have been appointed by holy spirit. These hardworking men care for much "necessary business." For example, elders may coordinate practical help for faithful older ones who have a genuine need. (Jas. 1:27) Some elders are very involved in constructing Kingdom Halls, organizing conventions, or doing hospital liaison work. Ministerial servants care for many duties that do not directly involve shepherding or teaching. All such qualified men must balance congregational and organizational responsibilities with the God-assigned obligation to preach the good news of the Kingdom. —1 Cor. 9:16.

Like the apostles, we preach "from house to house"

"The Word of God Went On Growing" (Acts 6:7)

²¹ With Jehovah's backing, the fledgling congregation survived persecution from without and a potentially divisive problem from within. Jehovah's blessing was evident, for we are told: "The word of God went on growing, and the number of the disciples kept multiplying in Jerusalem very much; and a great crowd of priests began to be obedient to the faith." (Acts 6:7) This is just one of a number of progress reports found in the book of Acts. (Acts 9:31; 12:24; 16:5; 19:20; 28:31) Today, are we not encouraged when we hear reports about the progress of the Kingdom-preaching work in other parts of the world?

²² Back in the first century C.E., the infuriated religious leaders were not about to give up. A wave of persecution was on the horizon. Soon, Stephen was singled out for vicious opposition, as we will see in the next chapter.

---

* Although the congregation *recommended* the seven certified men, the actual *appointment* was made by the apostles.

21, 22. What shows that Jehovah blessed the fledgling congregation?

"GREAT PERSECUTION AROSE AGAINST THE CONGREGATION"
ACTS 8:1

Did first-century Christians allow mounting opposition to stop them from bearing witness about God's Kingdom? Quite the contrary. In this section, we will see that vicious persecution actually resulted in the expansion of the preaching work.

CHAPTER 6

Stephen—"Full of Graciousness and Power"

Learning from Stephen's bold witness before the Sanhedrin

Based on Acts 6:8–8:3

STEPHEN faces the court. In an imposing hall, likely near the temple in Jerusalem, 71 men are arranged in a large semicircle. This court, the Sanhedrin, sits today to judge Stephen. The judges are powerful, influential men, most of whom have little regard for this disciple of Jesus. In fact, the man who convened the court is High Priest Caiaphas, who was presiding when the Sanhedrin condemned Jesus Christ to death some months earlier. Is Stephen frightened?

² There is something remarkable about Stephen's countenance at this moment. The judges gaze at him and see that his face is "as an angel's face." (Acts 6:15) Angels bear messages from Jehovah God and thus have reason to be fearless, serene, and peaceful. So it is with Stephen—even those hate-filled judges can see that. How can he be so calm?

³ Christians today can learn much from the answer to that question. We need to know, too, just what brought Stephen to this climactic moment. How had he defended his faith before? And in what ways can we imitate him?

"They Stirred Up the People" (Acts 6:8-15)

⁴ We have already learned that Stephen was a precious asset to the fledgling Christian congregation. In the preceding chapter of this book, we saw that he was among those seven humble men who were willing to be of assistance to the apostles when called upon to render aid. His humility is more remarkable when we consider the gifts with which this man was blessed. At Acts 6:8, we read that he was enabled to perform "great portents and signs," as some of the apostles did. We are also told that he was "full of graciousness and power." What did that mean?

1-3. (a) Stephen faces what fearsome situation, yet how does he respond to it? (b) What questions will we consider?

4, 5. (a) Why was Stephen a precious asset to the congregation? (b) In what way was Stephen "full of graciousness and power"?

"At hearing these things they felt cut to their hearts and began to gnash their teeth at him."
—Acts 7:54

⁵ Stephen evidently had a kindly, gentle, winning way with people. He spoke in such a manner as to persuade many of his hearers, convincing them of the sincerity of his heart and the wholesomeness of the truths he discussed. He was full of power because Jehovah's spirit was at work in him, for he humbly submitted to its lead. Rather than getting puffed up over his own gifts and abilities, he directed all praise to Jehovah and showed loving concern for the people he addressed. Little wonder, then, that his opposers found him a force to be reckoned with!

⁶ Various men rose up to dispute with Stephen, but "they could not hold their own against the wisdom and the spirit with which he was speaking."* Frustrated, they "secretly induced" men to bring accusations against this innocent follower of Christ. They also "stirred up the people," the older men, and the scribes, so that Stephen was forcibly taken before the Sanhedrin. (Acts 6:9-12) The opposers leveled this twofold charge against him: He was blaspheming both God and Moses. In what ways?

⁷ The false accusers said that Stephen blasphemed God in that he spoke against "this holy place"—the temple in Jerusalem. (Acts 6:13) He blasphemed Moses, they charged, in that he spoke against the Mosaic Law, changing customs that Moses had handed down. This was a very serious charge, for the Jews at that time put great emphasis on the temple, the details of the Mosaic Law, and the many oral traditions that they had added to that Law. Thus, the charge meant that Stephen was a dangerous man, deserving of death!

⁸ Sadly, it is not unusual for religious people to use such tactics in order to bring trouble on servants of God. To this day, religious opposers at times stir up secular leaders to persecute Jehovah's Witnesses. How should we respond when faced with twisted or false accusations? We can learn much from Stephen.

Boldly Witnessing About "the God of Glory" (Acts 7:1-53)

⁹ As mentioned at the outset, Stephen's face was serene, angelic, as he heard the charges against him. Now Caiaphas turned to him and

---

* Some of these opposers belonged to the "Synagogue of the Freedmen." They may once have been captured by the Romans and later freed, or perhaps they were freed slaves who had become Jewish proselytes. Some were from Cilicia, as was Saul of Tarsus. The account does not reveal whether Saul was among those Cilicians who were unable to hold their own against Stephen.

6-8. (a) Stephen's opposers leveled what twofold charge against him, and why? (b) Why may Stephen's example prove useful to Christians today?

9, 10. Critics have made what claim about Stephen's speech before the Sanhedrin, and what do we need to keep in mind?

said: "Are these things so?" (Acts 7:1) It was Stephen's turn to speak. And speak he did!

[10] Some critics have attacked Stephen's speech, claiming that for all its length, it did not even answer the charge against him. In truth, though, Stephen set a sterling example for us of how to "make a defense" of the good news. (1 Pet. 3:15) Keep in mind that Stephen was charged with blaspheming God by denigrating the temple and with blaspheming Moses by speaking against the Law. Stephen's reply is a summary of three phases of the history of Israel, with certain points carefully emphasized. Let us consider these three phases of history one at a time.

[11] *The era of the patriarchs.* (*Acts 7:1-16*) Stephen began by talking about Abraham, whom the Jews respected for his faith. While starting on this important common ground, Stephen emphasized that Jehovah, "the God of glory," first revealed himself to Abraham in Mesopotamia. (Acts 7:2) In fact, that man was an alien resident in the Promised Land. Abraham had neither a temple nor the Mosaic Law. How could anyone insist that faithfulness to God must always depend on such arrangements?

[12] Abraham's descendant Joseph was also highly esteemed by Stephen's audience, but Stephen reminded them that Joseph's own brothers, the fathers of the tribes of Israel, persecuted that righteous man and sold him into slavery. Yet, he became God's instrument for saving Israel from famine. Stephen no doubt saw the clear similarities between Joseph and Jesus Christ, but he held back that comparison in order to keep his audience with him as long as possible.

[13] *The time of Moses.* (*Acts 7:17-43*) Stephen said much about Moses—wisely so, since many members of the Sanhedrin were Sadducees, who rejected all Bible books other than those written by Moses.

IN WHAT SENSE A "MARTYR"?

The English word "martyr" is derived from the Greek term *mar′tys,* meaning "witness" —that is, one who observes a deed or event. But the Greek word means more than that. The Biblical *mar′tys* is also "active," states one Greek lexicon, "called upon to tell what he has seen and heard, to proclaim what he knows." All true Christians have the obligation to bear witness to what they know about Jehovah and his purposes. (Luke 24:48; Acts 1:8) The Scriptures call Stephen a "witness" for speaking about Jesus.—Acts 22:20, *Kingdom Interlinear.*

Christian witnessing often means facing opposition, arrest, beatings, and even death. Thus, from as early as the second century C.E., "martyr" also came to signify one who suffers such consequences rather than renounce his faith. It is in this sense that Stephen may be called the first Christian martyr. Originally, though, a person was considered a "martyr" because he witnessed, not because he died.

11, 12. (a) How did Stephen make effective use of Abraham's example? (b) Why was Joseph relevant to Stephen's speech?

13. How did the discussion about Moses answer the charges against Stephen, and what theme did this help to develop?

Remember, too, the charge that Stephen had blasphemed Moses. Stephen's words answered that charge directly, for he showed that he had the greatest respect for Moses and for the Law. (Acts 7:38) He noted that Moses too was faced with rejection by those whom he endeavored to save. They rejected him when he was 40 years old. Over 40 years later, they challenged his leadership on a number of occasions.* Stephen thus steadily developed a key theme: God's people repeatedly rejected those whom Jehovah had appointed to lead them.

¹⁴ Stephen reminded his audience that Moses had foretold that a prophet like Moses would arise from Israel. Who would that be, and how would he be received? Stephen saved the answers for his conclusion. He made another key point: Moses had learned that any ground can be made holy, as in the case of the ground at the burning bush, where Jehovah had spoken to him. So, can worship of Jehovah be limited or confined to a single building, such as the temple in Jerusalem? Let us see.

¹⁵ *The tabernacle and the temple.* (*Acts 7:44-50*) Stephen reminded the court that before there was any temple in Jerusalem, God had Moses construct a tabernacle—a movable, tentlike structure for worship. Who would dare to argue that the tabernacle was inferior to the temple, since Moses himself had worshipped there?

¹⁶ Later, when Solomon built the temple in Jerusalem, he was inspired to convey a vital lesson in his prayer. As Stephen put it, "the Most High does not dwell in houses made with hands." (Acts 7:48; 2 Chron. 6:18) Jehovah may make use of a temple to further his purposes, but he is not confined to it. Why, then, should his worshippers feel that pure worship depends on a building made by human hands? Stephen brought this argument to a powerful conclusion by quoting the book of Isaiah: "The heaven is my throne, and the earth is my footstool. What sort of house will you build for me? Jehovah says. Or what is the place for my resting? My hand made all these things, did it not?" —Acts 7:49, 50; Isa. 66:1, 2.

¹⁷ As you review Stephen's speech to the Sanhedrin up to this point, would you not agree that he skillfully addressed the attitudes of his accusers? He showed that Jehovah's purpose is progressive and dynamic,

---

* Stephen's speech contains information we can find nowhere else in the Bible, such as facts about Moses' Egyptian education, his age when he first fled Egypt, and the length of his sojourn in Midian.

---

14. The use of Moses' example supported what points in Stephen's speech?

15, 16. (a) Why was the tabernacle important to the argument Stephen was developing? (b) How did Stephen use Solomon's temple in his discussion?

17. How had Stephen's speech (a) addressed the attitudes of his hearers and (b) responded to the charges against him?

not static and tradition-bound. Those who were mired in reverence for that lovely building in Jerusalem and for the customs and traditions that had grown up around the Mosaic Law had missed the whole purpose behind the Law and the temple! Indirectly, Stephen's speech raised the vital question: Do you not honor the Law and the temple best by obeying Jehovah? Really, Stephen's words provided an excellent defense of his own actions, for he had obeyed Jehovah as best he could.

[18] What can we learn from Stephen's speech? He was thoroughly familiar with the Scriptures. Likewise, we need to be serious students of God's Word if we are to handle "the word of the truth aright." (2 Tim. 2: 15) We can also learn about graciousness and tact from Stephen. His audience could hardly have been more hostile! Yet, for as long as possible, he maintained common ground with them by dwelling on things that those men held in high regard. He also addressed them with respect, calling the older men "fathers." (Acts 7:2) We too need to present the truths of God's Word with "a mild temper and deep respect."—1 Pet. 3:15.

[19] However, we do not hold back from sharing the truths of God's Word for fear of offending people; nor do we soften Jehovah's judgment messages. Stephen is a case in point. He could no doubt see that all the evidence that he had laid before the Sanhedrin had little effect on those hardhearted judges. So, moved by holy spirit, he concluded his talk by fearlessly showing them that they were just like their forefathers who had rejected Joseph, Moses, and all the prophets. (Acts 7:51-53) In fact, these judges of the Sanhedrin had murdered the Messiah, whose very coming Moses and all the prophets had foretold. Really, they had transgressed the Mosaic Law in the worst possible way!

"Lord Jesus, Receive My Spirit" (Acts 7:54–8:3)

[20] The undeniable truth of Stephen's words filled those judges with rage. Losing any semblance of dignity, they gnashed their teeth at Stephen. That faithful man must have seen that he would receive no mercy, any more than had his Master, Jesus.

[21] Stephen needed courage to face what lay ahead, and he no doubt received much encouragement from the vision that Jehovah then kindly granted him. Stephen saw God's glory, and he saw Jesus standing at His Father's right hand! As Stephen described the vision, his judges put their hands over their ears. Why? Earlier, Jesus had told

---

18. In what ways should we try to imitate Stephen?

19. How did Stephen courageously deliver Jehovah's judgment message to the Sanhedrin?

20, 21. How did the Sanhedrin react to Stephen's words, and how did Jehovah strengthen him?

that same court that he was the Messiah and that he would soon be at his Father's right hand. (Mark 14:62) Stephen's vision proved that Jesus spoke the truth. That Sanhedrin had, in fact, betrayed and murdered the Messiah! With one accord, they rushed to have Stephen stoned to death.*

22 Stephen died in much the same way his Master had died, with a heart at peace, full of trust in Jehovah and forgiveness for his killers. He said, "Lord Jesus, receive my spirit," perhaps because he could still see in vision the Son of man with His Father. No doubt, Stephen knew Jesus' encouraging words: "I am the resurrection and the life." (John 11:25) Finally, Stephen prayed directly to God in a loud voice: "Jehovah, do not charge this sin against them." After saying this, he fell asleep in death.—Acts 7:59, 60.

23 Stephen thus became the first martyr on record among Christ's followers. (See the box "In What Sense a 'Martyr,'?" on page 48.) Sadly, though, he would hardly be the last. Right down to our day, some faithful servants of Jehovah have been put to death by religious fanatics, political zealots, and other vicious opposers. Still, we have reason to be just as confident as Stephen was. Jesus is reigning as King now, wielding the marvelous power his Father has granted him. Nothing will prevent him from resurrecting his faithful followers.—John 5:28, 29.

24 Observing all of this was a young man named Saul. He approved of Stephen's murder, even watching over the garments of those casting the stones. Shortly thereafter, he spearheaded a wave of vicious persecution. But the death of Stephen would cast a long shadow. His example would only strengthen other Christians to remain faithful and achieve a similar victory. Furthermore, Saul—in later years most often called Paul—would come to look back on his role in Stephen's death with profound regret. (Acts 22:20) He had helped to put Stephen to death, but he would later come to realize: "I was a blasphemer and a persecutor and an insolent man." (1 Tim. 1:13) Clearly, Paul never forgot Stephen and the powerful speech he gave that day. In fact, some of Paul's speeches and writings developed themes touched on in Stephen's speech. (Acts 7:48; 17:24; Heb. 9:24) In time, Paul fully learned to follow the example of faith and courage set by Stephen, a man "full of graciousness and power." The question is, Will we?

---

* It is doubtful that the Sanhedrin had the authority under Roman law to order an execution. (John 18:31) At any rate, Stephen's death seems to have been a murder carried out by an enraged mob, rather than a judicial act.

22, 23. Stephen's death was like that of his Master in what ways, and how can Christians today be as confident as Stephen was?

24. How did Saul contribute to the martyrdom of Stephen, and what were some long-term effects of that faithful man's death?

CHAPTER 7

Declaring "the Good News About Jesus"

Philip sets an example as an evangelizer

Based on Acts 8:4-40

A WAVE of bitter persecution has struck, and Saul begins to "deal outrageously" with the congregation—an expression that in the original language describes brutal cruelty. (Acts 8:3) The disciples flee, and it may seem to some that Saul's goal of snuffing out Christianity will be realized. However, something unexpected results from the dispersion of Christians. What is it?

[2] Those who are scattered begin "declaring the good news of the word" in the lands to which they have fled. (Acts 8:4) Just imagine! Not only has persecution failed to silence the good news but it has actually helped to spread the message! By scattering the disciples, the persecutors have unwittingly enabled the Kingdom-preaching work to expand into far-flung territories. As we will see, something similar has happened in modern times.

"Those Who Had Been Scattered" (Acts 8:4-8)

[3] One of "those who had been scattered" was Philip.* (Acts 8:4; see the box "Philip 'the Evangelizer,'" on page 53.) He went to Samaria, a city that was largely untouched by the preaching work, for Jesus had at one time instructed the apostles: "Do not enter into a Samaritan city; but, instead, go continually to the lost sheep of the house of Israel." (Matt. 10:5, 6) However, Jesus knew that, in time, Samaria would receive a thorough witness, for prior to his ascension to heaven, he said: "You will be witnesses of me both in Jerusalem and in all Judea and Samaria and to the most distant part of the earth."—Acts 1:8.

---

* This is not the apostle Philip. Rather, it is the Philip who, as noted in Chapter 5 of this book, was among the "seven certified men" appointed to organize the daily distribution of food among the Greek-speaking and the Hebrew-speaking Christian widows in Jerusalem.—Acts 6:1-6.

1, 2. How did efforts to silence the good news have the opposite effect in the first century?

3. (a) Who is Philip? (b) Why was Samaria largely untouched by the preaching work, and yet what had Jesus foretold would happen to that territory?

⁴ Philip found that Samaria was "white for harvesting." (John 4:35) His message was a breath of fresh air to those living there, and it is easy to see why. The Jews had no dealings with Samaritans, many even showing disdain for them. In contrast, the Samaritans found that the message of the good news ignored class distinctions, and thus it differed greatly from the narrow-minded thinking of the Pharisees. By zealously and impartially witnessing to the Samaritans, Philip showed that he was not tainted by the prejudice of those who looked down on them. It is hardly surprising, then, that crowds of Samaritans listened to Philip "with one accord."—Acts 8:6.

⁵ Today, as in the first century, persecution of God's people has not silenced their preaching. Time and again, forcing Christians to move from one place to another—either prison or another land—has only helped to introduce the Kingdom message to people in the new location. For instance, during World War II, Jehovah's Witnesses were able to give an outstanding witness in Nazi concentration camps. A Jew who

---

4. How do the Samaritans respond to Philip's preaching, and what factor may have contributed to their reaction?

5-7. Give examples of how the dispersion of Christians has led to the spread of the good news.

PHILIP "THE EVANGELIZER"

When Christ's followers were scattered because of persecution, Philip went to Samaria. Evidently, he worked in close cooperation with the first-century governing body, for "when the apostles in Jerusalem heard that Samaria had accepted the word of God, they dispatched Peter and John to them." The result was that the new believers there received the free gift of holy spirit.—Acts 8:14-17.

After the events recorded in Acts chapter 8, Philip is mentioned just once more. Some 20 years after Philip's initial preaching, the apostle Paul and his traveling companions were making their way to Jerusalem at the end of Paul's third missionary journey. The group disembarked at Ptolemais. "The next day," recounts Luke, "we set out and arrived in Caesarea, and we entered into the house of Philip the evangelizer, who was one of the seven men, and we stayed with him. This man had four daughters, virgins, that prophesied."—Acts 21:8, 9.

Apparently, Philip had settled in his preaching territory and was a family man. The fact that Luke refers to him as "the evangelizer" is significant. The Scriptures use this term to describe those who left their homes to preach the good news in unworked areas. Obviously, then, Philip's zeal for the ministry remained strong. And the fact that he had four daughters who prophesied surely indicates that Philip taught his family to love and serve Jehovah.

"Now when Simon saw that through the laying on of the hands of the apostles the spirit was given, he offered them money."
—Acts 8:18

encountered the Witnesses there relates: "The fortitude of prisoners who were Jehovah's Witnesses convinced me that their faith was based on the Scriptures—and I became a Witness myself."

6 In some cases, even persecutors received a witness and responded to it. For example, when a Witness named Franz Desch was transferred to the Gusen concentration camp in Austria, he was able to study the Bible with an SS officer. Imagine their joy when years later the two men were reunited at a convention of Jehovah's Witnesses and *both* were proclaimers of the good news!

7 Something similar happened when persecution caused Christians to flee from one country to another. In the 1970's, for example, a great witness was given in Mozambique when Malawian Witnesses were forced to flee there. Even when opposition later arose in Mozambique, the preaching work went on. "True, some of us were apprehended and arrested a number of times for our preaching activity," says Francisco Coana. "Yet, when many responded to the Kingdom message, we were confident that God was helping us, just as he helped first-century Christians."

8 Of course, persecution has not been the only reason for the growth of Christianity in foreign territories. In recent decades, political and economic changes have also opened up opportunities for the Kingdom message to spread to people of many languages and national groups. Some from war zones and economically depressed areas have fled to more stable places and have begun to study the Bible in the land to which they have relocated. An influx of refugees has caused foreign-speaking territories to open up. In one city—San Diego, California, U.S.A.—more than a hundred languages are spoken, and many foreign-language congregations of Jehovah's Witnesses have been established there. Are you striving to witness to people "out of all nations and tribes and peoples and tongues" in your territory?—Rev. 7:9.

"Give Me Also This Authority" (Acts 8:9-25)

9 Philip performed many signs in Samaria. For example, he healed those with disabilities and even cast out wicked spirits. (Acts 8:6-8) One man was particularly impressed with Philip's miraculous gifts. He was Simon, a magician who was so highly regarded that people said of him: "This man is the Power of God." Simon was now an eyewitness to the *real* power of God, as evidenced in the miracles performed by Philip, and Simon became a believer. (Acts 8:9-13) Later, though, Simon's motives were tested. How?

---

8. How have political and economic changes had an impact on the preaching work?
9. Who was Simon, and what evidently drew him to Philip?

¹⁰ When the apostles became aware of the increase that was taking place in Samaria, they sent Peter and John there. (See the box "Peter Uses the 'Keys of the Kingdom,'" on this page.) Upon arriving, the two apostles laid their hands on the new disciples, whereupon each one received the holy spirit.* When Simon saw this, he was intrigued. "Give me also this authority," he told the apostles, "that anyone upon whom I lay my hands may receive holy spirit." Simon even offered them money, hoping to buy this sacred privilege!—Acts 8:14-19.

¹¹ Peter's reply to Simon was firm. "May your silver perish with you," said the apostle, "because you thought through money to get possession of the free gift of God. You have neither part nor lot in this matter, for your heart is not straight in the sight of God." Peter then urged Simon to repent and to pray for forgiveness. "Supplicate Jehovah," said Peter, "that, if possible, the device of your heart ["this scheme of yours," *New Jerusalem Bible*] may be forgiven you." Evidently, Simon was not a wicked man; he *wanted* to do what was right, but he was momentarily misguided. So he pleaded with the apostles: "You men, make supplica-

---

* Evidently, new disciples at that time were usually anointed by, or received, holy spirit at their baptism. This put them in line for the future hope of ruling as kings and priests with Jesus in heaven. (2 Cor. 1:21, 22; Rev. 5:9, 10; 20:6) However, in this particular case, the new disciples were not anointed at baptism. *Receiving* the holy spirit—and the miraculous gifts that were associated with it—took place only after Peter and John laid their hands on the newly baptized Christians.

---

10. (a) What did Peter and John do in Samaria? (b) What did Simon do upon seeing that new disciples received the holy spirit when Peter and John laid their hands on them?

11. What admonition does Peter give to Simon, and how does Simon respond?

PETER USES THE "KEYS OF THE KINGDOM"

Jesus told Peter: "I will give you the keys of the kingdom of the heavens." (Matt. 16:19) What did Jesus mean? His reference to "keys" indicated that Peter would open up knowledge and opportunities for distinct groups to enter the Messianic Kingdom. On what occasions did Peter use these keys?

• Peter used the first key at Pentecost 33 C.E. when he urged *Jews and Jewish proselytes* to repent and be baptized. Some 3,000 did so and became prospective heirs of the Kingdom.—Acts 2:1-41.

• The second key was used not long after the martyrdom of Stephen. In this instance, Peter and John laid their hands upon recently baptized *Samaritans*, after which these new converts received holy spirit.—Acts 8:14-17.

• Peter used the third key in 36 C.E. In that year, he extended the hope of the heavenly inheritance to uncircumcised *Gentiles*. This occurred when the apostle gave a witness to Cornelius, the first uncircumcised Gentile to become a Christian disciple.—Acts 10:1-48.

tion for me to Jehovah that none of the things you have said may come upon me."—Acts 8:20-24.

¹² The rebuke that Peter gave Simon stands as a warning to Christians today. In fact, the English word "simony" was coined as a result of this incident. "Simony" refers to the buying or selling of positions, specifically in a religious context. The history of apostate Christendom is rife with examples of this practice. Indeed, the ninth edition of *The Encyclopædia Britannica* (1878) noted: "A study of the history of the Papal conclaves leaves the student with the conviction that no election untainted by simony has ever yet been made, while in a great number of instances the simony practised in the conclave has been of the grossest, most shameless, and most overt kind."

¹³ Christians must guard against the sin of simony. For instance, they should not try to gain favors by showering generous gifts or excessive praise on those who appear able to grant individuals added privileges in the congregation. On the other hand, those who are thought to be in a position to grant favors should be on guard against showing favoritism toward wealthy ones. Both situations involve simony. Really, all of God's servants should conduct themselves as 'lesser ones,' waiting on Jehovah's spirit to make appointments to privileges of service. (Luke 9:48) There is no place in God's organization for those who try to "search out their own glory."—Prov. 25:27.

A "EUNUCH" IN WHAT SENSE?

The Greek term *eu·nou'khos,* rendered "eunuch," can refer either to a man deprived of his ability to procreate or simply to a high-ranking court official. Court officials who oversaw the harem of a king may actually have been castrated, but emasculation was not a requirement for other officials, such as a king's cupbearer or treasury overseer. The Ethiopian eunuch whom Philip baptized was evidently that type of official, for he oversaw a royal treasury. In effect, he was a minister of finance.

The Ethiopian was also a proselyte—that is, a non-Jew who had embraced the worship of Jehovah. Indeed, he had just been to Jerusalem to worship. (Acts 8:27) Because of this, we can conclude that the Ethiopian could not have been a eunuch in the literal sense, for the Mosaic Law forbade castrated men from becoming part of the congregation of Israel.—Deut. 23:1.

"Do You Actually Know What You Are Reading?" (Acts 8:26-40)

¹⁴ Jehovah's angel now instructed Philip to travel along the road leading from Jerusalem to Gaza. Any question in Philip's mind as to why he should go there was answered soon after he encountered an Ethiopian

12. What is "simony," and how has it proved to be a snare in Christendom?

13. In what ways must Christians be on guard against simony?

14, 15. (a) Who was the "Ethiopian eunuch," and how did Philip locate him? (b) How did the Ethiopian man respond to Philip's message, and why was his baptism not an impulsive act? (See footnote.)

eunuch who was "reading aloud the prophet Isaiah." (See the box "A 'Eunuch' in What Sense?" on page 57.) Jehovah's holy spirit moved Philip to approach the man's chariot. "Do you actually know what you are reading?" he asked the Ethiopian while running beside the chariot. "How could I ever do so," the Ethiopian replied, "unless someone guided me?"—Acts 8:26-31.

¹⁵ The Ethiopian invited Philip into the chariot. Just imagine the discussion that followed! The identity of the "sheep," or "servant," of Isaiah's prophecy had long been a mystery. (Isa. 53:1-12) Yet, as they traveled on, Philip explained to the Ethiopian eunuch that this prophecy was fulfilled in Jesus Christ. Like those who were baptized at Pentecost 33 C.E., the Ethiopian—who was already a Jewish proselyte—immediately knew what he should do. "Look!" he said to Philip. "A body of water; what prevents me from getting baptized?" The Ethiopian was baptized by Philip without delay!* (See the box "Baptism in 'a Body of Water.'") Afterward, Philip was led to a new assignment in Ashdod, where he continued declaring the good news.—Acts 8:32-40.

¹⁶ Christians today are privileged to share in work like that done by Philip. Often, they are able to present the Kingdom message to those they meet in informal settings, such as when traveling. In many cases, it is apparent that their meeting up with an honesthearted individual is no coincidence. This is to be expected, for the Bible makes clear that the angels are directing the preaching work so that the message reaches "every nation and tribe and tongue and people." (Rev. 14:6) Angelic direction in the preaching work is precisely what Jesus foretold.

BAPTISM IN "A BODY OF WATER"

How is Christian baptism performed? Some believe that it is sufficient to pour or sprinkle water on a person's head. However, the Ethiopian eunuch was baptized in "a body of water." The account says: "They both *went down into* the water, both Philip and the eunuch." (Acts 8:36, 38) If pouring or sprinkling water was all that was needed, it would not have been necessary for the eunuch to halt his chariot at a body of water. Even a minimal amount of water, such as that contained in a skin bottle, would have been enough. In fact, he probably had such a bottle because he was traveling on "a desert road."—Acts 8:26.

According to *A Greek-English Lexicon,* by Liddell and Scott, the Greek word *bapti′zo*—from which the English "baptize" is derived—means "to dip, to plunge." Biblical references to baptism harmonize with this definition. John 3:23 states that John "was baptizing in Aenon near Salim, because there was a *great quantity* of water there." Likewise, the account of Jesus' baptism says: "On *coming up out of the water* [Jesus] saw the heavens being parted." (Mark 1:9, 10) So true Christians are appropriately baptized by complete immersion in water.

---

* This was not an impulsive act. Since he was a Jewish proselyte, the Ethiopian already had a knowledge of the Scriptures, including the Messianic prophecies. Now that he had information about Jesus' role in God's purpose, he could get baptized without delay.

16, 17. How are angels involved in the preaching work today?

"God, whoever you are, please help me"

In his illustration about the wheat and weeds, Jesus said that during the harvesttime—the conclusion of the system of things—"the reapers are angels." He added that these spirit creatures would "collect out from his kingdom all things that cause stumbling and persons who are doing lawlessness." (Matt. 13:37-41) At the same time, the angels would gather prospective heavenly heirs of the Kingdom—and later "a great crowd" of "other sheep"—whom Jehovah wants to draw to his organization.—Rev. 7:9; John 6:44, 65; 10:16.

[17] As evidence that this is taking place, some of those whom we approach in our ministry say that they had been praying for spiritual guidance. Consider one experience in which two Kingdom publishers were accompanied by a small child. At the end of the morning, the two Witnesses were about to stop their preaching work, but the child was unusually eager to go to the next home. In fact, he went by himself and knocked on the door! When a young lady opened the door, the two adult Witnesses approached to talk to her. To their surprise, the woman explained that she had just been praying for someone to call on her to help her understand the Bible. A Bible study was arranged!

[18] As a member of the Christian congregation, you have the privilege of working along with the angels as the modern-day preaching work takes place on an unprecedented scale. Never take that privilege for granted. By persevering in your efforts, you will find great joy as you continue to declare "the good news about Jesus."—Acts 8:35.

---

18. Why should we never take our ministry for granted?

CHAPTER 8

The Congregation "Entered Into a Period of Peace"

The vicious persecutor Saul becomes a zealous minister

Based on Acts 9:1-43

THE grim travelers are approaching Damascus, where they intend to carry out an evil plan. They will tear the hated disciples of Jesus from their homes, bind them, humiliate them, and drag them to Jerusalem to face the wrath of the Sanhedrin.

[2] The mob leader, named Saul, already has blood on his hands.* Recently, he watched with approval as fellow zealots stoned to death Stephen, a devout disciple of Jesus. (Acts 7:57–8:1) Not content with raging against the followers of Jesus who live in Jerusalem, Saul becomes a firebrand ready to spread the flames of persecution. He wants to eradicate the pestilent sect known as "The Way."—Acts 9:1, 2; see the box "Saul's Mandate in Damascus," on page 61.

[3] Suddenly, a brilliant light engulfs Saul. His traveling companions see the light but are speechless with shock. Saul, struck blind, collapses. Unable to see, Saul hears a voice from heaven say: "Saul, Saul, why are you persecuting me?" Stunned, Saul asks: "Who are you, Lord?" The answer Saul receives must strike him to the very core: "I am Jesus, whom you are persecuting."—Acts 9:3-5; 22:9.

[4] What can we learn from Jesus' initial words to Saul? How can we benefit from reviewing the events surrounding the conversion of Saul? And what lessons can we draw from the way the congregation used the period of peace that settled in after Saul's conversion?

"Why Are You Persecuting Me?" (Acts 9:1-5)

[5] When Jesus stopped Saul on the road to Damascus, He did not ask: "Why are you persecuting my disciples?" As noted above, he said:

---

* See the box "Saul the Pharisee," on page 62.

1, 2. What did Saul intend to do in Damascus?

3, 4. (a) What happened to Saul? (b) What questions will we consider?

5, 6. What can we learn from Jesus' words to Saul?

"Why are you persecuting *me?*" (Acts 9:4) Yes, Jesus personally feels the trials experienced by his followers.—Matt. 25:34-40, 45.

⁶ If you are being oppressed because of your faith in Christ, be assured that both Jehovah and Jesus are aware of your situation. (Matt. 10:22, 28-31) At present, the trial may not be removed. Remember, Jesus watched Saul's involvement in Stephen's death, and He saw Saul drag faithful disciples from their homes in Jerusalem. (Acts 8:3) Yet, Jesus did not intervene at that time. Even so, Jehovah, through Christ, gave Stephen and the other disciples the strength they needed to remain faithful.

⁷ You too can endure persecution if you do the following: (1) Resolve to remain loyal, come what may. (2) Ask for Jehovah's help. (Phil. 4:6, 7) (3) Leave vengeance in Jehovah's hands. (Rom. 12:17-21) (4) Trust that Jehovah will provide you with the strength to endure until he sees fit to remove the trial.—Phil. 4:12, 13.

"Saul, Brother, the Lord . . . Has Sent Me Forth" (Acts 9:6-17)

⁸ After answering Saul's question, "Who are you, Lord?" Jesus said to him: "Rise and enter into the city, and what you must do will be told you." (Acts 9:6) The sightless Saul was led to his lodgings in Damascus, where he fasted and prayed for three days. Meanwhile, Jesus spoke about Saul to a disciple in that city, a man named Ananias, who was "well reported on by all the Jews" dwelling in Damascus.—Acts 22:12.

⁹ Think of the mixed emotions Ananias must have felt! Here, the Head of the congregation, the resurrected Jesus Christ, was speaking to him personally, singling him out for a special assignment. What an honor, but what an assignment! When told that he must speak to Saul, Ananias responded: "Lord, I have heard from many about this man, how

---

7. What must you do in order to endure persecution?

8, 9. How might Ananias have felt about his assignment?

SAUL'S MANDATE IN DAMASCUS

How did Saul get authority to arrest Christians in a foreign city? The Sanhedrin and the high priest exercised moral authority over Jews everywhere, and the high priest's powers apparently included authority to extradite criminals. Thus, letters from the high priest would elicit the cooperation of the elders of the Damascus synagogues.—Acts 9:1, 2.

The Romans, moreover, had granted the Jews the right to manage their own judicial affairs. This explains how five times the Jews could inflict "forty strokes less one" on the apostle Paul. (2 Cor. 11:24) The book of 1 Maccabees also mentions a letter written by a Roman consul to Ptolemy VIII of Egypt in 138 B.C.E. that demanded: "If any pestilent men have fled to you from their country [Judaea], hand them over to Simon the high priest, that he may punish them according to their law." (1 Macc. 15:21) In 47 B.C.E., Julius Caesar confirmed the privileges previously granted to the high priest along with his right to settle any questions that arose over Jewish customs.

many injurious things he did to your holy ones in Jerusalem. And here he has authority from the chief priests to put in bonds all those calling upon your name."—Acts 9:13, 14.

[10] Jesus did not reprove Ananias for expressing his concern. However, Jesus did provide him with clear direction. And He dignified him by telling him the reason why He wanted him to perform this unusual task. Jesus said of Saul: "This man is a chosen vessel to me to bear my name to the nations as well as to kings and the sons of Israel. For I shall show him plainly how many things he must suffer for my name." (Acts 9:15, 16) Ananias promptly obeyed Jesus. He sought out the per-

---

10. What do we learn about Jesus from the way he dealt with Ananias?

SAUL THE PHARISEE

The "young man called Saul" who appears in the Acts account at the stoning of Stephen was from Tarsus. It was the capital of the Roman province of Cilicia, in the south of modern-day Turkey. (Acts 7:58) A sizable Jewish community dwelled in that city. According to his own writings, Saul was "circumcised the eighth day, out of the family stock of Israel, of the tribe of Benjamin, a Hebrew born from Hebrews; as respects law, a Pharisee." That was viewed as an impeccable Jewish pedigree! —Phil. 3:5.

Saul's home was in a large, prosperous trading city, a center of Greek culture. Growing up in Tarsus, Saul knew Greek. It is likely that he would have received his primary education in a Jewish school. Saul learned to be a tentmaker, a skill typical of his native area. In all probability, while still a youth, Saul acquired this trade from his father.—Acts 18:2, 3.

The Acts account also reveals that Saul was born a Roman citizen. (Acts 22:25-28) This means that one of his forebears had already acquired that distinction. How Saul's family obtained Roman citizenship is unknown. Whatever the case, that privilege would place them among the social elite of their province. Saul's background and education, then, gave him a firm foothold in three different cultures —Jewish, Greek, and Roman.

Likely, when he was no older than 13, Saul moved 520 miles to Jerusalem to continue his education. In that city, Saul studied at the feet of Gamaliel, a highly esteemed teacher in the Pharisaic tradition.—Acts 22:3.

These additional studies, comparable to going to a university today, would consist of instruction in and memorization of both Scripture and Jewish oral law. A successful student of Gamaliel would have a promising career before him, and apparently Saul was just such a student. He later wrote: "I was making greater progress in Judaism than many of my own age in my race, as I was far more zealous for the traditions of my fathers." (Gal. 1:14) Of course, Saul's zeal for Jewish tradition was what turned him into a notorious persecutor of the fledgling Christian congregation.

secutor Saul and said to him: "Saul, brother, the Lord, the Jesus that appeared to you on the road over which you were coming, has sent me forth, in order that you may recover sight and be filled with holy spirit."—Acts 9:17.

[11] Several facts become evident from the events involving Jesus, Ananias, and Saul. For example, Jesus plays an active role in directing the preaching work, just as he promised he would. (Matt. 28:20) Although he does not speak directly to individuals today, Jesus does direct the preaching work by means of the faithful slave class, whom he has now appointed over all his belongings. (Matt. 24:45-47) The slave class, represented by its Governing Body, sends out publishers, pioneers, and missionaries to find those who want to know more about Christ. As mentioned in the preceding chapter, many of such ones have prayed for guidance and have then been contacted by Jehovah's Witnesses.—Acts 9:11.

[12] Ananias obediently accepted an assignment and was blessed. Do you obey the command to bear thorough witness, even if the assignment causes you some apprehension? For some, going from house to house and meeting strangers can cause anxiety. Others find it a challenge to preach to people at their places of business, on the street, or via telephone. Ananias overcame his fear and had the honor of helping Saul receive the holy spirit.* Ananias was successful because he trusted Jesus and he viewed Saul as his brother. We can overcome our fears if, like Ananias, we trust that Jesus is directing the preaching work, we have empathy for people, and we view even the most intimidating individuals as our potential brothers.—Matt. 9:36.

"He Began to Preach Jesus" (Acts 9:18-30)

[13] Saul acted swiftly on what he learned. After he was healed, he submitted to baptism and began associating closely with the disciples in Damascus. But he did more. "Immediately in the synagogues he began to preach Jesus, that this One is the Son of God."—Acts 9:20.

[14] If you are studying the Bible but are not yet baptized, will you be like Saul and act decisively on what you learn? Granted, Saul

---

* As a general rule, the gifts of the holy spirit were passed on through the apostles. In this unusual situation, however, it appears that Jesus authorized Ananias to transmit the gifts of the spirit to His "chosen vessel," Saul. After his conversion, Saul was separated for a considerable time from contact with the 12 apostles. However, it is likely that he was active throughout that period. So Jesus apparently saw to it that Saul had the power he needed in order to carry out his preaching assignment.

11, 12. What do we learn from the events involving Jesus, Ananias, and Saul?

13, 14. If you are studying the Bible but are not yet baptized, what can you learn from Saul's example?

witnessed firsthand a miracle performed by Christ, and this no doubt helped to motivate him to action. But others also witnessed miracles performed by Jesus. For instance, one group of Pharisees watched as he cured a man's withered hand, and a large number of the Jews in general knew that Jesus raised Lazarus from the dead. Yet, many of them remained apathetic, even antagonistic. (Mark 3:1-6; John 12:9, 10) By contrast, Saul was transformed. Why did Saul respond when others failed to do so? Because he feared God more than man and he deeply appreciated the mercy Christ had shown to him. (Phil. 3:8) If you respond similarly, you will let nothing stop you from joining in the preaching work and from becoming qualified for baptism.

¹⁵ Can you picture the surprise, shock, and anger that must have rippled through the crowds when Saul began to preach about Jesus in the synagogues? "Is this not the man that ravaged those in Jerusalem who call upon this name?" they asked. (Acts 9:21) When explaining his change of heart about Jesus, Saul "proved logically that this is the Christ." (Acts 9:22) But logic is not a universal key. It cannot unlock every mind shackled by tradition or every heart bound by pride. Still, Saul did not give up.

¹⁶ Three years later, the Jews in Damascus were still contending with Saul. Finally, they sought to kill him. (Acts 9:23; 2 Cor. 11:32, 33; Gal. 1: 13-18) When the plot became known, Saul chose the discreet course and left the city by allowing himself to be lowered in a basket through an opening in the city wall. Luke describes those who helped Saul escape that night as being "his [Saul's] disciples." (Acts 9:25) This wording seems to indicate that at least some who heard Saul speak in Damascus responded to his preaching and became followers of Christ.

¹⁷ When you first started to tell your family, friends, and others about the good things you were learning, you may have expected that everyone would accept the sheer logic of Bible truth. Some may have done so, whereas many did not. Indeed, members of your own household may have treated you as an enemy. (Matt. 10:32-38) However, if you continue to improve in your ability to reason from the Scriptures and if you maintain Christian conduct, even those who oppose you might eventually have a change of heart.—Acts 17:2; 1 Pet. 2:12; 3:1, 2, 7.

¹⁸ When Saul entered Jerusalem, the disciples were understandably

---

15, 16. What did Saul do in the synagogues, and how did the Jews in Damascus respond?

17. (a) In what ways do people respond to Bible truth? (b) What should we continue to do, and why?

18, 19. (a) When Barnabas vouched for Saul, what was the effect? (b) How can we imitate Barnabas and Saul?

skeptical of his claims that he was now a disciple. However, when Barnabas vouched for Saul, the apostles accepted him, and he remained with them for a time. (Acts 9:26-28) Saul was discreet, but he was not ashamed of the good news. (Rom. 1:16) He boldly preached in Jerusalem, the very place from which he had launched vicious persecution against the disciples of Jesus Christ. To their horror, the Jews in Jerusalem realized that their champion had defected, and they now sought to kill him. "When the brothers detected this," states the account, "they brought [Saul] down to Caesarea and sent him off to Tarsus." (Acts 9: 30) Saul submitted to Jesus' direction as expressed through the congregation. Both Saul and the congregation benefited.

[19] Notice that Barnabas took the initiative to assist Saul. No doubt this kind act helped to foster the warm friendship that developed between these zealous servants of Jehovah. Do you, like Barnabas, willingly assist new ones in the congregation, working with them in the field service and helping them to progress spiritually? You will be richly rewarded if you do. If you are a new publisher of the good news, do you, like Saul, accept the help that is offered to you? By working along with more experienced publishers, you will improve in your skill in the ministry, your joy will increase, and you will form bonds of friendship that can last a lifetime.

"Many Became Believers" (Acts 9:31-43)

[20] After Saul's conversion and safe departure, "the congregation throughout the whole of Judea and Galilee and Samaria entered into a period of peace." (Acts 9:31) How did the disciples use this "favorable season"? (2 Tim. 4:2) The account says that they were "being built up." The apostles and other responsible brothers reinforced the faith of the disciples and took the lead as the congregation "walked in the fear of Jehovah and in the comfort of the holy spirit." For example, Peter used the time to strengthen the disciples in the town of Lydda in the Plain of Sharon. His efforts caused many who lived in the vicinity to turn "to the Lord." (Acts 9:32-35) The disciples did not become sidetracked by other pursuits but exerted themselves caring for one another and preaching the good news. The result was that the congregation "kept on multiplying."

[21] Toward the end of the 20th century, Jehovah's Witnesses in many countries entered into a similar "period of peace." Regimes that had oppressed God's people for decades suddenly came to an end, and certain bans on the preaching work were eased or lifted. Tens of thousands of Witnesses seized the opportunity to preach publicly, with spectacular

---

20, 21. How have God's servants past and present made the most of 'periods of peace'?

results. For instance, when Jehovah's Witnesses in Russia received official recognition in 1991, there were fewer than 16,000 Kingdom publishers in that country. Just 16 years later, in 2007, more than 150,000 were zealously preaching the good news.

²² Are you making good use of the freedom you possess? If you live in a country that enjoys religious freedom, Satan would love to induce you to pursue material riches, not Kingdom interests. (Matt. 13:22) Do not be sidetracked. Use productively any periods of relative peace that you may now enjoy. View them as opportunities to bear thorough witness and to build up the congregation. Remember, your circumstances can change abruptly.

²³ Consider what happened to a disciple named Tabitha, or Dorcas. She lived in Joppa, a town not far from Lydda. This faithful sister used her time and assets wisely, abounding "in good deeds and gifts of mercy." Suddenly, though, she fell ill and died.* Her death caused great grief among the disciples in Joppa, especially among the widows who had been touched by her kindness. When Peter arrived at the house where her body was being prepared for burial, he performed a miracle unprecedented among the apostles of Jesus Christ. Peter prayed and then raised Tabitha from the dead! Can you imagine the joy of the widows and other disciples when Peter called them back into the room and presented Tabitha to them alive? How these events must have strengthened them for the trials that lay ahead! Understandably, the miracle "became known throughout all Joppa, and many became believers on the Lord."—Acts 9:36-42.

²⁴ We learn two important points from this heartwarming account involving Tabitha. (1) Life is fleeting. How vital it is, then, that we make a good name with God while we are able to do so! (Eccl. 7:1) (2) The resurrection hope is sure. Jehovah noticed the numerous acts of kindness that Tabitha had performed, and he rewarded her. He will remember our hard

How can you imitate Dorcas?

---

* See the box "Dorcas—'She Abounded in Good Deeds,'" on page 67.

---

22. How can you make the most of the freedom that you possess?

23, 24. (a) What points do we learn from the account involving Tabitha? (b) What should be our resolve?

work and will resurrect us if our life should end before Armageddon. (Heb. 6:10) So whether we are currently enduring a "troublesome season" or are enjoying "a period of peace," let us persevere in bearing thorough witness to Christ.—2 Tim. 4:2.

DORCAS—"SHE ABOUNDED IN GOOD DEEDS"

Dorcas was a member of the Christian congregation in the seaport town of Joppa. Her fellow believers loved her because "she abounded in good deeds and gifts of mercy." (Acts 9:36) Like many Jews who lived in areas having a mixed Jewish and Gentile population, Dorcas had two names—one Hebrew or Aramaic and the other Greek or Latin. Her Greek name, Dorcas, was rendered "Tabitha" in Aramaic. Both names mean "Gazelle."

It appears that Dorcas fell sick and suddenly died. As was the custom, her body was washed in preparation for burial. It was laid out in an upper chamber, possibly in her own house. The hot climate of the Middle East required that burials take place either on the day of a person's death or on the next day. The Christians in Joppa had heard that the apostle Peter was in nearby Lydda. There was enough time for Peter to come to Joppa before Dorcas would have to be buried, since the distance between the two cities was only 11 miles—about a four-hour walk. So the congregation dispatched two men to ask Peter to come without delay. (Acts 9: 37, 38) Says one scholar: "It was a regular practice in early Judaism to send out emissaries in pairs, in part so that one could validate the testimony of the other."

What happened when Peter arrived? The account tells us: "They led him up into the upper chamber; and all the widows presented themselves to him weeping and exhibiting many inner garments and outer garments that Dorcas used to make while she was with them." (Acts 9:39) Among the factors that endeared Dorcas to the members of her congregation was that she was in the habit of sewing for them. She made tunics, worn next to the body, and cloaks or robes, which were worn over the tunic. Whether Dorcas paid for all the material herself or just provided her labor is not stated. In any case, she was loved for her kindness and "gifts of mercy."

What Peter saw in that upper chamber must have moved him. "This was mourning which was far different from that manifested in the house of Jairus with its noisy, hired mourning women and flute-blowers," says scholar Richard Lenski. "This was not such artificial mourning as that." (Matt. 9:23) It was genuine and heartfelt. The fact that no mention is ever made of a husband leads many to conclude that Dorcas was single.

When Jesus commissioned his apostles, he gave them power to "raise up dead persons." (Matt. 10:8) Peter had seen Jesus perform such miracles, including the resurrection of Jairus' daughter, but we have no record prior to this of an apostle performing a resurrection. (Mark 5: 21-24, 35-43) But now Peter put onlookers out of the upper chamber, and then he prayed earnestly, with the result that Tabitha opened her eyes and sat up. What joy there must have been among the Christians in Joppa when Peter was then able to present to the holy ones and the widows their beloved Dorcas—alive!—Acts 9:40-42.

"PEOPLE OF THE NATIONS... RECEIVED THE WORD OF GOD"

ACTS 11:1

Would the Jewish followers of Jesus be willing to preach the good news to uncircumcised Gentiles? In this section, we will see how Jehovah's spirit opened hearts and enabled Christians to overcome prejudice, giving great impetus to the work of bearing witness to all the nations.

CHAPTER 9

"God Is Not Partial"

The preaching work opens up to uncircumcised Gentiles

Based on Acts 10:1–11:30

THE year is 36 C.E. The autumn sun warms Peter as he prays on the flat rooftop of a house near the sea in the harbor city of Joppa. He has been a guest in this home for some days now. His willingness to stay here reveals, to an extent, an unprejudiced attitude. The owner, a certain Simon, is a tanner by trade, and not every Jew would lodge with such a man.* Still, Peter is about to learn a vital lesson regarding Jehovah's impartiality.

2 While Peter is praying, he falls into a trance. What he sees in a vision would disturb any Jew. Descending from heaven is a sheetlike vessel containing animals unclean according to the Law. Told to slaughter and eat, Peter replies: "Never have I eaten anything defiled and unclean." Not once but three times he is told: "You stop calling defiled the things God has cleansed." (Acts 10:14-16) The vision leaves Peter confused but not for long.

3 What did Peter's vision mean? It is important that we grasp its significance, for at the heart of this vision is a profound truth about the way Jehovah views people. As true Christians, we cannot bear thorough witness about God's Kingdom unless we learn to share God's view of people. To unlock the meaning of Peter's vision, let us examine the dramatic events that surrounded it.

Making "Supplication to God Continually" (Acts 10:1-8)

4 Little did Peter know that the preceding day in Caesarea, about 30 miles north, a man named Cornelius had also received a divine vision. Cornelius, a centurion in the Roman army, was "a devout man."#

---

* Some Jews looked down on a tanner because his trade brought him into contact with the hides and carcasses of animals and with the loathsome materials required for his work. Tanners were considered unfit to appear at the temple, and their place of business had to be no less than 50 cubits, or somewhat over 70 feet, from a town. This, in part, may explain why Simon's house was "by the sea."—Acts 10:6.

See the box "Cornelius and the Roman Army," on page 70.

1-3. What vision does Peter receive, and why do we need to grasp its significance?

4, 5. Who was Cornelius, and what happened while he was praying?

He was also an exemplary family man, for he was "one fearing God together with all his household." Cornelius was not a Jewish proselyte; he was an uncircumcised Gentile. Yet, he showed compassion to needy Jews, giving them material help. This sincere man "made supplication to God continually."—Acts 10:2.

5 At about 3:00 p.m., Cornelius was praying when he saw a vision in which an angel told him: "Your prayers and gifts of mercy have ascended as a remembrance before God." (Acts 10:4) As directed by the angel, Cornelius dispatched men to summon the apostle Peter. As an uncircumcised Gentile, Cornelius was about to enter a door that up to then had been closed to him. He was about to receive the message of salvation.

6 Does God answer the prayers of sincere ones today who want to find out the truth about him? Consider an experience. A woman in Albania accepted a copy of The Watchtower containing an article about raising children.* She told the Witness who called at her door: "Would you believe that I was praying to God for help in raising my daughters? He sent you! You touched my heart in the exact spot where I needed it!" The woman and her daughters began studying, and her husband later joined in the study.

7 Is this an isolated example? By no means! This type of experience has been repeated over and over again around the world—far too often to be attributed to mere chance. What, then, can we conclude? First, Jehovah answers the prayers of sincere individuals who search for him. (1 Ki. 8:41-43; Ps. 65:2) Second, we have angelic support for our preaching work.—Rev. 14:6, 7.

* The article, entitled "Reliable Advice for Raising Children," appeared in the November 1, 2006, issue, pages 4 to 7.

CORNELIUS AND THE ROMAN ARMY

Administrative and military headquarters for the Roman province of Judea were located in Caesarea. The troops under the governor's command consisted of 500 to 1,000 cavalry and five cohorts of infantry, the size of which could be varied from 500 to 1,000 soldiers each. These troops were usually recruited from among provincials rather than Roman citizens. Most served in Caesarea, but small garrisons were scattered throughout Judea. One cohort was permanently based in the Tower of Antonia in Jerusalem in order to police the Temple Mount and the city. The Roman presence in that city would be reinforced during Jewish festivals to deal with possible disturbances.

A cohort was divided into six centuries, nominally of 100 men, each commanded by a centurion. The Greek text of Acts 10:1 says that Cornelius was a centurion of the so-called Italian Band, probably based in Caesarea. This unit may have been the Second Italian Cohort of Roman Citizen Volunteers.* Centurions had considerable social and military status, as well as wealth. Their pay was perhaps 16 times that of regular soldiers.

* In Latin, Cohors II Italica voluntariorum civium Romanorum. Its presence in Syria in 69 C.E. is attested.

6, 7. (a) Relate an experience showing that God answers the prayers of sincere ones who want to find out the truth about him. (b) What can we conclude from such experiences?

"Peter Was in Great Perplexity" (Acts 10:9-23a)

8 Still on the rooftop, "Peter was in great perplexity" over the meaning of the vision when messengers from Cornelius approached the house. (Acts 10:17) Would Peter, who had three times said that he would refuse to eat foods considered unclean according to the Law, be willing to go with these men and enter into the home of a Gentile? In some way holy spirit made God's will known in this matter. Peter was told: "Look! Three men are seeking you. However, rise, go downstairs and be on your way with them, not doubting at all, because I have dispatched them." (Acts 10:19, 20) The vision of the sheetlike vessel that Peter had received no doubt prepared him to yield to the leadings of the holy spirit.

9 Learning that Cornelius had been divinely instructed to send for him, Peter invited the Gentile messengers into the house "and entertained them." (Acts 10:23a) The obedient apostle was already adjusting to new developments in the outworking of God's will.

10 To this day, Jehovah leads his people progressively. (Prov. 4:18) By means of his holy spirit, he is guiding "the faithful and discreet slave" and its Governing Body. (Matt. 24:45) At times, we may receive clarifications in our understanding of God's Word or changes in certain organizational procedures. We do well to ask ourselves: 'How do I respond to such refinements? Do I submit to the leadings of God's spirit in these matters?'

Peter "Commanded Them to Be Baptized" (Acts 10:23b-48)

11 The day after his vision, Peter and nine others—the three messengers sent by Cornelius and "six [Jewish] brothers" from Joppa—headed up to Caesarea. (Acts 11:12) Expecting Peter, Cornelius had assembled "his relatives and intimate friends"—evidently all Gentiles. (Acts 10:24) Upon arriving, Peter did something once unthinkable for him: He entered the home of an uncircumcised Gentile! Peter explained: "You well know how unlawful it is for a Jew to join himself to or approach a man of another race; and yet God has shown me I should call no man defiled or unclean." (Acts 10:28) By now Peter had come to discern that the vision he had received was intended to teach a lesson that was not limited to the types of foods one should eat. He should "call no *man* [not even a Gentile] defiled."

8, 9. What did the spirit make known to Peter, and how did he respond?

10. How does Jehovah lead his people, and what questions may we need to ask ourselves?

11, 12. What did Peter do upon arriving in Caesarea, and what had he learned?

[12] A receptive audience awaited Peter. "We are all present before God to hear all the things you have been commanded by Jehovah to say," explained Cornelius. (Acts 10:33) Imagine how you would feel if you heard such words from an interested person! Peter began with this powerful statement: "For a certainty I perceive that God is not partial, but in every nation the man that fears him and works righteousness is acceptable to him." (Acts 10:34, 35) Peter had learned that God's view of people is not determined by race, nationality, or any other external factors. Peter proceeded to bear witness about Jesus' ministry, death, and resurrection.

[13] Something unprecedented now happened: "While Peter was yet speaking," the holy spirit was poured out upon those "people of the nations." (Acts 10:44, 45) This is the only reported case in the Scriptures of the spirit's being poured out *before* baptism. Recognizing this sign of God's approval, Peter "commanded them [that group of Gentiles] to be baptized." (Acts 10:48) The conversion of these Gentiles in 36 C.E. marked the end of the period of special favor to the Jews. (Dan. 9:24-27) Taking the lead on this occasion, Peter used the third and final 'key of the kingdom.' (Matt. 16:19) This key opened the door for uncircumcised Gentiles to become spirit-anointed Christians.

[14] As Kingdom proclaimers today, we recognize that "there is no partiality with God." (Rom. 2:11) It is his will that "all sorts of men should be saved." (1 Tim. 2:4) So we must never judge people on the basis of external characteristics. Our commission is to bear thorough witness about God's Kingdom, and that involves preaching to *all* people, regardless of their race, nationality, appearance, or religious background.

"They Acquiesced, and They Glorified God" (Acts 11:1-18)

[15] No doubt eager to report what had happened, Peter headed for Jerusalem. Evidently, the news that uncircumcised Gentiles had "received the word of God" preceded him. Soon after Peter arrived, "the supporters of circumcision began to contend with him." They were disturbed because he had entered "the house of men that were not circumcised and had eaten with them." (Acts 11:1-3) The issue was not whether Gentiles could become followers of Christ. Rather, those Jewish disciples were really insisting that Gentiles needed to observe the Law—including circumcision—in order to worship Jehovah acceptably.

13, 14. (a) What was significant about the conversion of Cornelius and other Gentiles in 36 C.E.? (b) Why should we not judge people on the basis of external characteristics?

15, 16. Why did some Jewish Christians contend with Peter, and how did he explain his actions?

Clearly, some Jewish disciples had difficulty letting go of the Mosaic Law.

¹⁶ How did Peter explain his actions? According to Acts 11:4-16, he recounted four evidences of heavenly direction: (1) the divine vision he had received (Verses 4-10); (2) the spirit's command (Verses 11, 12); (3) the angel's visit to Cornelius (Verses 13, 14); and (4) the pouring out of the holy spirit upon the Gentiles. (Verses 15, 16) Peter concluded with a most compelling question: "If, therefore, God gave the same free gift [of holy spirit] to them [believing Gentiles] as he also did to us [Jews] who have believed upon the Lord Jesus Christ, who was I that I should be able to hinder God?"—Acts 11:17.

¹⁷ Peter's testimony posed a crucial test for those Jewish Christians. Would they be able to put aside any traces of prejudice and accept the newly baptized Gentiles as their fellow Christians? The account tells us: "Now when they [the apostles and other Jewish Christians] heard these things, they acquiesced, and they glorified God, saying: 'Well, then, God has granted repentance for the purpose of life to people of the nations also.'" (Acts 11:18) That positive attitude preserved the unity of the congregation.

¹⁸ Maintaining unity today can be challenging, for true worshippers have come "out of all nations and tribes and peoples and tongues." (Rev. 7:9) We thus find a diversity of races, cultures, and backgrounds in many congregations. We do well to ask ourselves: 'Have I rooted out of my heart any traces of prejudice? Am I determined never to let this world's divisive traits—including nationalism, tribalism, pride in culture, and racism—influence the way I treat my Christian brothers?' Recall what happened to Peter (Cephas) some years after the conversion of the first Gentiles. Yielding to the prejudice of others, he "went

ANTIOCH OF SYRIA

Antioch of Syria was located on the river Orontes, about 18 miles upstream from the Mediterranean seaport of Seleucia and some 350 miles north of Jerusalem. (Acts 13:4) Seleucus I Nicator, first ruler of the Seleucid Empire, founded Antioch in 300 B.C.E. As the capital of that empire, Antioch soon acquired great importance. In 64 B.C.E., Roman General Pompey made Syria a Roman province, with Antioch as its capital. By the first century C.E., the metropolis ranked third in size and wealth among the cities of the Roman Empire, after Rome and Alexandria.

Antioch was a commercial as well as a political center. The wares of all of Syria passed through it before being exported to the rest of the Mediterranean basin. "Since it was near the frontier between the settled Graeco-Roman area and the eastern states," says one scholar, "it was even more cosmopolitan than most Hellenistic cities." There was a large Jewish community in Antioch, and according to Jewish historian Flavius Josephus, they "made proselytes of a great many of the Greeks" who lived there.

17, 18. (a) Peter's testimony posed what test for Jewish Christians? (b) Why can it be a challenge to preserve the unity of the congregation, and what questions do we do well to ask ourselves?

withdrawing and separating himself" from Gentile Christians and had to be corrected by Paul. (Gal. 2:11-14) Let us keep ever on guard against the snare of prejudice.

"A Great Number . . . Became Believers" (Acts 11:19-26a)

[19] Did Jesus' followers start preaching to uncircumcised Gentiles? Notice what happened later in Antioch of Syria.* This city had a large Jewish community, but there was little hostility between Jews and Gentiles. So Antioch offered a favorable atmosphere for preaching to Gentiles. It was here that some Jewish disciples began declaring the good news to "the Greek-speaking people." (Acts 11:20) This preaching was directed not only to Greek-speaking Jews but also to uncircumcised Gentiles. Jehovah blessed the work, and "a great number . . . became believers."—Acts 11:21.

[20] To care for this ripe field, the Jerusalem congregation sent Barnabas to Antioch. The thriving interest evidently was more than he could handle alone. Who was better suited to help out than Saul, who was to become the apostle to the nations? (Acts 9:15; Rom. 1:5) Would Barnabas see Saul as a rival? On the contrary, Barnabas showed due modesty. He took the initiative to go to Tarsus, look for Saul, and bring him back to Antioch to help. Together they spent a year building up the disciples in the congregation there.—Acts 11:22-26a.

[21] How can we show modesty in fulfilling our ministry? This quality involves acknowledging our limitations. We all have different strengths and abilities. For example, some may be effective in placing literature but have difficulty making return visits or starting Bible studies. If you would like to improve in some aspect of the ministry, why not ask for help? By taking such initiative, you may become more productive and reap greater joy in the ministry.—1 Cor. 9:26.

Sending "a Relief Ministration" (Acts 11:26b-30)

[22] It was first in Antioch that "the disciples were by divine providence called Christians." (Acts 11:26b) That God-approved name aptly describes those whose way of life is modeled on that of Christ. As people of the nations became Christians, did a bond of brotherhood form

---

* See the box "Antioch of Syria," on page 73.

---

19. Jewish Christians in Antioch began preaching to whom, and with what result?

20, 21. How did Barnabas show due modesty, and how can we show similar modesty when fulfilling our ministry?

22, 23. The brothers in Antioch made what expression of brotherly love, and how do God's people today act similarly?

"Cornelius, of course, was expecting them
and had called together his relatives and intimate friends."
—Acts 10:24

between Jewish and Gentile believers? Consider what happened when a great famine occurred about 46 C.E.* In ancient times, famines sorely affected the poor, who had neither reserves of money nor extra food. During this famine, the Jewish Christians living in Judea, many of whom apparently were poor, were in need of provisions. Learning of the need, the brothers in Antioch—including Gentile Christians—sent "a relief ministration" to the brothers in Judea. (Acts 11:29) What a genuine expression of brotherly love!

²³ It is no different among God's people today. When we learn that our brothers—in another land or in our own area—are in need, we willingly reach out to help them. Branch Committees quickly organize the formation of relief committees to look after our brothers who may be affected by natural disasters, including hurricanes, earthquakes, and tsunamis. All such relief efforts demonstrate the genuineness of our brotherhood.—John 13:34, 35; 1 John 3:17.

²⁴ As true Christians, we take to heart the meaning of the vision that Peter received on the rooftop in Joppa over 1,900 years ago. We worship an impartial God. It is his will that we bear thorough witness about his Kingdom, which involves preaching to others regardless of their race, national origin, or social standing. Let us, then, be determined to give all who will listen an opportunity to respond to the good news.—Rom. 10:11-13.

---

* The Jewish historian Josephus refers to this "great famine" during the reign of Emperor Claudius (41-54 C.E.).

---

24. How can we show that we take to heart the meaning of the vision that Peter received?

When our brothers are in need, we willingly reach out to help

CHAPTER 10

"The Word of Jehovah Went On Growing"

Peter is delivered, and persecution fails to stop the spread of the good news

Based on Acts 12:1-25

WITH a resounding clang, the massive iron gate swings shut behind Peter. Shackled between two Roman guards, he is led off to his cell. He then endures long hours, perhaps days, of waiting to learn what is to be done with him. There is little for his gaze to fall on but his prison walls and bars, his chains, and his guards.

² The news, when it comes, is grim. King Herod Agrippa I is determined to see Peter dead.* In fact, Peter is to be presented to the people after the Passover, his death sentence a gift to delight the crowds. This is no empty threat. One of Peter's fellow apostles—James—has recently been executed by this same ruler.

³ It is the evening before the scheduled execution. What is Peter thinking in the gloom of his prison cell? Does he recall that years before, Jesus revealed that Peter would one day be bound and led against his will—to his death? (John 21:18, 19) Perhaps Peter wonders if that time has arrived.

⁴ If you were in Peter's situation, how would you feel? Many would despair, thinking that all hope is lost. For a genuine follower of Jesus Christ, however, is any situation truly hopeless? What can we learn from how Peter and his fellow Christians reacted to the persecution that befell them? Let us see.

"Prayer . . . Was Being Carried On Intensely" (Acts 12:1-5)

⁵ As we learned in the preceding chapter of this publication, the conversion of the Gentile Cornelius and his family was a thrilling development for the Christian congregation. But nonbelieving Jews must have

---

* See the box "King Herod Agrippa I," on page 79.

1-4. What difficult situation does Peter face, and how would you feel if you were in his place?

5, 6. (a) Why and how did King Herod Agrippa I attack the Christian congregation? (b) Why was the death of James a trial for the congregation?

been shocked to learn that many Jewish Christians were now worshipping freely with non-Jews.

[6] Herod, a canny politician, saw in this an opportunity to curry favor with the Jews, so he set about mistreating the Christians. No doubt, he learned that the apostle James had been especially close to Jesus Christ. Hence, Herod "did away with James the brother of John by the sword." (Acts 12:2) What a trial for the congregation! James was one of the three who had witnessed Jesus' transfiguration and other miracles not revealed to the other apostles. (Matt. 17:1, 2; Mark 5:37-42) Jesus had called James and his brother John "Sons of Thunder" because of their fiery enthusiasm. (Mark 3:17) So the congregation lost a bold, faithful witness and beloved apostle.

[7] The execution of James pleased the Jews, just as Agrippa had hoped. Thus emboldened, he went after Peter next. As described at the outset, he had Peter arrested. Agrippa likely recalled, though, that prisons had not always proved effective in containing the apostles, as noted in Chapter 5 of this book. Taking no chances, Herod had Peter chained between 2 guards, with 16 guards working in shifts day and night to make sure that this apostle did not escape. If he did, those guards would themselves face Peter's sentence. Under such dire circumstances, what could Peter's fellow Christians do?

[8] The congregation knew well what to do. Acts 12:5 reads: "Consequently Peter was being kept in the prison; but prayer to God for

7, 8. How did the congregation respond to Peter's imprisonment?

We pray in behalf of our brothers in prison for their faith

him was being carried on intensely by the congregation." Yes, their prayers in behalf of their beloved brother were intense, heartfelt pleas. The death of James had not plunged them into despair; nor had it caused them to view prayer as valueless. Prayers mean a great deal to Jehovah. If they are in harmony with his will, he will answer them. (Heb. 13:18, 19; Jas. 5:16) This is a lesson that Christians today will want to take to heart.

⁹ Do you know of fellow believers who are beset by trials? They may be enduring persecution, governmental bans, or natural disasters. Why not make them the subject of your heartfelt prayers? You may also know of some who are undergoing less noticeable forms of hardship, such as family troubles, discouragement, or some challenge to their faith. If you meditate before praying, you may think of a number of people to mention by name as you speak to Jehovah, the "Hearer of prayer." (Ps. 65:2) After all, you need your brothers and sisters to do the same for you, should you come upon hard times.

"Keep Following Me" (Acts 12:6-11)

¹⁰ Was Peter anxious about the danger he faced? We cannot say for sure, but during that final night in prison, he was fast asleep between his two vigilant guards. This man of faith surely knew that whatever tomorrow might bring, he was safe with Jehovah. (Rom. 14:7, 8) At any rate, Peter could not have anticipated the amazing events that were about to unfold. Suddenly, a bright light filled his cell. An angel stood there,

---

9. What can we learn from the example set by Peter's fellow Christians in the matter of prayer?

10, 11. Describe the way that Jehovah's angel delivered Peter from imprisonment.

KING HEROD AGRIPPA I

Herod Agrippa I, who had James executed and Peter imprisoned, was the grandson of Herod the Great. The Herods were a dynasty of political rulers over the Jews. The family was Idumaean, that is, Edomite. The Idumaeans were nominally Jewish, since circumcision had been forced upon them in about 125 B.C.E.

Born in 10 B.C.E., Herod Agrippa I was educated in Rome. He cultivated friendships with various members of the imperial family. One of those friends was Gaius, better known as Caligula, who became emperor in 37 C.E. He soon proclaimed Agrippa king over Ituraea, Trachonitis, and Abilene. Later, Caligula expanded Agrippa's domain to include Galilee and Perea.

Agrippa was in Rome when Caligula was assassinated in 41 C.E. Reportedly, Agrippa played an important role in resolving the crisis that ensued. He participated in the tense negotiations between another powerful friend, Claudius, and the Roman Senate. The result was that Claudius was proclaimed emperor and civil war was averted. To reward Agrippa for his mediation, Claudius granted him kingship also over Judea and Samaria, which had been administered by Roman procurators since 6 C.E. Thus Agrippa came to be in charge of territories equaling those of Herod the Great.

Agrippa's capital was Jerusalem, where he won the favor of the religious leaders. He is said to have observed Jewish law and traditions scrupulously by, among other things, offering sacrifices in the temple daily, reading the Law publicly, and playing "the role of zealous protector of the Jewish faith." However, he belied his claim of being a worshipper of God by arranging gladiatorial combats and pagan spectacles in the theater. Agrippa's character has been described as "treacherous, superficial, extravagant."

evidently unseen by the guards, and urgently awakened Peter. And those chains binding his hands—chains that had seemed so unbreakable—simply fell off!

[11] The angel gave Peter a series of terse commands: "Rise quickly! . . . Gird yourself and bind your sandals on. . . . Put your outer garment on." Peter readily complied. Finally, the angel said: "Keep following me," and Peter did so. They left the cell, walked right by the sentinel guards stationed outside, and made their way silently to the massive iron gate. How could they get through that? If such a thought even formed in Peter's mind, it was short-lived. As they approached the gate, it opened "of its own accord." Before Peter knew it, they passed through the gate and into the street, and then the angel vanished. Peter was left there, and the realization dawned on him that all of this had really happened. This was no vision. He was free!—Acts 12:7-11.

[12] Is it not comforting to contemplate Jehovah's limitless power to rescue his servants? Peter was held captive by a king who was backed by the strongest governmental power the world had ever seen. Yet, Peter walked right out of prison! Granted, Jehovah does not perform such miracles for all his servants. He had not done so for James; nor did He do so for Peter later, when Jesus' words about this apostle were finally fulfilled. Christians today do not expect miraculous deliverance. However, we keep in mind that Jehovah has not changed. (Mal. 3:6) And he will soon use his Son to free countless millions from that most unyielding of prisons, death. (John 5:28, 29) We can draw tremendous courage from such promises when we face trials today.

"They Saw Him and Were Astonished" (Acts 12:12-17)

[13] Peter stood in the dark street, deciding where to go next. Then he knew. Living nearby was a Christian woman named Mary. Evidently a widow of some means, Mary owned a house that was large enough to accommodate a congregation. She was the mother of John Mark, whom the Acts account mentions for the first time here and who eventually became like a son to Peter. (1 Pet. 5:13) On this night, many in that congregation were at Mary's house despite the late hour, praying earnestly. No doubt they were praying for Peter's release—but they were not prepared for Jehovah's answer!

[14] Peter knocked at the door of the gateway, which opened into a courtyard in front of the house. A servant girl named Rhoda—a com-

---

12. Why may we find it comforting to contemplate Jehovah's rescue of Peter?

13-15. (a) How did the congregation members meeting at Mary's house react to Peter's arrival? (b) To what does the book of Acts shift its focus, but what effect did Peter continue to have on his spiritual brothers and sisters?

mon Greek name meaning "Rose"—came to the gate. She could not believe her ears. It was Peter's voice! Instead of opening the gate, the excited girl left Peter standing in the street, ran back into the house, and tried to convince the congregation that Peter was there. They said she was mad, but she was not the type to be dissuaded. She kept asserting what she knew to be true. Giving in a bit, some suggested that it might be an angel who was representing Peter. (Acts 12:12-15) All the while, Peter kept knocking until, finally, they went to the gate and opened it.

¹⁵ At the gate, "they saw him and were astonished"! (Acts 12:16) Peter had to quiet their happy hubbub so that he could tell his story, direct that it be passed along to the disciple James and the brothers, and then take his leave before Herod's soldiers could find him. Peter went off to continue his faithful service somewhere safer. Except for his contribution toward resolving the circumcision issue, as mentioned in Acts chapter 15, he exits the account. The book of Acts next turns its focus to the work and travels of the apostle Paul. However, we can be sure that Peter strengthened the faith of his brothers and sisters wherever he went. When he left that group at Mary's house, they were certainly in a joyful frame of mind.

¹⁶ Sometimes Jehovah gives his servants more than they could possibly expect, leaving them almost incredulous with joy. That was how Peter's spiritual brothers and sisters felt that night. It is how we may at times feel when we experience Jehovah's rich blessing today. (Prov. 10: 22) In the future, we will see all of Jehovah's promises being fulfilled on a global scale. The glorious realities will surely far exceed anything we can imagine today. So, as long as we remain faithful, we can count on many happy times ahead.

"The Angel of Jehovah Struck Him" (Acts 12:18-25)

¹⁷ Peter's escape also astonished Herod—but his was no pleasant surprise. Herod quickly ordered a thorough search, then had Peter's guards interrogated. They were "led off to punishment," likely execution. (Acts 12:19) Herod Agrippa will not be remembered for compassion or mercy. Was this cruel man ever punished?

¹⁸ Agrippa may have felt humiliated over his failure to execute Peter, but he soon found solace for his wounded pride. A diplomatic function arose wherein some of his enemies had to sue for peace, and he was no doubt eager to make a speech before a large audience. Luke reported that in preparation, "Herod clothed himself with royal raiment." The

16. Why is the future sure to bring us many occasions for rejoicing?

17, 18. What led up to the flattering of Herod?

Jewish historian Josephus wrote that Herod's garment was made of silver, so that when the light fell upon the king, he seemed to be lit up with glory. The pompous politician then gave a speech. The fawning crowd cried out: "A god's voice, and not a man's!"—Acts 12:20-22.

¹⁹ Such glory belonged to God, and God was watching! Herod had a chance to avoid disaster. He could have rebuked the crowd or could at least have disagreed with them. Instead, he became a vivid illustration of the proverb: "Pride is before a crash." (Prov. 16:18) "Instantly the angel of Jehovah struck him," causing that puffed-up egomaniac to suffer a gruesome death. Herod "became eaten up with worms and expired." (Acts 12:23) Josephus too noted that Agrippa was stricken suddenly and added that the king concluded that he was dying because of accepting the flattery of the crowd. Josephus wrote that Agrippa lingered for five days before he expired.*

²⁰ Sometimes it may seem that ungodly people get away with all manner of wickedness. That should not surprise us, since "the whole world is lying in the power of the wicked one." (1 John 5:19) Still, faithful servants of God are sometimes troubled when evil people seem to escape justice. That is one reason why accounts such as this one are comforting. In effect, we see Jehovah stepping in, reminding all his servants that he is a lover of justice. (Ps. 33:5) Sooner or later, his justice will prevail.

²¹ This account concludes with an even more encouraging lesson: "The word of Jehovah went on growing and spreading." (Acts 12:24) This progress report on the expansion of the preaching work may remind us of the way that Jehovah has blessed the same work in modern times. Clearly, the record contained in Acts chapter 12 is not primarily about the death of one apostle and the escape of another. It is about Jehovah and his thwarting of Satan's attempts to crush the Christian congregation and to quell its zealous preaching work. Those attacks failed, just as all such schemes must fail. (Isa. 54:17) On the other hand, those who side with Jehovah and Jesus Christ are part of a work that will never fail. Is that not an encouraging thought? What a privilege we have to help spread "the word of Jehovah" today!

---

* One doctor and author wrote that the symptoms described by Josephus and Luke might have been caused by roundworms forming a deadly intestinal obstruction. Such worms are sometimes vomited up, or they crawl from the patient's body at the time of death. Notes one reference work: "Luke's professional exactness as a physician brings out the horror of [Herod's] death."

19, 20. (a) Why was Herod punished by Jehovah? (b) What comfort may we find in the account of Herod Agrippa's sudden demise?

21. What is the primary lesson contained in Acts chapter 12, and why may it comfort us today?

"They got to the iron gate leading into the city, and this opened to them of its own accord."

—Acts 12:10

"SENT OUT BY THE HOLY SPIRIT"
ACTS 13:4

In this section, we will follow the apostle Paul on his first missionary journey. In city after city, the apostle was persecuted. Yet, led by holy spirit, he continued to bear witness, establishing new congregations. This exciting record will surely stimulate us to manifest even greater zeal in our ministry.

CHAPTER 11

"Filled With Joy and Holy Spirit"

Paul's example in dealing with hostile, unresponsive people

Based on Acts 13:1-52

IT IS an exciting day for the Antioch congregation. Of all the prophets and teachers here, Barnabas and Saul have been chosen by holy spirit to take the good news to faraway places.* (Acts 13:1, 2) True, qualified men have been sent out before. In the past, though, missionaries had journeyed to areas where Christianity had already taken root. (Acts 8: 14; 11:22) This time, Barnabas and Saul—along with John Mark, who will serve as an attendant—will be sent to lands where people are largely unfamiliar with the good news.

² Some 14 years earlier, Jesus had said to his followers: "You will be witnesses of me both in Jerusalem and in all Judea and Samaria and to the most distant part of the earth." (Acts 1:8) The appointment of Barnabas and Saul to serve as missionaries will spur on the fulfillment of Jesus' prophetic words!#

Set Apart "for the Work" (Acts 13:1-12)

³ Today, thanks to such inventions as the automobile and the airplane, people can travel quite a distance in just an hour or two. Such was not the case in the first century C.E. Back then, the main mode of travel on land was to walk, often over rough terrain. A day's journey, perhaps covering just 20 miles, was exhausting!△ Thus, while Barnabas and Saul no doubt eagerly looked forward to their assignment, they surely realized that considerable effort and self-sacrifice would be involved.—Matt. 16:24.

---

* See the box "Barnabas—'Son of Comfort,'" on page 86.

At this point, congregations can already be found as far away as Syrian Antioch—some 350 miles north of Jerusalem.

△ See the box "On the Road," on page 87.

1, 2. What is unique about the journey that Barnabas and Saul are about to make, and how will their work help fulfill Acts 1:8?

3. What made long journeys difficult in the first century?

⁴ But why did the holy spirit specifically direct that Barnabas and Saul be set apart "for the work"? (Acts 13:2) The Bible does not say. We do know that the holy spirit directed the choosing of these men. There is no indication that the prophets and teachers in Antioch contested the decision. Instead, they fully supported the appointment. Imagine how Barnabas and Saul must have felt as their spiritual brothers, without envy, "fasted and prayed and laid their hands upon them and let them go." (Acts 13:3) We too should support those who receive theocratic assignments, including men appointed as congregation overseers. Rather than being envious of those who receive such privileges, we should "give them more than extraordinary consideration in love because of their work."—1 Thess. 5:13.

⁵ After walking to Seleucia, a harbor near Antioch, Barnabas and Saul sailed to the island of Cyprus, a journey of about 120 miles.* As a native of Cyprus, Barnabas no doubt was eager to bring the good

---

* In the first century, a ship could travel about a hundred miles in a day if winds were favorable. In unfavorable conditions, such a journey could take much longer.

---

4. (a) What directed the choosing of Barnabas and Saul, and how did fellow believers react to the appointment? (b) How can we give support to those who receive theocratic assignments?

5. Describe what was involved in witnessing on the island of Cyprus.

BARNABAS—"SON OF COMFORT"

A prominent member of the early Jerusalem congregation was Joseph, a Levite and a native of Cyprus. The apostles gave him an additional name, descriptive of his personality—Barnabas, meaning "Son of Comfort." (Acts 4: 36) When Barnabas saw a need among his fellow believers, he hastened to meet it.

At Pentecost 33 C.E., 3,000 new disciples were baptized. It is likely that many of these had traveled to Jerusalem for the festival and had not planned to stay in the city for as long as they did. The congregation needed resources to care for this multitude. Therefore, Barnabas sold a piece of land and generously brought the money to the apostles as a contribution.—Acts 4:32-37.

As a mature Christian overseer, Barnabas was eager to help others. It was he who aided newly converted Saul of Tarsus when all the other disciples feared him because of his reputation as a persecutor. (Acts 9:26, 27) Barnabas responded humbly when Paul gave him and Peter strong counsel concerning the proper relationship between Jewish and Gentile Christians. (Gal. 2:9, 11-14) These few examples show that Barnabas truly lived up to his name —"Son of Comfort."

news to those in his home territory. Upon arriving at Salamis, a city on the eastern shore of the island, these men wasted no time. Immediately, "they began publishing the word of God in the synagogues of the Jews."* (Acts 13:5) Barnabas and Saul made their way from one end of Cyprus to the other, likely witnessing in key cities along the way. Depending on the route they took, these missionaries may have walked about 140 miles!

⁶ First-century Cyprus was steeped in false worship. This became particularly apparent when Barnabas and Saul reached Paphos, on the western coast of the island. There, they met up with "a sorcerer, a false prophet, a Jew whose name was Bar-Jesus, and he was with the proconsul Sergius Paulus, an intelligent man."# In the first century, many sophisticated Romans—even "an intelligent man," such as Sergius Paulus—often turned to a sorcerer or an astrologer for help in making important decisions. Nevertheless, Sergius Paulus was intrigued by the Kingdom message and "earnestly sought to hear the word of God." This did not sit well with Bar-Jesus, who was also known by his professional title Elymas, meaning "Sorcerer."—Acts 13:6-8.

ON THE ROAD

In the ancient world, overland travel was slower, more tiring, and probably more expensive than sailing. However, the only way to get to many places was on foot.

A traveler could walk about 20 miles a day. He would be exposed to the elements —sun, rain, heat, and cold—and to the danger of being accosted by thieves. The apostle Paul noted that he was "in journeys often, in dangers from rivers, in dangers from highwaymen."—2 Cor. 11:26.

A vast network of paved roads traversed the Roman Empire. Along the main highways, travelers would find inns spaced a day's walking distance apart. Between these were taverns where one could obtain basic supplies. Contemporary writers describe inns and taverns as being dirty, overcrowded, humid, and flea-infested. They were disreputable places, frequented by the worst elements of society. Innkeepers often robbed travelers and included prostitution among the services offered.

Christians no doubt avoided such places as much as possible. When traveling in lands where they had no family or friends, though, they would likely have had little alternative.

⁷ Bar-Jesus was opposed to the Kingdom message. Indeed, the only way he could protect his influential position as adviser to Sergius Paulus was to "turn the proconsul away from the faith." (Acts 13:8) But Saul was not about to watch a court magician divert the interest of Sergius Paulus. So, what did Saul do? The account states: "Saul, who is also Paul, becoming filled with holy spirit, looked at him

* See the box "In the Synagogues of the Jews," on page 89.

Cyprus was under the rule of the Roman Senate. The principal administrator of the island was a provincial governor with the rank of proconsul.

6, 7. (a) Who was Sergius Paulus, and why did Bar-Jesus attempt to dissuade him from listening to the good news? (b) How did Saul counteract the opposition from Bar-Jesus?

Like Paul, we boldly defend the truth in the face of opposition

[Bar-Jesus] intently and said: 'O man full of every sort of fraud and every sort of villainy, you son of the Devil, you enemy of everything righteous, will you not quit distorting the right ways of Jehovah? Well, then, look! Jehovah's hand is upon you, and you will be blind, not seeing the sunlight for a period of time.' Instantly a thick mist and darkness fell upon him, and he went around seeking men to lead him by the hand."* The result of this miraculous event? "The proconsul, upon seeing what had happened, became a believer, as he was astounded at the teaching of Jehovah."—Acts 13: 9-12.

8 Paul was not intimidated by Bar-Jesus. Likewise, we should not cower when opposers try to subvert the faith of those who show interest in the Kingdom message. Of course, we should let our expressions "be always with graciousness, seasoned with salt." (Col. 4:6) At the same time, we would not want to jeopardize the spiritual welfare of an interested person just to avoid conflict. Nor should we fearfully hold back from exposing false religion, which continues "distorting the right ways of Jehovah" as Bar-Jesus did. (Acts 13: 10) Like Paul, may we boldly declare the truth and appeal to honesthearted ones. And even though God's support may not be as obvious as it was in the case of Paul, we can be sure that Jehovah will use his holy spirit to draw deserving ones to the truth.—John 6:44.

A "Word of Encouragement" (Acts 13:13-43)

9 Evidently, a change took place when the men left Paphos and set sail for Perga, on the coast of Asia Minor, about 150 miles away by sea. At Acts 13:13, the group is identified as "the men, together with Paul."

---

* From this point on, Saul is referred to as Paul. Some have suggested that he adopted the Roman name in honor of Sergius Paulus. However, the fact that he retained the name Paul even after leaving Cyprus points to a different explanation—that Paul, "an apostle to the nations," decided henceforth to use his Roman name. He may also have used the name Paul because the Greek pronunciation of his Hebrew name, Saul, is very similar to that of a Greek word that has a bad connotation.—Rom. 11:13.

---

8. How can we imitate Paul's boldness today?

9. How did Paul and Barnabas set a fine example for those taking the lead in the congregation today?

The wording suggests that Paul now took the lead in the group's activities. However, there is no indication that Barnabas became envious of Paul. On the contrary, these two men continued to work together to accomplish God's will. Paul and Barnabas set a fine example for those who take the lead in the congregation today. Rather than vying for prominence, Christians remember Jesus' words: "All you are brothers." He added: "Whoever exalts himself will be humbled, and whoever humbles himself will be exalted."—Matt. 23:8, 12.

¹⁰ Upon arriving at Perga, John Mark withdrew from Paul and Barnabas and returned to Jerusalem. The reason for his sudden departure is not explained. Paul and Barnabas continued on, traveling from Perga to Antioch in Pisidia, a city in the province of Galatia. This was no easy trek, since Pisidian Antioch is about 3,600 feet above sea level. The treacherous mountain passages were also known for the prevalence of bandits. As if this were not enough, it is likely that at this point Paul was experiencing health problems.*

¹¹ In Antioch of Pisidia, Paul and Barnabas entered the synagogue on the Sabbath. The account relates: "After the public reading of the Law and of the Prophets the presiding officers of the synagogue sent out to them, saying: 'Men, brothers, if there is any word of encouragement for the people that you have, tell it.'" (Acts 13: 15) Paul stood up to speak.

¹² Paul started out by addressing his audience: "Men, Israelites and you others that fear God." (Acts 13:16) Paul's audience was made up of Jews and

---

* Paul's letter to the Galatians was written several years later. In that letter, Paul wrote: "It was through a sickness of my flesh I declared the good news to you the first time."—Gal. 4:13.

10. Describe the journey from Perga to Pisidian Antioch.

11, 12. In speaking in the synagogue in Antioch of Pisidia, how did Paul appeal to his audience?

IN THE SYNAGOGUES OF THE JEWS

Literally, "synagogue" means "a bringing together." It referred to an assembly or congregation of Jews and eventually took on the meaning of the place or building where the assembly was held.

It is believed that synagogues were instituted either during or immediately after the Jews' 70-year exile in Babylon. Synagogues served as places for instruction, worship, the reading of the Scriptures, and spiritual exhortation. In the first century C.E., each town in Palestine had its own synagogue. Larger cities had more than one, and Jerusalem had many.

Following the Babylonian exile, however, not all the Jews returned to Palestine. Many traveled abroad for business reasons. As early as the fifth century B.C.E., Jewish communities existed throughout the 127 jurisdictional districts of the Persian Empire. (Esther 1:1; 3:8) In time, Jewish quarters also developed in cities all around the Mediterranean. These scattered Jews came to be known as the Diaspora, or Dispersion, and they too established synagogues wherever they settled.

In the synagogues, the Law was read and expounded every Sabbath. Readings were delivered from an elevated platform, surrounded on three sides by seats. Participation in reading, preaching, and exhortation was open to any devout Jewish male.

proselytes. How did Paul appeal to these listeners, who did not recognize Jesus' role in God's purpose? First, Paul outlined the history of the Jewish nation. He explained how Jehovah "exalted the people during their alien residence in the land of Egypt" and how after their release God "put up with their manner of action in the wilderness" for 40 years. Paul also related how the Israelites were able to take possession of the Promised Land and how Jehovah "distributed the land of them by lot." (Acts 13:17-19) It has been suggested that Paul may have been alluding to certain Scriptural passages that had been read aloud moments before as part of the Sabbath observance. If that is so, this is yet another example showing that Paul knew how to "become all things to people of all sorts."—1 Cor. 9:22.

[13] We too should strive to appeal to those to whom we preach. For example, knowing the religious background of a person can help us choose topics that will be of particular interest to him. Also, we can quote portions of the Bible with which the individual might be familiar. It may be effective to have the person read from his personal copy of the Bible. Look for ways to appeal to the hearts of your listeners.

[14] Paul next discussed how the line of Israelite kings led to "a savior, Jesus," whose forerunner was John the Baptizer. Then Paul described how Jesus had been put to death and raised up from the dead. (Acts 13:20-37) "Let it therefore be known to you," Paul stated, "that through this One a forgiveness of sins is being published to you . . . Everyone who believes is declared guiltless by means of this One." The apostle then provided his listeners with this warning: "See to it that what is said in the Prophets does not come upon you, 'Behold it, you scorners, and wonder at it, and vanish away, because I am working a work in your days, a work that you will by no means believe even if anyone relates it to you in detail.'" The response to Paul's speech was amazing. "The people began entreating for these matters to be spoken to them on the following sabbath," the Bible reports. In addition, after the synagogue assembly was adjourned, "many of the Jews and of the proselytes who worshiped God followed Paul and Barnabas."—Acts 13:38-43.

"We Turn to the Nations" (Acts 13:44-52)

[15] On the next Sabbath, "nearly all the city" gathered to listen to Paul. This did not please certain Jews, who "began blasphemously contradicting the things being spoken by Paul." He and Barnabas boldly told them: "It was necessary for the word of God to be spoken first to you.

13. How can we appeal to the hearts of our listeners?

14. (a) How did Paul introduce the good news about Jesus, and what warning did he provide? (b) How did the crowd react to Paul's speech?

15. What happened on the Sabbath following Paul's speech?

*"They raised up a persecution against Paul and Barnabas...
And the disciples continued to be filled with joy and holy spirit."*
—Acts 13:50-52

Since you are thrusting it away from you and do not judge yourselves worthy of everlasting life, look! we turn to the nations. In fact, Jehovah has laid commandment upon us in these words, 'I have appointed you as a light of nations, for you to be a salvation to the extremity of the earth.'"—Acts 13:44-47; Isa. 49:6.

[16] Gentile listeners rejoiced, and "all those who were rightly disposed for everlasting life became believers." (Acts 13:48) The word of Jehovah soon spread throughout the country. The reaction of the Jews was quite different. In effect, the missionaries told them that although God's word had been spoken to them first, they had chosen to reject the Messiah and hence were in line for God's adverse judgment. The Jews stirred up the city's reputable women and principal men, "and they raised up a persecution against Paul and Barnabas and threw them outside their boundaries." How did Paul and Barnabas respond? They "shook the dust off their feet against them and went to Iconium." Was that the end of Christianity in Pisidian Antioch? Hardly! The disciples who were left behind "continued to be filled with joy and holy spirit."—Acts 13:50-52.

[17] The manner in which these faithful ones responded to opposition provides a valuable lesson for us. We do not stop preaching, even when prominent people of the world try to dissuade us from proclaiming our message. Note, too, that when the people of Antioch rejected their message, Paul and Barnabas "shook the dust off their feet"—a gesture that indicated not anger but a disclaiming of responsibility. These missionaries realized that they could not control how others would respond. What they *could* control was whether they would continue to preach. And preach they did as they moved on to Iconium!

[18] What about the disciples left in Antioch? True, they were in hostile territory. But their joy was not dependent on a positive response. Jesus said: "Happy are those hearing the word of God and keeping it!" (Luke 11:28) And that is precisely what the disciples in Pisidian Antioch resolved to do.

[19] Like Paul and Barnabas, may we always remember that our responsibility is to preach the good news. The decision to accept or reject the message rests squarely with our listeners. If those to whom we preach seem unresponsive, we can take a lesson from the first-century disciples. By appreciating the truth and allowing ourselves to be led by holy spirit, we too can be joyful, even in the face of opposition.—Gal. 5: 18, 22.

---

16. How did the Jews react to the strong words of the missionaries, and how did Paul and Barnabas respond to the opposition?

17-19. In what ways can we imitate the fine example set by Paul and Barnabas, and how will our doing so contribute to our joy?

CHAPTER 12

"Speaking With Boldness by the Authority of Jehovah"

Paul and Barnabas display humility, perseverance, and boldness

Based on Acts 14:1-28

CHAOS reigns in Lystra. A man lame from birth leaps about with joy after two strangers heal him. People gasp in wonder, and a priest brings garlands for the two men whom the crowd believe to be gods. Bulls snort and bellow as a priest of Zeus prepares to slaughter them. Cries of protest rise from the throats of Paul and Barnabas. Ripping their garments apart, they leap into the crowd and beg not to be worshipped, barely restraining the adoring throng.

² Then, Jewish opposers arrive from Pisidian Antioch and Iconium. With venomous slander, they poison the minds of the people of Lystra. The once-worshipful crowd now swirl around Paul and pelt him with stones until he is unconscious. Their anger spent, they drag Paul's battered body outside the city gates, leaving him for dead.

³ What led up to this dramatic incident? What can present-day proclaimers of the good news learn from the events involving Barnabas, Paul, and the fickle inhabitants of Lystra? And how can Christian elders imitate the example set by Barnabas and Paul as those faithful men persevered in their ministry, "speaking with boldness by the authority of Jehovah"?—Acts 14:3.

"A Great Multitude . . . Became Believers" (Acts 14:1-7)

⁴ Not many days earlier, Paul and Barnabas were thrown out of the Roman city of Pisidian Antioch after Jewish opposers stirred up trouble for them. Instead of becoming discouraged, however, the two men "shook the dust off their feet" against the city's unresponsive inhabitants. (Acts 13:50-52; Matt. 10:14) Paul and Barnabas peacefully departed and left those resisters to the consequences that would come from God. (Acts 18:5, 6; 20:26) With undiminished joy, the two missionaries

1, 2. What series of events unfolds while Paul and Barnabas are in Lystra?

3. What questions will we consider in this chapter?

4, 5. Why did Paul and Barnabas travel to Iconium, and what happened there?

*"Turn from these vain things to the living God,
who made the heaven and the earth."*
—Acts 14:15

continued their preaching tour. Trekking about 100 miles southeast, they reached a fertile plateau cupped between the Taurus and Sultan mountain ranges.

[5] Initially, Paul and Barnabas stopped at Iconium, an enclave of Greek culture and one of the principal cities of the Roman province of Galatia.* This city sheltered an influential Jewish population and a large number of non-Jewish proselytes. According to their custom, Paul and Barnabas entered the synagogue and began preaching. (Acts 13:5, 14) They "spoke in such a manner that a great multitude of both Jews and Greeks became believers."—Acts 14:1.

[6] Why was the manner in which Paul and Barnabas spoke so effective? Paul was a storehouse of Scriptural wisdom. He masterfully linked references to history, prophecy, and the Mosaic Law in order to prove that Jesus was the promised Messiah. (Acts 13:15-31; 26:22, 23) Barnabas radiated concern for people. (Acts 4:36, 37; 9:27; 11:23, 24) Neither man relied on his own understanding but spoke "by the authority of Jehovah." How can you imitate those missionaries in your preaching activity? By doing the following: Become thoroughly familiar with God's Word. Select Scriptural references that are most likely to appeal to your listeners. Look for practical ways to comfort those to whom you preach. And always base your teaching on the authority of Jehovah's Word, not on your own wisdom.

[7] However, not all in Iconium were happy to hear what Paul and Barnabas had to say. "Jews that did not believe," continued Luke, "stirred up and wrongly influenced the souls of people of the nations against the brothers." Paul and Barnabas discerned the need to stay and defend the good news, and they "spent considerable time speaking with boldness." As a result, "the multitude of the city was split, and some were for the Jews but others for the apostles." (Acts 14:2-4) Today, the good news produces similar effects. For some it is a force for unity; for others, a cause for division. (Matt. 10:34-36) If your family is divided because you are obedient to the good news, remember that opposition is often a reaction to unfounded rumor or outright slander. Your fine conduct could become the antidote to such poison and may eventually soften the hearts of those who oppose you.—1 Pet. 2:12; 3:1, 2.

[8] After some time, opposers in Iconium hatched a plot to stone Paul

---

* See the box "Iconium—City of the Phrygians," on page 96.

---

6. Why were Paul and Barnabas effective teachers, and how can we imitate them?

7. (a) The good news produces what effects? (b) If your family is divided because of your obedience to the good news, what should you remember?

8. Why did Paul and Barnabas leave Iconium, and what lesson do we learn from their example?

and Barnabas. When these two missionaries were informed of it, they chose to move to other witnessing territory. (Acts 14:5-7) Kingdom proclaimers use similar discretion today. When faced with verbal attacks, we speak with boldness. (Phil. 1:7; 1 Pet. 3:13-15) But when violence looms, we avoid doing something foolhardy that would unnecessarily endanger our lives or the lives of fellow believers.—Prov. 22:3.

"Turn . . . to the Living God" (Acts 14:8-19)

9 Paul and Barnabas headed for Lystra, a Roman colony about 20 miles to the southwest of Iconium. Lystra maintained strong ties with Pisidian Antioch but, unlike that city, did not have a prominent Jewish community. While the inhabitants likely spoke Greek, their mother tongue was Lycaonian. Possibly because the city contained no synagogue, Paul and Barnabas began preaching in a public area. While in Jerusalem, Peter had healed a man born disabled. In Lystra, Paul healed a man who was lame from birth. (Acts 14:8-10) Because of the miracle Peter had performed, a great crowd had become believers. (Acts 3:1-10) The miracle Paul performed led to a drastically different outcome.

10 As described at the outset of this chapter, when the lame man leaped to his feet, the pagan crowd in Lystra immediately drew the wrong conclusion. They referred to Barnabas as Zeus, the chief of the gods, and to Paul as Hermes, the son of Zeus and spokesman for the gods. (See the box "Lystra and the Cult of Zeus and Hermes," on page 97.) Barnabas and Paul, however, were determined to make the crowd understand that they spoke and acted not by the authority of pagan

ICONIUM—CITY OF THE PHRYGIANS

Iconium was located on a high, well-watered, and fertile plateau. The city stood at a crossroads on an important trade route linking Syria with Rome, Greece, and the Roman province of Asia.

The local religion in Iconium was worship of the Phrygian fertility goddess Cybele, which included elements adopted from Greek worship during the Hellenistic period. The city came under Roman influence in 65 B.C.E., and in the first century C.E., it was a large and prosperous center of trade and agriculture. Although Iconium was home to an influential Jewish population, the city seems to have retained its Hellenistic character. The Acts account, in fact, refers to resident Jews and to "Greeks."—Acts 14:1.

Iconium lay on the border between the Galatian regions of Lycaonia and Phrygia. Certain ancient writers, including Cicero and Strabo, called Iconium a city of Lycaonia, and from a geographic standpoint, the city did belong to that region. The Acts account, however, distinguishes Iconium from Lycaonia, where "the Lycaonian tongue" was spoken. (Acts 14:1-6, 11) For this reason, critics argued that the book of Acts was inaccurate. In 1910, though, archaeologists found inscriptions in the city indicating that Phrygian was indeed the language used in Iconium for two centuries following the visit of Paul and Barnabas. Hence, the writer of Acts was correct in distinguishing Iconium from the cities of Lycaonia.

9, 10. Where was Lystra located, and what do we know about its inhabitants?

gods but by the authority of Jehovah, the one true God.—Acts 14:11-14.

[11] Despite the dramatic circumstances, Paul and Barnabas still sought to reach the hearts of their audience in the best way. With this incident, Luke recorded an effective way to preach the good news to pagans. Note how Paul and Barnabas appealed to their listeners: "Men, why are you doing these things? We also are humans having the same infirmities as you do, and are declaring the good news to you, for you to turn from these vain things to the living God, who made the heaven and the earth and the sea and all the things in them. In the past generations he permitted all the nations to go on in their ways, although, indeed, he did not leave himself without witness in that he did good, giving you rains from heaven and fruitful seasons, filling your hearts to the full with food and good cheer."—Acts 14:15-17.

[12] What lessons can we learn from these thought-provoking words? First, Paul and Barnabas did not consider themselves superior to their audience. They did not pretend to be something that they were not. Instead, they humbly admitted to having the same weaknesses as their pagan listeners. True, Paul and Barnabas had received the holy spirit and had been freed from false teachings. They had also been blessed with the hope of ruling with Christ. But they realized that the inhabitants of Lystra could receive these very same gifts by obeying Christ.

11-13. (a) What did Paul and Barnabas say to the inhabitants of Lystra? (b) What is one lesson that we can learn from the statements made by Paul and Barnabas?

LYSTRA AND THE CULT OF ZEUS AND HERMES

Lystra was located in a secluded valley off the main highways. Caesar Augustus designated the city a Roman colony, naming it Julia Felix Gemina Lustra. Its garrison was to defend the province of Galatia from local mountain tribes. The city was thus administered according to traditional Roman civic organization, with its officials bearing Latin titles. Even so, Lystra retained much of its local character. It remained more Lycaonian than Roman, and indeed, the Lystran protagonists in the Acts account spoke the Lycaonian tongue.

Among the archaeological finds in the vicinity of ancient Lystra are inscriptions referring to "priests of Zeus" and a statue of the god Hermes. An altar dedicated to Zeus and Hermes has also been discovered in that area.

A legend recorded by the Roman poet Ovid (43 B.C.E. to 17 C.E.) provides further background for the Acts account. According to Ovid, Jupiter and Mercury, the Roman counterparts of the Greek gods Zeus and Hermes, visited the hill country of Phrygia disguised as mortal men. They sought hospitality in a thousand homes, but everyone turned them away. Only an elderly couple, named Philemon and Baucis, welcomed them into their humble cottage. As a result, Zeus and Hermes transformed that home into a temple of marble and gold, made the elderly couple its priest and priestess, and destroyed the homes of those who had refused them lodging. "If the people of Lystra remembered such a legend when they saw Paul and Barnabas heal the lame man," says *The Book of Acts in Its Graeco-Roman Setting,* "it is not surprising that they would want to welcome them with sacrifices."

¹³ What is our attitude toward those to whom we preach? Do we view them as our equals? As we help others learn truths from God's Word, do we, like Paul and Barnabas, avoid seeking adulation? Charles Taze Russell, an outstanding teacher who took the lead in the preaching work in the late 19th and early 20th centuries, set an example in this regard. He wrote: "We want no homage, no reverence, for ourselves or our writings; nor do we wish to be called Reverend or Rabbi." Brother Russell's humble attitude reflected that of Paul and Barnabas. Likewise, our purpose in preaching is not to bring glory to ourselves but to help people to turn to "the living God."

¹⁴ Consider a second lesson we can learn from this speech. Paul and Barnabas were adaptable. Unlike the Jews and proselytes in Iconium, the inhabitants of Lystra had little or no knowledge of the Scriptures or of God's dealings with the nation of Israel. Even so, those listening to Paul and Barnabas were part of an agricultural community. Lystra was blessed with a mild climate and fertile fields. Those people could see ample evidence of the Creator's qualities as revealed in such things as fruitful seasons, and the missionaries used this common ground in their appeal to reason.—Rom. 1:19, 20.

¹⁵ Can we likewise be adaptable? Although a farmer may plant the same type of seed in a number of his fields, he has to vary the methods he uses to prepare the soil. Some ground may already be soft and ready to accept the seed. Other soil may need more preparation. Similarly, the seed we plant is always the same—the Kingdom message found in God's Word. However, if we are like Paul and Barnabas, we will try to discern the circumstances and religious background of the people to whom we preach. Then we will allow this knowledge to influence the way we present the Kingdom message.—Luke 8:11, 15.

¹⁶ We can learn a third lesson from the account involving Paul, Barnabas, and the inhabitants of Lystra. Despite our best efforts, the seed we plant is sometimes snatched away or falls on rocky soil. (Matt. 13:18-21) If that happens, do not despair. As Paul later reminded the disciples in Rome, "each of us [including each individual with whom we discuss God's Word] will render an account for himself to God." —Rom. 14:12.

"They Committed Them to Jehovah" (Acts 14:20-28)

¹⁷ After Paul was dragged outside Lystra and left for dead, the disciples surrounded him and he got up and found shelter in the city over-

---

14-16. What second and third lessons can we learn from what Paul and Barnabas said to the inhabitants of Lystra?

17. After leaving Derbe, where did Paul and Barnabas travel, and why?

night. The next day, Paul and Barnabas began the 60-mile journey to Derbe. We can only imagine the discomfort Paul felt during this arduous trip, having been pelted with stones just hours earlier. Still, he and Barnabas persevered, and when they arrived in Derbe, they made "quite a few disciples." Then, rather than taking the shorter route back to their home base in Syrian Antioch, "they returned to Lystra and to Iconium and to [Pisidian] Antioch." For what purpose? To strengthen "the souls of the disciples, encouraging them to remain in the faith." (Acts 14:20-22) What an example those two men set! They placed the interests of the congregation ahead of their own comfort. Traveling overseers and missionaries in modern times have imitated their example.

[18] In addition to strengthening the disciples by their words and example, Paul and Barnabas appointed "older men for them in each congregation." Although "sent out by the holy spirit" on this missionary journey, Paul and Barnabas still prayed and fasted when "they committed them [the older men] to Jehovah." (Acts 13:1-4; 14:23) A similar pattern is followed today. Before recommendations for appointments are made, the local body of elders prayerfully reviews a brother's Scriptural qualifications. (1 Tim. 3:1-10, 12, 13; Titus 1:5-9) The length of time he has been a Christian is not the main determining factor. Instead, the brother's speech, conduct, and reputation give evidence of the degree to which holy spirit operates in his life. His meeting the requirements for overseers as set out in the Scriptures determines whether he is qualified to serve as a shepherd of the flock.—Gal. 5:22, 23.

[19] Appointed elders know that they are accountable to God for the way that they treat the congregation. (Heb. 13:17; 1 Pet. 5:1-3) Like Paul and Barnabas, elders take the lead in the preaching work. They strengthen fellow disciples with their words. And they are willing to place the interests of the congregation ahead of their own comfort. —Phil. 2:3, 4.

[20] When Paul and Barnabas finally returned to their missionary base in Syrian Antioch, they reported "the many things God had done by means of them, and that he had opened to the nations the door to faith." (Acts 14:27) As we read about the faithful work of our Christian brothers and see how Jehovah blessed their efforts, we will be encouraged to keep on "speaking with boldness by the authority of Jehovah."

---

18. What is involved in the appointment of older men?

19. Elders know that they have what accountability, and how do they imitate Paul and Barnabas?

20. How do we benefit from reading reports about the faithful work of our brothers?

"THE APOSTLES AND THE OLDER MEN GATHERED TOGETHER"

ACTS 15:6

A heated issue arose that threatened the peace and unity of the congregations. To whom did the congregations look for direction and guidance to resolve the dispute? In this section, we will gain insight into the way the first-century congregation was organized, which sets a pattern for God's people today.

CHAPTER 13

"There Had Occurred No Little Dissension"

The issue of circumcision goes before the governing body

Based on Acts 15:1-12

ELATED, Paul and Barnabas have just returned to the Syrian city of Antioch from their first missionary tour. They are thrilled that Jehovah has "opened to the nations the door to faith." (Acts 14:26, 27) Indeed, Antioch itself is abuzz with the good news and "a great number" of Gentiles are being added to the congregation here.—Acts 11:20-26.

[2] The exciting news about this influx soon reaches Judea. But instead of bringing joy to all, this development forces into prominence the ongoing debate about circumcision. What should be the relationship between Jewish and non-Jewish believers, and how should the latter view the Mosaic Law? The issue causes dissension that becomes so serious that it threatens to split the Christian congregation into factions. How will this matter be resolved?

[3] As we consider this account in the book of Acts, we will learn many valuable lessons. These may help us to act wisely should potentially divisive issues arise in our day.

"Unless You Get Circumcised" (Acts 15:1)

[4] The disciple Luke wrote: "Certain men came down [to Antioch] from Judea and began to teach the brothers: 'Unless you get circumcised according to the custom of Moses, you cannot be saved.'" (Acts 15:1) Whether these "certain men" had been Pharisees before converting to Christianity is not stated. At the very least, they appear to have been influenced by that Jewish sect's legalistic thinking. Also, they may have wrongly claimed to speak for the apostles and older men in Jerusalem. (Acts 15:23, 24) Why, though, were Jewish believers still promoting circumcision some 13 years after the apostle Peter, as directed by

---

1-3. (a) What developments threaten to divide the early Christian congregation? (b) How may we benefit from studying this account in the book of Acts?

4. What wrong views were certain believers promoting, and what question does this raise?

God, had welcomed uncircumcised Gentiles into the Christian congregation?*—Acts 10:24-29, 44-48.

⁵ The reasons may have been many. For one thing, male circumcision had been instituted by Jehovah himself, and it was a sign of a special relationship with him. Predating the Law covenant but later becoming part of it, circumcision began with Abraham and his household.# (Lev. 12:2, 3) Under the Mosaic Law, even aliens had to be circumcised before they could enjoy certain privileges, such as eating the Passover meal. (Ex. 12:43, 44, 48, 49) Indeed, in the Jewish mind, for a man to be uncircumcised was to be unclean, contemptible.—Isa. 52:1.

⁶ Thus, it required faith and humility on the part of Jewish believers to adjust to revealed truth. The Law covenant had been replaced by the new covenant, so birth as a Jew no longer automatically made one a member of God's people. And for Jewish Christians who lived in Jewish communities—as did the believers in Judea—it took courage to confess Christ and to accept as fellow believers Gentiles who had not been circumcised.—Jer. 31:31-33; Luke 22:20.

⁷ Of course, God's standards had not changed. Reflecting this truth, the new covenant incorporated the *spirit* of the Mosaic Law. (Matt. 22:36-40) In regard to circumcision, for example, Paul later wrote: "He is a Jew who is one on the inside, and his circumcision is that of the heart by spirit, and not by a written code." (Rom. 2:29; Deut. 10:16) The "certain men" from Judea had not grasped these truths but asserted that God had never revoked the law of circumcision. Would they listen to reason?

"Dissension and Disputing" (Acts 15:2)

⁸ Luke continued: "When there had occurred no little dissension and disputing by Paul and Barnabas with them [the "certain men"], they [the elders] arranged for Paul and Barnabas and some others of them to go up to the apostles and older men in Jerusalem regarding this

---

* See the box "The Teachings of the Judaizers," on page 103.

The covenant of circumcision was not part of the Abrahamic covenant, which remains in force to this day. The Abrahamic covenant went into effect in 1943 B.C.E. when Abraham (then Abram) crossed the Euphrates on his way to Canaan. He was then 75 years of age. The covenant of circumcision was made later, in 1919 B.C.E., when Abraham was 99 years old.—Gen. 12:1-8; 17:1, 9-14; Gal. 3:17.

5, 6. (a) Why may some Jewish Christians have wanted to cling to circumcision? (b) Was the covenant of circumcision part of the Abrahamic covenant? Explain. (See footnote.)

7. What truths had "certain men" failed to grasp?

8. Why was the issue of circumcision taken to the governing body in Jerusalem?

dispute."* (Acts 15:2) The "dissension and disputing" reflected strong feelings and firm convictions on both sides, and the congregation in Antioch could not resolve it. In the interests of peace and unity, the congregation wisely arranged to take the question to "the apostles and older men in Jerusalem," who made up the governing body. What can we learn from the elders in Antioch?

9 One valuable lesson we learn is that we need to trust God's organization. Consider: The brothers in Antioch knew that the governing body was made up entirely of Christians of Jewish background. Yet, they trusted that body to settle the question of circumcision in harmony with the Scriptures. Why? The congregation was confident that Jehovah would direct matters by means of his holy spirit and the Head of the Christian congregation, Jesus Christ. (Matt. 28:18, 20; Eph. 1:22, 23) When serious issues arise today, let us imitate the fine example of the believers in Antioch by trusting God's organization and its Governing Body of anointed Christians, who represent "the faithful and discreet slave."—Matt. 24:45.

10 We are also reminded of the value of humility and patience. Paul and Barnabas had been personally appointed by holy spirit to go to the nations, yet they did not invoke that authority to settle the issue of circumcision then and there in Antioch. (Acts 13:2, 3) Moreover, Paul later wrote: "I went up [to Jerusalem] as a result of a revelation"—indicating divine direction in the matter. (Gal. 2:2) Elders today strive to have the same humble, patient attitude when potentially divisive questions arise. Instead of being contentious, they look to Jehovah by consulting

---

* Titus, a Greek Christian who later became a trusted companion and emissary of Paul, appears to have been a member of the delegation. (Gal. 2:1; Titus 1:4) This man was a fine example of an uncircumcised Gentile anointed by holy spirit.—Gal. 2:3.

9, 10. In what way did the brothers in Antioch as well as Paul and Barnabas set a fine example for us today?

THE TEACHINGS OF THE JUDAIZERS

Even after the first-century governing body settled the circumcision issue, certain individuals who claimed to be Christians stubbornly kept the question alive. The apostle Paul called them "false brothers" who wanted "to pervert the good news about the Christ."—Gal. 1:7; 2:4; Titus 1:10.

The Judaizers' objective was apparently to appease the Jews, to keep them from opposing Christianity so violently. (Gal. 6: 12, 13) The Judaizers argued that righteousness was established by works of the Mosaic Law in such matters as diet, circumcision, and Jewish festivals.—Col. 2:16.

Understandably, those who held to these views felt uncomfortable in the presence of Gentile believers. Sadly, such unwholesome feelings were even manifest among a number of reputable Christians of Jewish background. For example, when representatives from the Jerusalem congregation visited Antioch, they kept separate from their Gentile brothers. Even Peter, who until then had freely socialized with the Gentiles, withdrew—not even eating with them. Yes, he went against the very principles he had earlier defended. As a result, Peter received strong counsel from Paul.—Gal. 2:11-14.

the Scriptures and the instruction and guidance provided by the slave class.—Phil. 2:2, 3.

[11] In some instances, we may have to wait for Jehovah to shed light on a certain matter. Remember that the brothers in Paul's time had to wait until about 49 C.E.—some 13 years from the time of Cornelius' anointing in 36 C.E.—before Jehovah brought the issue of whether Gentiles should be circumcised to a resolution. Why so long? Perhaps God wanted to allow sufficient time for sincere Jews to adjust to such a major change in viewpoint. After all, the termination of the 1,900-year-old covenant of circumcision made with their beloved forefather Abraham was no minor matter!—John 16:12.

[12] What a privilege it is to be instructed and molded by our patient and kind heavenly Father! The results are always good and always to our advantage. (Isa. 48:17, 18; 64:8) So let us never proudly push ahead with our own ideas or react negatively to organizational changes or to adjusted explanations of certain scriptures. (Eccl. 7:8) If you detect even a hint of such a tendency in yourself, why not meditate prayerfully on the timely principles found in Acts chapter 15?*

[13] The need for patience may arise when we study the Bible with people who find it hard to abandon cherished false beliefs or unscriptural customs. In such cases, we may need to allow a reasonable amount of time for God's spirit to work on the heart of the student. (1 Cor. 3:6, 7) Also, we do well to make the subject a matter of prayer. In one way or another and at the right time, God will help us to know the wise course to take.—1 John 5:14.

They Related Encouraging Experiences "in Detail" (Acts 15:3-5)

[14] Luke's narrative continues: "After being conducted partway by the congregation, these men continued on their way through both Phoenicia and Samaria, relating in detail the conversion of people of the nations, and they were causing great joy to all the brothers." (Acts 15:3) That the congregation conducted Paul, Barnabas, and the other travelers partway was an act of Christian love that honored them, showing that the congregation wished them God's blessing. Again, what a fine example the brothers in Antioch set for us! Do you show honor to your spiritual brothers and sisters, "especially those [older men] who

---

* See the box "Jehovah's Witnesses Build Their Beliefs on the Bible," on page 105.

11, 12. Why is it important to wait on Jehovah?

13. How can we reflect Jehovah's patience in our ministry?

14, 15. How did the congregation in Antioch honor Paul, Barnabas, and the other travelers, and how did their presence prove to be a blessing to fellow believers?

work hard in speaking and teaching"? —1 Tim. 5:17.

¹⁵ En route, the travelers proved to be a blessing to fellow Christians in Phoenicia and Samaria by sharing with them "in detail" experiences about the work in the Gentile field. The listeners possibly included Jewish believers who had fled to those regions after Stephen's martyrdom. Likewise today, reports of Jehovah's blessing on the disciple-making work are a source of encouragement to our brothers, especially those undergoing trials. Do you benefit fully from such reports by attending Christian meetings, assemblies, and conventions as well as by reading the experiences and life stories published in our literature?

¹⁶ After traveling south some 350 miles, the delegation from Antioch finally reached their destination. Luke wrote: "On arriving in Jerusalem they were kindly received by the congregation and the apostles and the older men, and they recounted the many things God had done by means of them." (Acts 15:4) In response, however, "some of those of the sect of the Pharisees that had believed rose up from their seats and said: 'It is necessary to circumcise them and charge them to observe the law of Moses.'" (Acts 15:5) Clearly, the question of the circumcision of non-Jewish Christians had become a major issue, and it had to be settled.

"The Apostles and the Older Men" Met Together (Acts 15:6-12)

¹⁷ "With those consulting together there is wisdom," says Proverbs 13:10. In harmony with that sound principle, "the apostles and the older men gathered together to see about [the question of circumcision]." (Acts 15:6) "The apostles and the older men" acted in a representative way for the entire Christian congregation, just as the Governing Body does today. Why were "the older men" serving along with the apostles? Remember that the apostle James had been executed, and at least for a period, the apostle Peter had been imprisoned. Might

'JEHOVAH'S WITNESSES BUILD THEIR BELIEFS ON THE BIBLE'

As amply demonstrated in the case of the early Christian congregation, the history of true worship is a record of progressive spiritual enlightenment. (Prov. 4:18; Dan. 12: 4, 9, 10; Acts 15:7-9) Today, too, Jehovah's people adjust their beliefs to conform to revealed truth; they do not force the Scriptures to fit their views. Impartial observers have recognized this fact. In his book *Truth in Translation,* Jason David BeDuhn, associate professor of religious studies at Northern Arizona University in the United States, wrote that Jehovah's Witnesses approach the Bible "with a kind of innocence, and [build] their system of belief and practice from the raw material of the Bible without predetermining what was to be found there."

---

16. What shows that circumcision had become a major issue?

17. Who made up the governing body in Jerusalem, and why may "the older men" have been included?

similar eventualities befall other apostles? The presence of other qualified anointed men would help to ensure the orderly continuance of oversight.

[18] Luke continued: "Now when much disputing had taken place, Peter rose and said . . . : 'Men, brothers, you well know that from early days God made the choice among you that through my mouth people of the nations should hear the word of the good news and believe; and God, who knows the heart, bore witness by giving them the holy spirit, just as he did to us also. And he made no distinction at all between us and them, but purified their hearts by faith.'" (Acts 15:7-9) According to one reference work, the Greek word translated "disputing" in verse 7 also denotes "a seeking," 'a questioning.' Apparently, the brothers had honest differences of opinion, which they openly expressed.

[19] Peter's powerful words reminded all that he himself was present when the first uncircumcised Gentiles—Cornelius and his household—were anointed with holy spirit in 36 C.E. So if Jehovah had ceased making a distinction between Jew and non-Jew, by what authority should humans do otherwise? Moreover, faith in Christ, not compliance with the Mosaic Law, purifies a believer's heart.—Gal. 2:16.

[20] On the basis of the unassailable witness of both the word of God and the holy spirit, Peter concluded: "Now, therefore, why are you making a test of God by imposing upon the neck of the disciples a yoke that neither our forefathers nor we were capable of bearing? On the contrary, we trust to get saved through the undeserved kindness of the Lord Jesus in the same way as those people also." (Acts 15:10, 11) Promoters of circumcision were, in fact, "making a test of God," or 'straining his patience,' as another translation renders it. They were trying to impose on Gentiles a code that the Jews themselves could not fully comply with and that therefore condemned them to death. (Gal. 3:10) Instead, Peter's Jewish listeners should have been thankful for God's undeserved kindness expressed through Jesus.

[21] Evidently, Peter's words struck home, for "the entire multitude became silent." Thereafter, Barnabas and Paul related "the many signs and portents that God did through them among the nations." (Acts 15: 12) Now, at last, the apostles and older men were in a position to evaluate all the evidence and make a decision that clearly reflected the will of God on the matter of circumcision.

18, 19. What powerful words did Peter speak, and what conclusion should his listeners have reached?

20. How were the promoters of circumcision "making a test of God"?

21. Barnabas and Paul contributed what to the discussion?

22 Today, too, when the members of the Governing Body meet, they look to God's Word for direction and pray earnestly for holy spirit. (Ps. 119:105; Matt. 7:7-11) To that end, each member of the Governing Body receives an agenda ahead of time so that he can give the items prayerful thought. (Prov. 15:28) At the meeting, these anointed brothers freely and respectfully express themselves. The Bible is used frequently during the discussions.

23 Congregation elders should imitate that example. And if after consideration at an elders' meeting a serious matter remains unresolved, the body may consult the local branch office or its appointed representatives, such as traveling overseers. The branch, in turn, may write to the Governing Body if necessary.

24 Yes, Jehovah blesses those who respect the theocratic arrangement and who display humility, loyalty, and patience. As we shall see in the following chapter, the God-given rewards for doing so are genuine peace, spiritual prosperity, and Christian unity.

22-24. (a) How does the Governing Body today follow the example of the early governing body? (b) How can all elders show respect for theocratic authority?

Some insisted: "It is necessary to . . . charge [the Gentiles] to observe the law of Moses"

CHAPTER 14

"We Have Come to a Unanimous Accord"

How the governing body reached a decision and the unifying effect it had on the congregations

Based on Acts 15:13-35

SUSPENSE fills the air. The apostles and older men occupying this room in Jerusalem look at one another, sensing that they have reached a pivotal moment. The issue of circumcision has raised serious questions. Are Christians under the Mosaic Law? Is there to be any distinction between Jewish and Gentile Christians?

[2] The men taking the lead have considered much evidence. They have in mind God's prophetic Word as well as powerful firsthand testimony revealing Jehovah's blessing. They have expressed themselves fully. The evidence that has mounted regarding the issue at hand is overwhelming. Jehovah's spirit is clearly pointing the way. Will these men respond to that direction?

[3] It will take real faith and courage to accept the spirit's guidance in this case. They risk intensifying the hatred of the Jewish religious leaders. And they face resistance from men within the congregation who are determined to lead God's people back to reliance on the Mosaic Law. What will the governing body do? Let us see. In the process, we will see how those men set a pattern that is followed by the Governing Body of Jehovah's Witnesses today. It is a pattern that we too need to follow as we face decisions and challenges in our life as Christians.

"The Words of the Prophets Agree" (Acts 15:13-21)

[4] The disciple James, the half brother of Jesus, spoke up.* It seems that on this occasion he was acting as chairman of the meeting. His

---

* See the box "James—'The Brother of the Lord,'" on page 112.

1, 2. (a) What serious questions face the governing body of the first-century Christian congregation? (b) What help do those brothers receive in order to reach the right conclusion?

3. How may we benefit from examining the account in Acts chapter 15?

4, 5. What insight from God's prophetic Word did James bring into the discussion?

words crystallized the consensus that the body as a whole appears to have reached. To the assembled men, James said: "Symeon has related thoroughly how God for the first time turned his attention to the nations to take out of them a people for his name. And with this the words of the Prophets agree."—Acts 15:14, 15.

⁵ The speech by Symeon, or Simon Peter, and the evidence submitted by Barnabas and Paul probably brought to James' mind pertinent scriptures that shed light on the subject under discussion. (John 14:26) After saying that "the words of the Prophets agree," James quoted the words of Amos 9:11, 12. That book was listed in the part of the Hebrew Scriptures commonly called "the Prophets." (Matt. 22:40; Acts 15:16-18) You will note that the words quoted by James are somewhat different from those we find in the book of Amos today. It is likely that James quoted from the *Septuagint*, a Greek translation of the Hebrew Scriptures.

⁶ Through the prophet Amos, Jehovah foretold that the time would come when He would raise up "the booth of David," that is, the royal line leading to the Messianic Kingdom. (Ezek. 21:26, 27) Would Jehovah once again deal exclusively with fleshly Jews as a nation? No. The prophecy adds that "people of *all the nations*" would be brought together as "people who are called by [God's] name." Remember, Peter had just testified that God "made no distinction at all between us [Jewish Christians] and them [Gentile believers], but purified their hearts by faith." (Acts 15:9) In other words, it is God's will that Jews and Gentiles alike be brought into the Kingdom as heirs. (Rom. 8:17; Eph. 2:17-19) Nowhere did such inspired prophecies suggest that the Gentile believers must first be circumcised in the flesh or become proselytes.

⁷ Moved by such Scriptural evidence and the powerful testimony he had heard, James went on to offer these words for consideration: "Hence my decision is not to trouble those from the nations who are turning to God, but to write them to abstain from things polluted by idols and from fornication and from what is strangled and from blood. For from ancient times Moses has had in city after city those who preach him, because he is read aloud in the synagogues on every sabbath."—Acts 15:19-21.

⁸ When James said "hence my decision is," was he asserting his authority—perhaps as chairman of the meeting—over the other brothers and arbitrarily deciding what was to be done? Not at all! The Greek expression rendered "my decision is" may also mean "I judge" or "I give an opinion." Far from ruling over the entire body, James was proposing for

---

6. How did the Scriptures shed light on the discussion?

7, 8. (a) What did James propose? (b) How should we understand James' words?

Like the first-century Christians, Jehovah's Witnesses today are directed by a Governing Body of dedicated, spirit-anointed men representing "the faithful and discreet slave." (Matt. 24:45) The Governing Body meets weekly as a group. Its members are also organized into the following six committees, each having its own responsibilities.

- The *Coordinators' Committee* consists of the coordinators of each of the other committees and a secretary who is also a member of the Governing Body. It helps all the committees to operate smoothly and efficiently. This committee oversees legal matters and the use of the media when necessary to convey an accurate picture of our beliefs. It also responds to disasters, outbreaks of persecution, and other emergencies affecting Jehovah's Witnesses anywhere in the world.

- The *Personnel Committee* oversees arrangements for the spiritual and personal welfare of the volunteers who serve in the branch offices of Jehovah's Witnesses earth wide. In addition, this committee supervises the inviting of additional volunteers to serve at branch offices.

- The *Publishing Committee* supervises the printing, publishing, and shipping of Bible literature. It oversees the printeries and properties owned and operated by the corporations used by Jehovah's Witnesses and the construction of branch facilities, as well as Kingdom Halls and Assembly Halls in lands with limited resources. This committee also supervises the use of donated funds.

- The *Service Committee* oversees the preaching work along with matters affecting congregation elders, traveling overseers, and full-time evangelizers. It supervises the preparation of *Our Kingdom Ministry*. This committee also invites and assigns students of Gilead School, for the training of missionaries, and students of the Ministerial Training School, designed for the instruction of unmarried congregation elders and ministerial servants.

- The *Teaching Committee* oversees the instruction provided at assemblies, conventions, and congregation meetings, as well as the development of audio and video programs. It prepares curriculums for Gilead School, the Pioneer Service School, and other schools and arranges spiritual programs for branch office volunteers.

- The *Writing Committee* supervises the production of spiritual food in written form for the congregations and for the general public. It also answers Bible questions, oversees translation work worldwide, and approves such material as drama scripts and talk outlines.

The Governing Body relies on God's holy spirit for direction. Its members do not regard themselves as the leaders of Jehovah's people. Rather, like all anointed Christians on earth, they "keep following the Lamb [Jesus Christ] no matter where he goes."—Rev. 14:4.

their consideration a course of action based on the evidence heard and on what the Scriptures say about the matter.

⁹ Was James' proposal a good one? Obviously it was, for the apostles and the older men later adopted it. With what benefits? On the one hand, the recommended course would not "trouble," or "make it difficult for," Gentile Christians by imposing upon them the requirements of the Mosaic Law. (Acts 15:19; *New International Version*) On the other hand, this decision would show respect for the conscience of Jewish Christians, who over the years had heard "Moses . . . read aloud in the synagogues on every sabbath."* (Acts 15:21) The recommended course would surely strengthen the bond between Jewish and Gentile Christians. Above all, it would please Jehovah God, reflecting his advancing purpose. What a fine way to resolve a problem that threatened the unity and well-being of the entire congregation of God's people! And what an excellent example this is for the Christian congregation today!

Albert Schroeder speaking at a **1998** international convention

¹⁰ As mentioned in the preceding chapter, like its first-century counterpart, the Governing Body of Jehovah's Witnesses today looks to Jehovah, the Universal Sovereign, and Jesus Christ, the Head of the congregation, for direction in all matters.# (1 Cor. 11:3) How is this done? Albert D. Schroeder, who served on the Governing Body from 1974 until he finished his earthly course in March 2006, explained: "The Governing Body meets every Wednesday, opening the meeting with prayer and asking for the direction of Jehovah's spirit. A real effort is made to see that every matter that is handled and every decision that is made is in harmony with God's Word the Bible." Similarly, Milton G. Henschel, a longtime member of the Governing Body who finished his earth-

---

* James wisely referred to the writings of Moses, which included not only the Law code but also a record of God's dealings and indications of His will that predated the Law. For example, God's view of blood, adultery, and idolatry can be plainly seen in Genesis. (Gen. 9:3, 4; 20:2-9; 35:2, 4) Jehovah thus revealed principles that are binding on all of mankind, whether Jew or Gentile.

See the box "How the Governing Body Is Organized Today," on page 110.

---

9. James' proposal offered what benefits?

10. How does the Governing Body today follow the pattern set by its first-century counterpart?

James, a son of Joseph and Mary, is listed first among Jesus' younger half brothers. (Matt. 13:54, 55) He may therefore have been Mary's second-oldest child. James grew up with Jesus, observed his ministry, and at least knew of Jesus' "powerful works," whether he actually witnessed them or not. During Jesus' ministry, however, James and his brothers "were, in fact, not exercising faith in him," their older brother. (John 7:5) James may even have shared the sentiments of some of Jesus' other relatives, who said of Jesus: "He has gone out of his mind." —Mark 3:21.

All of that changed with Jesus' death and resurrection. Although three others named James are mentioned in the Greek Scriptures, it was evidently to his half brother James that Jesus appeared personally during the 40 days after He was raised. (1 Cor. 15:7) This experience might have led James to the right conclusion about his older brother's true identity. In any case, less than ten days after Jesus ascended to heaven, James, his mother, and his brothers were gathered with the apostles in an upper room to pray.—Acts 1:13, 14.

James eventually became a highly respected member of the congregation in Jerusalem, apparently being regarded as an apostle, or "one sent forth," of that congregation. (Gal. 1:18, 19) James' prominence was evident when the apostle Peter, after being miraculously released from prison, told the disciples: "Report these things to James and the brothers." (Acts 12:12, 17) When the circumcision issue came before "the apostles and the older men" in Jerusalem, James seems to have presided over the discussion. (Acts 15:6-21) And the apostle Paul noted that James along with Cephas (Peter) and the apostle John "seemed to be pillars" of the Jerusalem congregation. (Gal. 2:9) Even years later when Paul returned to Jerusalem from his third missionary tour, he reported back "to James; and all the older men were present."—Acts 21:17-19.

This James, whom Paul called "the brother of the Lord," evidently wrote the letter, or Bible book, bearing his name. (Gal. 1:19) In that letter, James humbly identifies himself, neither as an apostle nor as Jesus' brother, but as "a slave of God and of the Lord Jesus Christ." (Jas. 1:1) The letter of James shows that like Jesus, James was a keen observer of the natural world and of human nature. To illustrate spiritual truths, James drew on familiar natural phenomena, including windblown seas, starry skies, the scorching sun, fragile flowers, wildfires, and tame animals. (Jas. 1:6, 11, 17; 3:5, 7) His divinely inspired insights into people's attitudes and actions provided excellent counsel on maintaining healthy relationships.—Jas. 1:19, 20; 3:2, 8-18.

Paul's words recorded at 1 Corinthians 9:5 suggest that James was married. The Bible does not report on the time or circumstances of James' death. However, Jewish historian Josephus wrote that shortly after the death of Roman Governor Porcius Festus, about 62 C.E., and before his successor, Albinus, took office, Ananus (Ananias) the high priest "convened the judges of the Sanhedrin and brought before them a man named James, the brother of Jesus who was called the Christ, and certain others." According to Josephus, Ananus "accused them of having transgressed the law and delivered them up to be stoned."

ly course in March 2003, presented a fundamental question to the graduating students of the 101st class of the Watchtower Bible School of Gilead. He asked, "Is there another organization on earth whose Governing Body consults God's Word, the Bible, before making important decisions?" The answer is obvious.

"Sending Chosen Men" (Acts 15:22-29)

[11] The governing body in Jerusalem had reached a unanimous decision on the issue of circumcision. For the brothers in the congregations to act in unity, however, that decision had to be communicated to them clearly and in a positive, encouraging way. How could this best be done? The account explains: "The apostles and the older men together with the whole congregation favored sending chosen men from among them to Antioch along with Paul and Barnabas, namely, Judas who was called Barsabbas and Silas, leading men among the brothers." In addition, a letter was prepared and sent along with these men so that it could be read in all the congregations in Antioch, Syria, and Cilicia. —Acts 15:22-26.

[12] As "leading men among the brothers," Judas and Silas were fully qualified to act as representatives of the governing body. The delegation of four men would make it clear that the message they brought was, not simply a reply to the original inquiry, but the express direction of the governing body. The presence of these "chosen men" would forge a close bond between the Jewish Christians in Jerusalem and the Gentile Christians in the field. What a wise and loving arrangement! It no doubt promoted peace and harmony among God's people.

[13] The letter provided clear direction for Gentile Christians not only regarding the circumcision issue but also regarding what they must do in order to receive Jehovah's favor and blessing. The key part of the letter stated: "The holy spirit and we ourselves have favored adding no further burden to you, except these necessary things, to keep abstaining from things sacrificed to idols and from blood and from things strangled and from fornication. If you carefully keep yourselves from these things, you will prosper. Good health to you!"—Acts 15:28, 29.

[14] Today, harmony of belief and unity of action prevail among Jehovah's Witnesses, who total some 7,000,000 in well over 100,000 congregations around the earth. How is such unity possible, especially in

---

11. How was the governing body's decision communicated to the congregations?

12, 13. What good was accomplished by sending (a) Judas and Silas? (b) a letter from the governing body?

14. How is it possible for Jehovah's people to work in unity in today's divisive world?

view of the turmoil and divisive thinking prevalent in today's world? Principally, unity results from the clear and decisive direction that Jesus Christ, the Head of the congregation, provides through "the faithful and discreet slave," represented by its Governing Body. (Matt. 24:45-47) Unity also results from the way the worldwide brotherhood cooperates willingly with the direction of the Governing Body.

"They Rejoiced Over the Encouragement" (Acts 15:30-35)

[15] The account in Acts goes on to tell us that when the delegation of brothers from Jerusalem reached Antioch, "they gathered the multitude together and handed them the letter." How did the brothers there react to the direction from the governing body? "After reading [the letter], they rejoiced over the encouragement." (Acts 15:30, 31) In addition, Judas and Silas "encouraged the brothers with many a discourse and strengthened them." In that sense, the two men were "prophets," much as Barnabas, Paul, and others were called prophets—a term referring to those who declared or made known God's will.—Acts 13:1; 15:32; Ex. 7: 1, 2.

[16] Jehovah's blessing was clearly upon the entire arrangement, bringing the issue to a happy resolution. What was the key to the positive outcome? Unquestionably, it was the governing body's clear and timely direction, based on God's Word and on the guidance of the holy spirit. Added to that was the loving, personal way in which the decisions were communicated to the congregations.

[17] Following that pattern, the Governing Body of Jehovah's Witnesses today provides timely direction to the worldwide brotherhood. When decisions are made, they are communicated to the congregations in a clear and direct manner. One way is by visits of traveling overseers. These self-sacrificing brothers travel from one congregation to another, providing clear direction and warm encouragement. Like Paul and Barnabas, they spend much time in the ministry, "teaching and declaring, with many others also, the good news of the word of Jehovah." (Acts 15: 35) Like Judas and Silas, they 'encourage the brothers with many a discourse and strengthen them.'

[18] What about the congregations? What will enable the congregations throughout the earth to continue to enjoy peace and harmony in today's divisive world? Recall that it was the disciple James who later

---

15, 16. What was the outcome of the circumcision issue, and what accounted for such a result?

17. How was the pattern set for some features of visits by traveling overseers in our day?

18. How can God's people be certain to continue to receive Jehovah's blessing?

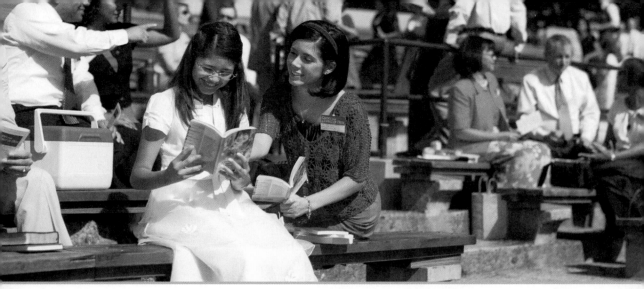

Modern-day Christians benefit from the spiritual provisions made available through the Governing Body and its representatives

wrote: "The wisdom from above is first of all chaste, then peaceable, reasonable, ready to obey . . . Moreover, the fruit of righteousness has its seed sown under peaceful conditions for those who are making peace." (Jas. 3:17, 18) Whether James had the meeting in Jerusalem in mind or not, we have no way of telling. But from our consideration of the events recorded in Acts chapter 15, it is certain that only when there is unity and cooperation can there be Jehovah's blessing.

¹⁹ That peace and unity now existed in the Antioch congregation was clearly evident. Rather than contending with the brothers from Jerusalem, the brothers in Antioch treasured the visit of Judas and Silas, for it was only after "they had passed some time, they were let go in peace by the brothers to those who had sent them out," that is, back to Jerusalem.* (Acts 15:33) We can be sure that the brothers in Jerusalem also rejoiced when they heard what the two men had to say about their journey. Thanks to Jehovah's undeserved kindness, their mission was happily accomplished!

²⁰ Paul and Barnabas, who remained in Antioch, could now focus their efforts on taking a strong lead in the evangelizing work, much as traveling overseers today do when they visit the congregations under their care. (Acts 13:2, 3) What a blessing for Jehovah's people! How, though, did Jehovah further use and bless these two zealous evangelizers? This we shall see in the next chapter.

---

* In verse 34, some Bible translations insert words to the effect that Silas chose to remain in Antioch. (*King James Version*) However, such words appear to be later additions.

19, 20. (a) How was it evident that peace and unity existed in the Antioch congregation? (b) What were Paul and Barnabas now able to do?

"LET US RETURN AND VISIT THE BROTHERS"
ACTS 15:36

What important role do traveling overseers have in the Christian congregation? What blessings result when we accept theocratic assignments with a willing spirit? How can we reason effectively from the Scriptures, and why do we need to adapt to our audience? We will learn the answers to these and other questions as we accompany the apostle Paul on his second missionary journey.

CHAPTER 15

"Strengthening the Congregations"

Traveling ministers assist the congregations to be made firm in the faith

Based on Acts 15:36–16:5

AS THEY make their way across the rugged terrain between towns, the apostle Paul looks thoughtfully at the young man walking beside him. His name is Timothy. Youthful and full of vigor, Timothy is perhaps in his late teens or early 20's. Each step of this new journey takes him farther from his home. As the day fades, the region of Lystra and Iconium steadily recedes in the distance behind them. What lies ahead? Paul has some idea, for this is his second missionary journey. He knows that there will be hazards and problems aplenty. How will the young man at his side fare?

2 Paul has confidence in Timothy, perhaps more than this humble young man has in himself. Recent events have made Paul more convinced than ever that he needs to have the right traveling companion. Paul knows that the work ahead—visiting the congregations and strengthening them—will require unswerving determination and unity of thought on the part of the traveling ministers. Why might Paul feel this way? One factor may be a disagreement that earlier caused a split between Paul and Barnabas.

3 In this chapter, we will learn much about the best way to handle disagreements. We will also learn why Paul chose Timothy as a traveling companion, and we will gain insight into the vital role of those who serve as traveling overseers today.

"Let Us Return and Visit the Brothers" (Acts 15:36)

4 In the preceding chapter, we saw how a delegation of four brothers —Paul, Barnabas, Judas, and Silas—built up the congregation at Antioch with the decision of the governing body regarding circumcision. What did Paul do next? He approached Barnabas with a new travel plan, saying: "Above all things, let us return and visit the brothers in

---

1-3. (a) Who is Paul's new traveling companion, and what is he like? (b) What will we learn in this chapter?

4. What did Paul intend to do during his second missionary journey?

Mark's Gospel relates that those who arrested Jesus also tried to seize "a certain young man" who escaped and "got away naked." (Mark 14: 51, 52) Since Mark, also known as John Mark, is the only one who records this story, the young man may have been the writer himself. If so, Mark had at least some personal contact with Jesus.

Some 11 years later, during Herod Agrippa's persecution of the Christians, "quite a few" members of the Jerusalem congregation gathered in the home of Mary, Mark's mother, to pray. It was to their home that the apostle Peter made his way when he was miraculously freed from prison. (Acts 12:12) Thus, Mark may have grown up in a house that was later used for Christian meetings. He no doubt knew Jesus' early disciples well, and they had a good influence on him.

Mark served side by side with a number of the overseers of early Christian congregations. His first service privilege, as far as we know, was that of working with his cousin Barnabas and the apostle Paul in their assignment at Antioch of Syria. (Acts 12:25) When Barnabas and Paul embarked on their first missionary journey, Mark traveled with them, first to Cyprus and then on to Asia Minor. From there, Mark returned to Jerusalem for unspecified reasons. (Acts 13: 4, 13) After a disagreement between Barnabas and Paul concerning Mark, as described in Acts chapter 15, Mark and Barnabas continued their missionary service in Cyprus.—Acts 15:36-39.

All memories of that disagreement must have been long put behind them by 60 or 61 C.E. when Mark was once again working alongside Paul, this time in Rome. Paul, who was a prisoner in that city, wrote to the congregation in Colossae: "Aristarchus my fellow captive sends you his greetings, and so does Mark the cousin of Barnabas, (concerning whom you received commands to welcome him if ever he comes to you)." (Col. 4:10) So Paul was thinking of sending John Mark from Rome to Colossae as his representative.

Sometime between 62 and 64 C.E., Mark worked with the apostle Peter in Babylon. As noted in Chapter 10 of this publication, they developed a close relationship, for Peter referred to the younger man as "Mark my son." —1 Pet. 5:13.

Finally, in about 65 C.E. when the apostle Paul was imprisoned for a second time in Rome, he wrote to his fellow worker Timothy, who was in Ephesus: "Take Mark and bring him with you, for he is useful to me for ministering." (2 Tim. 4:11) Doubtless, Mark responded readily to that invitation and made his way from Ephesus back to Rome. No wonder this man was highly appreciated by Barnabas, Paul, and Peter!

The greatest of all Mark's privileges was his being inspired by Jehovah to write a Gospel account. Tradition has it that Mark received much of his information from the apostle Peter. The facts seem to support this view, for Mark's account contains firsthand details that an eyewitness, such as Peter, would have known. However, it would appear that Mark penned his Gospel in Rome, not in Babylon when he was with Peter. Mark uses many Latin expressions and translates Hebrew terms that would otherwise be difficult for non-Jews to understand, so it seems that he wrote primarily for Gentile readers.

every one of the cities in which we published the word of Jehovah to see how they are." (Acts 15:36) Paul was not suggesting a mere social visit to these newly converted Christians. The book of Acts reveals the full purpose of Paul's second missionary journey. First, he would continue delivering the decrees that had been issued by the governing body. (Acts 16:4) Second, as a traveling overseer, Paul was determined to build up the congregations spiritually, helping them to grow firm in the faith. (Rom. 1:11, 12) How does the modern-day organization of Jehovah's Witnesses follow the pattern established by the apostles?

⁵ Today, Christ uses the Governing Body of Jehovah's Witnesses to direct his congregation. Through letters, printed literature, meetings, and other communication tools, these faithful anointed men impart guidance and encouragement to all the congregations around the world. The Governing Body also seeks to maintain close contact with each congregation. They thus use the traveling-overseer arrangement. The Governing Body has directly appointed thousands of qualified elders around the world to serve as traveling ministers.

⁶ Modern-day traveling overseers focus on giving personal attention and spiritual encouragement to all in the congregations they visit. How? By following the pattern set by such first-century Christians as Paul. He exhorted his fellow overseer: "Preach the word, be at it urgently in favorable season, in troublesome season, reprove, reprimand, exhort, with all long-suffering and art of teaching. . . . Do the work of an evangelizer."—2 Tim. 4:2, 5.

⁷ In harmony with those words, the traveling minister—along with his wife if he is married—joins the local publishers in various aspects of the field ministry. Such traveling preachers are zealous for the ministry and are skillful teachers—qualities that have a positive effect on the flock. (Rom. 12:11; 2 Tim. 2:15) Those in the traveling work are best known for their self-sacrificing love. They give freely of themselves, traveling in unfavorable weather and even in dangerous areas. (Phil. 2:3, 4) Traveling overseers also encourage, teach, and admonish each congregation by means of Bible-based talks. All in the congregation benefit by contemplating the conduct of these traveling ministers and imitating their faith.—Heb. 13:7.

"A Sharp Burst of Anger" (Acts 15:37-41)

⁸ Barnabas welcomed Paul's proposal to "visit the brothers." The two had worked well as traveling partners and both were already

---

5. How does the modern-day Governing Body impart direction and encouragement to the congregations?

6, 7. What are some of the responsibilities of traveling overseers?

8. How did Barnabas respond to Paul's invitation?

acquainted with the regions and the peoples to be visited. (Acts 13:2–14:28) So the idea of joining together for this assignment may have seemed sensible and practical. But a complication arose. Acts 15:37 reports: "For his part, Barnabas was determined to take along also John, who was called Mark." Barnabas was not simply offering a suggestion. He "was determined" to include his cousin Mark as a traveling partner on this missionary journey.

[9] Paul did not agree. Why? The account says: "Paul did not think it proper to be taking [Mark] along with them, seeing that he had departed from them from Pamphylia and had not gone with them to the work." (Acts 15:38) Mark had traveled with Paul and Barnabas on their first missionary tour but had not stayed the course. (Acts 12:25; 13:13) Early in the trip, while still in Pamphylia, Mark had left his assignment and gone home to Jerusalem. The Bible does not say why he left, but the apostle Paul evidently viewed Mark's action as irresponsible. Paul might have had questions about Mark's dependability.

[10] Still, Barnabas was adamant about taking Mark along. Paul was just as adamant about not doing so. "At this there occurred a sharp burst of anger, so that they separated from each other," says Acts 15:39. Barnabas sailed away to his home island of Cyprus, taking Mark along. Paul proceeded with his plans. The account reads: "Paul selected Silas and went off after he had been entrusted by the brothers to the undeserved kindness of Jehovah." (Acts 15:40) Together they traveled "through Syria and Cilicia, strengthening the congregations." —Acts 15:41.

[11] This account may remind us of our own imperfect nature. Paul and Barnabas had been appointed as special representatives of the governing body. Paul himself likely became a member of that body. Still, in this instance, imperfect human tendencies got the better of Paul and Barnabas. Did they allow this situation to create a lasting rift between them? Although imperfect, Paul and Barnabas were humble men, having the mind of Christ. No doubt, in time they manifested a spirit of Christian brotherhood and forgiveness. (Eph. 4:1-3) Later, Paul and Mark worked together in other theocratic assignments.*—Col. 4:10.

---

* See the box "Mark Enjoys Many Privileges," on page 118.

---

9. Why did Paul disagree with Barnabas?

10. To what did the disagreement between Paul and Barnabas lead, and with what result?

11. What qualities are essential to preventing a lasting rift from developing between us and someone who has offended us?

Timothy was a highly valued assistant to the apostle Paul. After the two men had worked side by side for some 11 years, Paul could write concerning Timothy: "I have no one else of a disposition like his who will genuinely care for the things pertaining to you. . . . You know the proof he gave of himself, that like a child with a father he slaved with me in furtherance of the good news." (Phil. 2:20, 22) Timothy readily gave of himself in order to promote the preaching work, thus endearing himself to Paul and setting a fine example for us.

The son of a Greek father and a Jewish mother, Timothy seems to have been raised in Lystra. From infancy, Timothy had been taught the Scriptures by his mother, Eunice, and his grandmother Lois. (Acts 16:1, 3; 2 Tim. 1:5; 3:14, 15) Along with them, Timothy likely accepted Christianity during Paul's first visit to Timothy's hometown.

By the time Paul returned some years later, Timothy, then possibly in his late teens or early 20's, was already "well reported on by the brothers in Lystra and Iconium." (Acts 16:2) God's spirit had inspired "predictions" about the young man, and in harmony with them, Paul and the local elders recommended that Timothy undertake a special form of service. (1 Tim. 1:18; 4:14; 2 Tim. 1:6) He was to accompany Paul as a missionary companion. Timothy would have to leave his family, and in order to eliminate a possible cause for complaint among the Jews whom Timothy would be visiting, he had to submit to circumcision.—Acts 16:3.

Timothy traveled extensively. He preached with Paul and Silas in Philippi, with Silas in Beroea, then alone in Thessalonica. When he again met up with Paul in Corinth, Timothy brought good news about the love and faithfulness shown by the Thessalonians despite their tribulation. (Acts 16:6–17:14; 1 Thess. 3:2-6) On receiving disturbing news about the Corinthians, Paul, then in Ephesus, considered sending Timothy back to Corinth. (1 Cor. 4:17) From Ephesus, Paul later dispatched Timothy and Erastus to Macedonia. But when Paul wrote to the Romans, Timothy was back with him in Corinth. (Acts 19:22; Rom. 16: 21) These are just some of the journeys that Timothy undertook for the sake of the good news.

That Timothy may have been somewhat hesitant in exercising his authority is indicated by Paul's encouragement: "Let no man ever look down on your youth." (1 Tim. 4:12) But Paul could confidently dispatch Timothy to a troubled congregation with the instructions: "*Command* certain ones not to teach different doctrine." (1 Tim. 1:3) Paul also gave Timothy authority to appoint overseers and ministerial servants in the congregation.—1 Tim. 5:22.

Timothy's excellent qualities endeared him to Paul. The Scriptures reveal that the younger man was a close, faithful, and affectionate companion, like a son. Paul could write that he remembered Timothy's tears, longed to see him, and prayed for him. Like a concerned father, Paul also gave Timothy advice about his "frequent cases of sickness"—apparently stomach problems.—1 Tim. 5:23; 2 Tim. 1:3, 4.

During Paul's first imprisonment in Rome, Timothy was by his side. At least for a period, Timothy too endured prison bonds. (Philem. 1; Heb. 13: 23) The depth of feeling between these two men can be gauged by the fact that when Paul perceived that his own death was near, he summoned Timothy: "Do your utmost to come to me shortly." (2 Tim. 4:6-9) Whether Timothy arrived in time to see his beloved mentor again is not revealed in the Scriptures.

[12] This one burst of anger was not characteristic of either Barnabas or Paul. Barnabas was known to be a warmhearted and generous man —so much so that rather than calling him by his given name, Joseph, the apostles surnamed him Barnabas, which means "Son of Comfort." Paul too was known for his tenderness and gentle demeanor. (1 Thess. 2:7, 8) In imitation of Paul and Barnabas, all Christian overseers today, including traveling ministers, should always strive to show humility and to treat fellow elders as well as the entire flock with tenderness. —1 Pet. 5:2, 3.

"He Was Well Reported On" (Acts 16:1-3)

[13] Paul's second missionary journey took him to the Roman province of Galatia, where a few congregations had been established. Eventually "he arrived at Derbe and also at Lystra." "And, look!" says the account, "a certain disciple was there by the name of Timothy, the son of a believing Jewish woman but of a Greek father."—Acts 16:1.*

[14] Evidently, Paul had met Timothy's family when first traveling to the area about the year 47 C.E. Now during his second visit two or three years later, Paul took special notice of the young man Timothy. Why? Because Timothy was "well reported on by the brothers." Not only was he well-liked by the brothers in his hometown but his reputation extended beyond the boundaries of his own congregation. The account explains that the brothers both in Lystra and in Iconium, some 20 miles away, had good things to say about him. (Acts 16:2) Guided by holy spirit, the elders entrusted young Timothy with a weighty responsibility—to assist Paul and Silas as a traveling minister.—Acts 16:3.

[15] What earned Timothy such a good reputation at his young age? Was it his intelligence, his physical appearance, or his natural abilities? Humans are often impressed by such qualities. Even the prophet Samuel was once unduly influenced by outward appearances. However, Jehovah reminded him: "Not the way man sees is the way God sees, because mere man sees what appears to the eyes, but as for Jehovah, he sees what the heart is." (1 Sam. 16:7) Rather than any personal attributes, Timothy had inner qualities that earned him a good name among his fellow Christians.

---

* See the box "Timothy Slaves 'in Furtherance of the Good News,'" on page 121.

---

12. What should characterize modern-day overseers, in imitation of Paul and Barnabas?

13, 14. (a) Who was Timothy, and under what circumstances may Paul have met him? (b) What led Paul to take special notice of Timothy? (c) What assignment did Timothy receive?

15, 16. What was it about Timothy that earned him such a good reputation?

[16] Years later, the apostle Paul made reference to some of Timothy's spiritual qualities. Paul described Timothy's good disposition, his self-sacrificing love, and his diligence in caring for theocratic assignments. (Phil. 2:20-22) Timothy was also known for having faith "without any hypocrisy."—2 Tim. 1:5.

[17] Today, many young ones imitate Timothy by cultivating godly qualities. They thereby make a good name with Jehovah and his people, even at an early age. (Prov. 22:1; 1 Tim. 4:15) They display faith without hypocrisy, refusing to lead a double life. (Ps. 26:4) As a result, many young ones can, like Timothy, play an important role in the congregation. How they encourage all lovers of Jehovah around them when they qualify as publishers of the good news and in due time make a dedication to Jehovah and get baptized!

"Made Firm in the Faith" (Acts 16:4, 5)

[18] Paul and Timothy worked together for years. As traveling ministers, they carried out various missions on behalf of the governing body. The Bible record says: "As they traveled on through the cities they would deliver to those there for observance the decrees that had been decided upon by the apostles and older men who were in Jerusalem." (Acts 16:4) Evidently, the congregations did follow the direction from the apostles and older men in Jerusalem. As a result of such obedience, "the congregations continued to be made firm in the faith and to increase in number from day to day."—Acts 16:5.

[19] Similarly, Jehovah's Witnesses today enjoy the blessings that come from submissively obeying the direction received from "those who are taking the lead" among them. (Heb. 13:17) Because the scene of the world is always changing, it is vital that Christians keep pace with the spiritual food provided by "the faithful and discreet slave." (Matt. 24:45; 1 Cor. 7:29-31) Doing so can prevent spiritual calamity and help us to remain without spot from the world.—Jas. 1:27.

[20] True, modern-day Christian overseers, including members of the Governing Body, are imperfect, as were Paul, Barnabas, Mark, and other anointed elders in the first century. (Rom. 5:12; Jas. 3:2) But because the Governing Body strictly follows God's Word and sticks to the pattern set by the apostles, they prove themselves trustworthy. (2 Tim. 1: 13, 14) As a result, the congregations are being strengthened and made firm in the faith.

---

17. How can young ones today imitate Timothy?

18. (a) What privileges did Paul and Timothy enjoy as traveling ministers? (b) How were the congregations blessed?

19, 20. Why should Christians be obedient to "those who are taking the lead"?

"Therefore we put out to sea from Troas."
—Acts 16:11

CHAPTER 16

"Step Over Into Macedonia"

Blessings result from accepting an assignment and meeting persecution with joy

Based on Acts 16:6-40

A GROUP of women leave the city of Philippi in Macedonia. Before long, they reach the narrow river Gangites. As is their custom, they sit down at the river bank to pray to the God of Israel. Jehovah observes them. —2 Chron. 16:9; Ps. 65:2.

² Meanwhile, more than 500 miles east of Philippi, a group of men leave the city of Lystra in southern Galatia. Days later, they reach a paved Roman highway leading westward to the most populated region of the district of Asia. The men—Paul, Silas, and Timothy—are eager to travel down that road so as to visit Ephesus and other cities where thousands of people need to hear about Christ. Yet, even before they can start the journey, the holy spirit stops them in some undisclosed manner. They are forbidden to preach in Asia. Why? Jesus—by means of God's spirit—wants to guide Paul's party all the way through Asia Minor, across the Aegean Sea, and onward to the banks of that little river named Gangites.

³ The way that Jesus guided Paul and his companions during that unusual journey into Macedonia contains valuable lessons for us today. Therefore, let us review some of the events that occurred during Paul's second missionary tour, which began in about 49 C.E.

"God Had Summoned Us" (Acts 16:6-15)

⁴ Prevented from preaching in Asia, Paul and his companions turned northward to preach in the cities of Bithynia. To get there, they may have walked for days on unpaved trails between the sparsely populated regions of Phrygia and Galatia. However, when they neared Bithynia, Jesus again used the holy spirit to block them. (Acts 16:6, 7) By then, the men must have been puzzled. They knew *what* to preach and *how* to preach, but they did not know *where* to preach. They had knocked, as it were, on the door leading to Asia—but in vain. They had knocked

1-3. (a) How did Paul and his companions experience the direction of the holy spirit? (b) What events will we consider?

4, 5. (a) What happened to Paul's party near Bithynia? (b) What decision did the disciples make, and with what result?

How can we "step over into Macedonia" today?

on the door leading to Bithynia—again in vain. Still, Paul was determined to keep on knocking until he found a door that would open. The men then made a decision that might have seemed erratic. They turned west and walked for 350 miles, bypassing city after city until they reached the port of Troas, the natural gateway to Macedonia. (Acts 16:8) There, for the third time, Paul knocked on a door, and—yes!—it swung wide open.

⁵ The Gospel writer Luke, who joined Paul's party at Troas, reports what happened: "During the night a vision appeared to Paul: a certain Macedonian man was standing and entreating him and saying: 'Step over into Macedonia and help us.' Now as soon as he had seen the vision, we sought to go forth into Macedonia, drawing the conclusion that God had summoned us to declare the good news to them."* (Acts 16:9, 10) Finally, Paul knew *where* to preach. How happy Paul must have felt that he had not given up halfway through the journey! Immediately, the four men sailed for Macedonia.

⁶ What lesson can we learn from that account? Note this: Only *after* Paul set out for Asia did God's spirit intervene, only *after* Paul neared Bithynia did Jesus step in, and only *after* Paul reached Troas did Jesus direct him to Macedonia. Jesus, as Head of the congregation,

---

* See the box "Luke—The Writer of Acts," on page 128.

6, 7. (a) What lesson can we learn from what took place during Paul's journey? (b) What assurance can we derive from Paul's experience?

may deal with us in a similar way today. (Col. 1:18) For instance, we may have been thinking for some time about serving as a pioneer or moving to an area where the need for Kingdom publishers is greater. However, it may well be only *after* we take definite steps to attain our goal that Jesus, through God's spirit, will guide us. Why? Think of this example: A driver can direct his car to turn left or right but only if the car is moving. Similarly, Jesus directs us in expanding our ministry, but only if we are moving—if we are putting forth real effort to do so.

[7] What, though, if our efforts do not bear fruit right away? Should we give up, thinking that God's spirit is not guiding us? No. Remember that Paul too encountered setbacks. Yet, he kept on searching until he found a door that opened. We can be sure that our perseverance in searching for "a large door that leads to activity" will be similarly rewarded.—1 Cor. 16:9.

[8] After arriving in the district of Macedonia, Paul's party traveled to Philippi—a city whose inhabitants were proud to be Roman citizens. For the retired Roman soldiers living there, the colony of Philippi was like a little Italy—a miniature Rome planted in Macedonia. Outside the city gate, beside a narrow river, the missionaries found an area where they thought there was "a place of prayer."* On the Sabbath, they went down to that spot and found several women who gathered there to worship God. The disciples sat down and spoke to them. A woman named Lydia "was listening, and Jehovah opened her heart wide." Lydia was so moved by what she learned from the missionaries that she and her household got baptized. Then she made Paul and his traveling companions come and stay at her home.#—Acts 16:13-15.

[9] Imagine the joy occasioned by Lydia's baptism! How glad Paul must have been that he had accepted the invitation to "step over into Macedonia" and that Jehovah had seen fit to use him and his companions to answer the prayers of those God-fearing women! Today, numerous brothers and sisters—young and old, single and married—likewise move to areas where the need for Kingdom publishers is greater. Granted, they cope with hardship, but this fades in comparison with the satisfaction they feel as they find people like Lydia, who embrace Bible

---

* Perhaps the Jews were forbidden to have a synagogue in the city because of Philippi's military character. Or the city might have lacked ten Jewish males—the minimum number required for establishing a synagogue.

See the box "Lydia—The Seller of Purple," on page 132.

---

8. (a) Describe the city of Philippi. (b) What joyful event resulted from Paul's preaching at "a place of prayer"?

9. How have many today imitated Paul's example, resulting in what blessings?

Up to chapter 16, verse 9, the book of Acts is narrated strictly in the third person. That is, the writer limits himself to reporting what others said and did. At Acts 16:10, 11, however, there is a change in that style. In verse 11, for instance, the writer says: *"We put out to sea from Troas and came with a straight run to Samothrace."* This is where Luke, the writer, joined the action. But since Luke's name does not appear anywhere in Acts of Apostles, how do we know that he was, in fact, the writer?

The answer lies in the introductions to the book of Acts and Luke's Gospel. Both introductions are addressed to a certain "Theophilus." (Luke 1:1, 3; Acts 1:1) The opening words of Acts read: "The first account, O Theophilus, I composed about all the things Jesus started both to do and to teach." Since ancient authorities agree that "the first account," the Gospel, was written by Luke, he must also have written Acts.

We do not know very much about Luke. His name appears only three times in the Bible. The apostle Paul calls Luke "the beloved physician" and one of his own "fellow workers." (Col. 4:14; Philem. 24) The "we" sections of the book of Acts—those in which Luke includes himself in the narrative—indicate that Luke first accompanied the apostle Paul from Troas to Philippi in about 50 C.E. but that when Paul left Philippi, Luke was no longer with him. The two men met up again in Philippi in about 56 C.E. and traveled with seven other brothers from Philippi to Jerusalem, where Paul was arrested. Two years later, Luke accompanied Paul, who was still in chains, from Caesarea to Rome. (Acts 16:10-17, 40; 20:5–21:17; 24: 27; 27:1–28:16) When Paul, who had been jailed for a second time in Rome, perceived that his execution was near, "Luke alone" was with him. (2 Tim. 4:6, 11) It is clear that Luke traveled long distances and was willing to suffer hardships for the sake of the good news.

Luke did not claim to have witnessed what he wrote about Jesus. On the contrary, he said that he undertook "to compile a statement of the facts" based on the accounts of "eyewitnesses." Moreover, he "traced all things from the start with accuracy, to write them in logical order." (Luke 1:1-3) The results of Luke's labors show that he was a careful researcher. Perhaps he conducted interviews with Elizabeth, with Jesus' mother, Mary, and with others in order to collect his material. Much of what he wrote is unique among the Gospel accounts.—Luke 1:5-80.

Paul stated that Luke was a physician, and a doctor's interest in those who suffer can be perceived in what he wrote. Just to mention a few examples: Luke noted that when Jesus cured a demon-possessed man, "the demon came out of him without hurting him"; that the apostle Peter's mother-in-law was distressed with "a high fever"; and that a woman whom Jesus helped had been afflicted with "a spirit of weakness for eighteen years, and she was bent double and was unable to raise herself up at all."—Luke 4:35, 38; 13:11.

Clearly, Luke put "the work of the Lord" first in his life. (1 Cor. 15:58) His objective was, not to pursue a secular career or prominence, but simply to help others know and serve Jehovah.

truths. Could you make adjustments that would enable you to "step over" into a territory where the need is greater? Blessings await you. For example, consider Aaron, a brother in his 20's who moved to a Central American country. He echoes the sentiments of many when he says: "Serving abroad has helped me to grow spiritually and to draw closer to Jehovah. And field service is great—I'm conducting eight Bible studies!"

"The Crowd Rose Up . . . Against Them" (Acts 16:16-24)

[10] Satan was surely furious that the good news had gained a foothold in a part of the world where he and his demons may have been unchallenged. No wonder, then, that demonic activity was involved in causing a turn of events for Paul and his companions! As they continued visiting the place of prayer, a demon-possessed servant girl, who earned money for her masters by making predictions, kept following Paul's party, shouting: "These men are slaves of the Most High God, who are publishing to you the way of salvation." The demon may have made the girl cry out these words to make it appear that her predictions and Paul's teachings came from the same source. In that way, onlookers' attention could be distracted from Christ's true followers. But Paul silenced the girl by expelling the demon.—Acts 16:16-18.

[11] When the owners of the slave girl found out that their source of easy income had vanished, they were enraged. They dragged Paul and Silas into the marketplace, where magistrates—officials representing Rome—held court. The owners appealed to the judges' prejudice and patriotism, saying, in effect: 'These Jews are causing a disturbance by teaching customs that we Romans cannot accept.' Their words had immediate results. "The crowd [in the marketplace] rose up together against them [Paul and Silas]," and the magistrates gave the order "to beat them with rods." After that, Paul and Silas were dragged to prison. The jailer threw the injured men into the inner prison and locked their feet in stocks. (Acts 16:19-24) When the jailer shut the door, the darkness in that prison hole was so thick that Paul and Silas could no doubt hardly see each other. Yet, Jehovah was watching.—Ps. 139:12.

[12] Years earlier, Jesus told his followers: "They will persecute you." (John 15:20) Thus, when Paul's party stepped over into Macedonia,

---

10. How was demon activity involved in causing a turn of events for Paul and his companions?

11. After the demon was expelled from the girl, what happened to Paul and Silas?

12. (a) How did Christ's disciples view persecution, and why? (b) What forms of opposition are still used by Satan and his agents?

they were prepared to face opposition. When persecution struck, they viewed it, not as a sign of Jehovah's disapproval, but as an expression of Satan's anger. Today, Satan's agents still employ methods similar to those used in Philippi. Deceitful opposers misrepresent us at school and in the workplace, fueling opposition. In some lands, religious opposers accuse us in court, saying, in effect: 'These Witnesses cause a disturbance by teaching customs that we "traditional believers" cannot accept.' In some places, our fellow worshippers are beaten and thrown into prison. Yet, Jehovah is watching.—1 Pet. 3:12.

"Baptized Without Delay" (Acts 16:25-34)

[13] Paul and Silas must have needed some time to absorb the tumultuous events of that day. By midnight, however, they had recovered from their beating to the point that they "were praying and praising God with song." Then, suddenly, an earthquake shook the prison! The jailer awoke, saw that the doors were opened, and feared that the prisoners had run away. Knowing that he would be punished for letting them escape, he "drew his sword and was about to do away with himself." But Paul cried out: "Do not hurt yourself, for we are all here!" The distressed jailer asked: "Sirs, what must I do to get saved?" Paul and Silas could not save him; only Jesus could. So they answered: "Believe on the Lord Jesus and you will get saved."—Acts 16:25-31.

[14] Was the jailer's question heartfelt? Paul did not doubt the man's sincerity. The jailer was a Gentile, unfamiliar with the Scriptures. Before he could become a Christian, he needed to learn and accept basic Scriptural truths. So Paul and Silas took time to speak "the word of Jehovah to him." While engrossed in teaching the Scriptures, the men perhaps forgot how they ached from the blows they had received. The jailer, though, noticed the deep cuts on their backs, and he cleansed their wounds. Then he and his household "were baptized without delay." What a blessing Paul and Silas received for meeting persecution with joy!—Acts 16:32-34.

[15] Like Paul and Silas, many Witnesses today have preached the good news while imprisoned for their faith, with fine results. For example, in one land where our activities were banned, at one time 40 percent of all Witnesses living there had learned the truth about Jehovah while in prison! (Isa. 54:17) Note, too, that the jailer asked for help only *after* the

---

13. What caused the jailer to ask: "What must I do to get saved?"

14. (a) What help did Paul and Silas give the jailer? (b) What blessing did Paul and Silas receive for meeting persecution with joy?

15. (a) How have numerous Witnesses today followed the example of Paul and Silas? (b) Why should we continue to revisit the homes of those living in our territory?

earthquake struck. Similarly, some individuals today who have never responded to the Kingdom message may do so after their personal world is suddenly shaken by a distressing event. By faithfully visiting and revisiting those living in our territory, we make sure that we are available to help them.

"Are They Now Throwing Us Out Secretly?" (Acts 16:35-40)

[16] The morning after the flogging, the magistrates ordered the release of Paul and Silas. But Paul said: "They flogged us publicly uncondemned, men who are Romans, and threw us into prison; and are they now throwing us out secretly? No, indeed! but let them come themselves and bring us out." Upon learning that the two men were Roman citizens, the magistrates "grew fearful," for they had violated the men's rights.* The tables were turned. The disciples had been beaten publicly; now the magistrates had to apologize publicly. They entreated Paul and Silas to leave Philippi. The two disciples complied, but first they took time to encourage the growing group of new disciples. Only then did they depart.

[17] If their rights as Roman citizens had been respected earlier, Paul and Silas might well have been spared the flogging. (Acts 22:25, 26) However, that could have given the disciples in Philippi the impression that the men had used their position to exempt themselves from suffering for Christ's sake. How would that have affected the faith of disciples who were not Roman citizens? After all, the law would not shield them from floggings. Hence, by enduring punishment, Paul and his companion showed the new believers by example that followers of Christ are able to stand firm under persecution. In addition, by demanding that their citizenship be recognized, Paul and Silas forced the magistrates to go on public record as having acted unlawfully. That, in turn, might hold them back from mistreating Paul's fellow believers and provide a measure of legal protection from similar attacks in the future.

[18] Today, overseers in the Christian congregation also lead by example. Whatever they expect their fellow believers to do, Christian shepherds are willing to do. Similarly, like Paul, we weigh carefully how and

---

* Roman law stated that a citizen was always entitled to a proper trial and was never to be punished in public uncondemned.

---

16. On the day after Paul and Silas were flogged, how were the tables turned?

17. What important lesson would the new disciples have learned by observing the endurance of Paul and Silas?

18. (a) How do Christian overseers today imitate Paul's example? (b) How do we 'defend and legally establish the good news' in our day?

when to use our legal rights to obtain protection. If needed, we appeal to local, national, and even international judicial courts to gain legal protection to carry out our worship. Our objective is, not social reform, but "the defending and legally establishing of the good news," as Paul wrote to the congregation in Philippi some ten years after his imprisonment there. (Phil. 1:7) Still, no matter what the outcome of such court cases may be, like Paul and his companions, we are determined to continue "to declare the good news" wherever God's spirit may lead us. —Acts 16:10.

LYDIA—THE SELLER OF PURPLE

Lydia lived in Philippi, a prominent city in Macedonia. She was originally from Thyatira, a city in the region called Lydia in western Asia Minor. To ply her trade as a seller of purple, Lydia had moved across the Aegean Sea. She likely traded in purple goods of various kinds—rugs, tapestries, fabrics, and even dyes. An inscription found in Philippi testifies to the presence of a guild of sellers of purple in that city.

Lydia is described as "a worshiper of God," likely meaning that she was a proselyte to Judaism. (Acts 16:14) She may have become acquainted with the worship of Jehovah in her home city. In contrast with Philippi, it hosted a Jewish meeting place. Some believe that Lydia was a nickname —meaning "Lydian Woman"—given to her in Philippi. However, there is documentary evidence to show that Lydia was also in use as a proper name.

The Lydians and their neighbors were famed for their skill in the dyeing of purple since the days of Homer, in the ninth or eighth century B.C.E. Indeed, Thyatira's water was reputed to produce "the brightest and the most permanent hues."

Purple materials were luxury items, accessible only to the rich. Although different sources for purple dye were known, the best and most expensive—used for treating fine linen—came from Mediterranean shellfish. A single drop of dye could be extracted from each mollusk, and some 8,000 shellfish had to be processed to obtain just one gram of the precious liquid; thus, cloth of that color was very costly.

Since Lydia's trade required substantial capital and she had a large house capable of hosting four men—Paul, Silas, Timothy, and Luke—in all likelihood she was a successful and wealthy merchant. The reference to her "household" could mean that she lived with relatives, but it may also imply that she had slaves and servants. (Acts 16:15) And the fact that before leaving the city, Paul and Silas met with some brothers in this hospitable woman's home suggests that it became a meeting place for the first Christians in Philippi.—Acts 16:40.

When Paul wrote to the Philippian congregation some ten years later, he made no mention of Lydia. So the details contained in Acts chapter 16 are all we know about her.

CHAPTER 17

"He Reasoned With Them From the Scriptures"

The basis of effective teaching; the Beroeans' fine example

Based on Acts 17:1-15

THE well-traveled road, built by skilled Roman engineers, cuts through the rugged mountains. Sounds along that road occasionally mingle —the braying of donkeys, the clatter of chariot wheels on thick flagstone, and the clamor of travelers of all sorts, likely including soldiers, merchants, and craftsmen. Three companions—Paul, Silas, and Timothy—are traveling more than 80 miles along this road, from Philippi to Thessalonica. The journey is far from easy, particularly for Paul and Silas. They are nursing the wounds they received in Philippi, where they were beaten with rods.—Acts 16:22, 23.

[2] How do these men keep their minds off the long miles that lie ahead? Conversation surely helps. Still fresh in their minds is the thrilling experience they had when that jailer back in Philippi and his family became believers. That experience has made these travelers even more determined to continue proclaiming the word of God. However, as they approach the coastal city of Thessalonica, they may wonder how the Jews in that city will treat them. Will they be attacked, even beaten, as they were in Philippi?

[3] Paul later made his feelings known in a letter he wrote to Christians in Thessalonica: "After we had first suffered and been insolently treated (just as you know) in Philippi, we mustered up boldness by means of our God to speak to you the good news of God with a great deal of struggling." (1 Thess. 2:2) Paul thus seems to suggest that he had misgivings about entering the city of Thessalonica, particularly after what happened in Philippi. Can you empathize with Paul? Do you ever find it a struggle to proclaim the good news? Paul relied on Jehovah to strengthen him, to help him muster up the boldness he needed. Studying Paul's example can help you to do the same.—1 Cor. 4:16.

1, 2. Who are journeying from Philippi to Thessalonica, and what might be on their minds?

3. How can Paul's example in mustering up boldness to preach be useful to us today?

"He Reasoned . . . From the Scriptures" (Acts 17:1-3)

⁴ The account tells us that while in Thessalonica, Paul preached in the synagogue for three Sabbaths. Does this mean that his visit to the city lasted just three weeks? Not necessarily. We do not know how soon after his arrival Paul first went to the synagogue. Further, Paul's letters disclose that while in Thessalonica, he and his companions worked to support themselves. (1 Thess. 2:9; 2 Thess. 3:7, 8) Also, during his stay, Paul twice received provisions from the brothers in Philippi. (Phil. 4:16) So his stay in Thessalonica was likely somewhat longer than three weeks.

⁵ Having mustered up boldness to preach, Paul spoke to those assembled in the synagogue. According to his custom, "he reasoned with them from the Scriptures, explaining and proving by references that it was necessary for the Christ to suffer and to rise from the dead, and saying: 'This is the Christ, this Jesus whom I am publishing to you.'" (Acts 17:2, 3) Note that Paul did not seek to stir up the emotions of his listeners; he appealed to their minds. He knew that those who attended the synagogue were familiar with and respected the Scriptures. What they lacked was understanding. Paul therefore reasoned, explained, and proved from the Scriptures that Jesus of Nazareth was the promised Messiah, or Christ.

⁶ Paul followed the standard set by Jesus, who used the Scriptures as the basis for his teaching. During his public ministry, for example, Jesus told his followers that according to the Scriptures, the Son of man must suffer, die, and be raised from the dead. (Matt. 16:21) After his resurrection, Jesus appeared to his disciples. Surely that alone would show that he had spoken the truth. Yet, Jesus gave them more. Concerning what he said to certain disciples, we read: "Commencing at Moses and all the Prophets he interpreted to them things pertaining to himself in all the Scriptures." With what result? The disciples exclaimed: "Were not our hearts burning as he was speaking to us on the road, as he was fully opening up the Scriptures to us?"—Luke 24:13, 27, 32.

⁷ The message of God's Word has power. (Heb. 4:12) Christians today thus base their teachings on that Word, as did Jesus, Paul, and the other apostles. We too reason with people, explain what the Scriptures

---

4. Why is it likely that Paul spent more than three weeks in Thessalonica?

5. In what way did Paul seek to appeal to people?

6. How did Jesus reason from the Scriptures, and with what result?

7. Why is it important to base our teaching on the Scriptures?

mean, and provide proof of what we teach by opening the Bible to show householders what it says. After all, the message we bring is not ours. By using the Bible liberally, we help people to discern that we proclaim, not our own ideas, but the teachings of God. Additionally, we do well to keep in mind that the message we preach is solidly founded on God's Word. It is completely reliable. Does knowing that not give you confidence to share the message boldly, as Paul did?

"Some . . . Became Believers" (Acts 17:4-9)

[8] Paul had already experienced the truthfulness of Jesus' words: "A slave is not greater than his master. If they have persecuted me, they will persecute you also; if they have observed my word, they will observe yours also." (John 15:20) In Thessalonica, Paul met just such a mixed response—some were eager to observe the word, while others resisted it. Concerning those who reacted favorably, Luke writes: "Some of them [the Jews] became believers [Christians] and associated themselves with Paul and Silas, and a great multitude of the Greeks who worshiped God and not a few of the principal women did so." (Acts 17:4) Surely these new disciples rejoiced to have the Scriptures opened to their understanding.

[9] Though some appreciated Paul's words, others gnashed their teeth at him. Some of the Jews in Thessalonica were jealous of Paul's success at winning over "a great multitude of the Greeks." Those Jews, intent on making Jewish proselytes, had instructed the Greek Gentiles in the teachings of the Hebrew Scriptures and looked upon those Greeks as belonging to them. Suddenly, though, it seemed that Paul was stealing these Greeks away, and right at the synagogue! The Jews were furious.

[10] Luke tells us what happened next: "The Jews, getting jealous, took into their company certain wicked men of the marketplace idlers and formed a mob and proceeded to throw the city into an uproar. And they assaulted the house of Jason and went seeking to have [Paul and Silas] brought forth to the rabble. When they did not find them they dragged Jason and certain brothers to the city rulers, crying out: 'These men that have overturned the inhabited earth are present here also, and Jason has received them with hospitality. And all these men act in opposition to the decrees of Caesar, saying there is another king, Jesus.'" (Acts 17:5-7) How would this mob action affect Paul and his companions?

8-10. (a) In what ways did people in Thessalonica respond to the good news? (b) Why were some of the Jews jealous of Paul? (c) How did the Jewish opposers act?

[11] A mob is an ugly thing. It rushes with the fury of a swollen river —violent and uncontrolled. This was the weapon that the Jews employed to try to rid themselves of Paul and Silas. Then, after the Jews had thrown the city "into an uproar," they tried to convince the rulers that the charges were weighty. The first charge was that Paul and his fellow Kingdom proclaimers had "overturned the inhabited earth," though Paul and his companions had not caused the uproar in Thessalonica! The second charge was far more serious. The Jews argued that the missionaries proclaimed another King, Jesus, thereby violating the decrees of the emperor.*

[12] Recall that the religious leaders brought a similar charge against Jesus. To Pilate they said: "This man we found subverting our nation . . . and saying he himself is Christ a king." (Luke 23:2) Possibly fearing that the emperor might conclude that Pilate condoned high treason, he sent Jesus to His death. Similarly, the charges against the Christians in Thessalonica could have brought serious consequences. One reference work states: "It is hard to exaggerate the danger to which this exposed them, for 'the very suggestion of treason against the Emperors often proved fatal to the accused.'" Would this hateful attack prove successful?

[13] The mob failed to put a stop to the preaching work in Thessalonica. Why? For one thing, Paul and Silas could not be found. Furthermore, the city rulers were evidently not convinced of the truthfulness of the charges. After requiring "sufficient security," perhaps in the form of bail, they released Jason and the other brothers who had been brought before them. (Acts 17:8, 9) Following Jesus' counsel to be "cautious as serpents and yet innocent as doves," Paul prudently kept out of harm's way so that he could continue preaching elsewhere. (Matt. 10:16) Clearly, the boldness that Paul mustered up did not mean recklessness. How can Christians today follow his example?

[14] In modern times, the clergy of Christendom have often incited mobs against Jehovah's Witnesses. With cries of sedition and trea-

---

* According to one scholar, there was at that time a decree of Caesar forbidding the making of any prediction "of the coming of a new king or kingdom, especially one that might be said to supplant or judge the existing emperor." Paul's enemies might well have misrepresented the apostle's message as a violation of such a decree. See the box "The Caesars and the Book of Acts," on page 137.

---

11. What charges were brought against Paul and his fellow Kingdom proclaimers, and what decree might the accusers have had in mind? (See footnote.)

12. What shows that the charges against Christians in Thessalonica could have brought serious consequences?

13, 14. (a) Why did the mob fail in its attack? (b) How did Paul demonstrate Christlike caution, and how can we imitate his example?

son, they have manipulated rulers to act against the Witnesses. Like those first-century persecutors, modern-day opposers are driven by jealousy. At any rate, true Christians do not court trouble. We avoid confrontations with such angry, unreasonable people whenever possible, seeking rather to continue our work in peace, perhaps returning later when things have calmed down.

They Were "More Noble-Minded" (Acts 17:10-15)

[15] For safety's sake, Paul and Silas were sent to Beroea, about 40 miles away. Upon arriving there, Paul went to the synagogue and spoke to those assembled. What a delight to find a receptive audience! Luke wrote that the Jews of Beroea were "more noble-minded than those in Thessalonica, for they received the word with the greatest eagerness of mind, carefully examining the Scriptures daily as to whether these things were so." (Acts 17:10, 11) Did those words reflect unfavorably on the ones in Thessalonica who had embraced the truth? Not at all. Paul later wrote to them: "We also thank God incessantly, because when you received God's word, which you heard from us, you accepted it, not as the word of men, but, just as it truthfully is, as the word of God, which is also at work in you believers." (1 Thess. 2:13) What, though, made those Jews in Beroea so noble-minded?

[16] Though the Beroeans were hearing something new, they were not suspicious

---

15. How did the Beroeans respond to the good news?

16. Why are the Beroeans fittingly described as "noble-minded"?

All of the events recorded in the book of Acts—and for that matter, in the entire Christian Greek Scriptures—take place within the borders of the Roman Empire. Thus, the supreme secular authority was always the Roman emperor. He was the one to whom the Thessalonian Jews referred when they spoke of "the decrees of Caesar." (Acts 17:7) Four emperors ruled during the period covered by Acts—Tiberius, Gaius, Claudius I, and Nero.

- *Tiberius* (14-37 C.E.) was emperor during all of Jesus' ministry and during the first few years of the existence of the Christian congregation. At Jesus' trial, it was to Tiberius that the Jews were referring when they shouted: "If you [Pilate] release this man, you are not a friend of Caesar. . . . We have no king but Caesar."—John 19:12, 15.
- *Gaius,* also known as *Caligula* (37-41 C.E.), is not mentioned in the Christian Greek Scriptures.
- *Claudius I* (41-54 C.E.) is named twice in the book of Acts. As foretold by the Christian prophet Agabus, "a great famine," dated about 46 C.E., came "upon the entire inhabited earth . . . in the time of Claudius." Moreover, in 49 or early 50 C.E., Claudius "ordered all the Jews to depart from Rome," a decree that prompted Aquila and Priscilla to move to Corinth, where they met the apostle Paul.—Acts 11:28; 18:1, 2.
- *Nero* (54-68 C.E.) was the Caesar to whom Paul appealed. (Acts 25:11) It is said that this emperor later blamed the Christians for the fire that destroyed much of Rome in about 64 C.E. Soon thereafter, in about 65 C.E., the apostle Paul suffered his second imprisonment in Rome and was executed.

or harshly critical; neither were they gullible. First, they listened carefully to what Paul had to say. Then, they verified what they had learned by turning to the Scriptures, which Paul had opened up to their understanding. Moreover, they diligently studied the Word of God, not just on the Sabbath, but daily. And they did so with great "eagerness of mind," devoting themselves to finding out what the Scriptures revealed in light of this new teaching. Then, they proved humble enough to make changes, for "many of them became believers." (Acts 17:12) No wonder Luke describes them as "noble-minded"!

¹⁷ Little did those Beroeans realize that the record of their reaction to the good news would be preserved in God's Word as a shining example of spiritual noble-mindedness. They did precisely what Paul had hoped they would do and what Jehovah God wanted them to do. Likewise, it is what we encourage people to do—to examine the Bible carefully so that their faith is solidly based on God's Word. After we become believers, though, does the need to be noble-minded come to an end? On the contrary, it becomes ever more important that we be eager to learn from Jehovah and quick to apply his teachings. In that way, we allow Jehovah to mold us and train us according to his will. (Isa. 64:8) We thus remain useful and fully pleasing to our heavenly Father.

¹⁸ Paul did not stay in Beroea for long. We read: "When the Jews from Thessalonica learned that the word of God was published also in Beroea by Paul, they came there also to incite and agitate the masses. Then the brothers immediately sent Paul off to go as far as the sea; but both Silas and Timothy remained behind there. However, those conducting Paul brought him as far as Athens and, after receiving a command for Silas and Timothy to come to him as quickly as possible, they departed." (Acts 17:13-15) How persistent those enemies of the good news were! It was not enough to chase Paul out of Thessalonica; they traveled to Beroea and tried to stir up the same sort of trouble there —all to no avail. Paul knew that his territory was vast; he simply moved on to preach elsewhere. May we today prove equally determined to frustrate the efforts of those who want to stop the preaching work!

¹⁹ Having borne thorough witness to the Jews in Thessalonica and Beroea, Paul had surely learned much about the importance of witnessing with boldness and reasoning from the Scriptures. We have too. Now, though, Paul was to face a different audience—the Gentiles of Athens. How would he fare in that city? In the next chapter, we will see.

---

17. Why is the example of the Beroeans so commendable, and how can we continue to imitate it long after becoming believers?

18, 19. (a) Why did Paul leave Beroea, yet how did he show perseverance that is worthy of imitation? (b) Whom was Paul to address next, and where?

"*They...went seeking to have them brought forth to the rabble.*"
—Acts 17:5

CHAPTER 18

"Seek God, . . . and Really Find Him"

Paul establishes common ground and adapts to his audience

Based on Acts 17:16-34

PAUL is greatly disturbed. He is in Athens, Greece, the center of learning where Socrates, Plato, and Aristotle once taught. Athens is a most religious city. All around him—in temples, in public squares, and on the streets—Paul sees an array of idols, for Athenians worship a pantheon of gods. Paul knows how Jehovah, the true God, views idolatry. (Ex. 20: 4, 5) The faithful apostle shares Jehovah's view—he abhors idols!

[2] What Paul sees upon entering the agora, or marketplace, is especially shocking. A large number of phallic statues of the god Hermes line the northwest corner, near the principal entrance. The marketplace is filled with shrines. How will the zealous apostle preach in this deeply idolatrous climate? Will he control his emotions and find common ground with his audience? Will he succeed in helping any to seek the true God and really find Him?

[3] Paul's speech to the learned men of Athens, as recorded at Acts 17:22-31, is a model of eloquence, tact, and discernment. By studying Paul's example, we can learn much about how to establish common ground, helping our listeners to reason.

Teaching "in the Marketplace" (Acts 17:16-21)

[4] Paul visited Athens on his second missionary journey, in about 50 C.E.* While waiting for Silas and Timothy to arrive from Beroea, Paul "began to reason in the synagogue with the Jews," as was his custom. He also sought out a territory where he could reach Athens' non-Jewish citizens—"in the marketplace," or agora. (Acts 17:17) Located northwest of the Acropolis, Athens' agora covered 12 acres or so. The marketplace was much more than a location for buying and selling; it

---

* See the box "Athens—Cultural Capital of the Ancient World," on page 142.

1-3. (a) Why is the apostle Paul greatly disturbed in Athens? (b) What can we learn by studying Paul's example?

4, 5. Where did Paul preach in Athens, and what challenging audience awaited him?

was the city's public square. One reference work notes that this place was "the economic, political and cultural heart of the city." Athenians delighted to convene there and engage in intellectual discussion.

⁵ Paul faced a challenging audience at the marketplace. Among his listeners were Epicureans and Stoics, members of rival schools of philosophy.* The Epicureans believed that life came into existence by accident. Their view of life was summed up as follows: "Nothing to fear in God; Nothing to feel in death; Good can be achieved; Evil can be endured." The Stoics stressed reason and logic and did not believe God to be a Person. Neither the Epicureans nor the Stoics believed in the resurrection as taught by Christ's disciples. Clearly, the philosophical views of these two groups were incompatible with the elevated truths of genuine Christianity, which Paul was preaching.

⁶ How did the Greek intellectuals react to Paul's teaching? Some used a word that means "chatterer," or "seed picker." (Acts 17:18; ftn.) Regarding this Greek term, one scholar states: "The word was originally used of a small bird that went around picking up grain, and later was applied to persons who picked up food scraps and other odds and ends in the market place. Still later it came to be used figuratively of any person who picked up odd bits of information, and especially of one who was unable to put them together properly." In effect, those learned men were saying that Paul was an ignorant plagiarist. Yet, as we will see, Paul was not intimidated by such name-calling.

⁷ It is no different today. As Jehovah's Witnesses, we have often been the target of name-calling because of our Bible-based beliefs. For example, some educators teach that evolution is a fact and insist that if you are intelligent, you must accept it. They, in effect, label as ignorant those who refuse to believe in it. Such learned men would have people think that we are 'seed pickers' when we present what the Bible says and point to the evidence of design in nature. But we are not intimidated. On the contrary, we speak with confidence when defending our belief that life on earth is the product of an intelligent Designer, Jehovah God.—Rev. 4:11.

⁸ Others who heard Paul's preaching in the marketplace had a different reaction. "He seems to be a publisher of foreign deities," they concluded. (Acts 17:18) Was Paul really introducing new gods to the Athenians? This was a serious matter, echoing one of the charges for which

---

* See the box "Epicureans and Stoics," on page 144.

6, 7. How did some of the Greek intellectuals react to Paul's teaching, and what similar reaction may we encounter today?

8. (a) Some who heard Paul's preaching had what reaction? (b) What might it mean that Paul was led to the Areopagus? (See footnote on page 142.)

Socrates had been tried and condemned to death centuries earlier. Not surprisingly, Paul was led to the Areopagus and asked to explain the teachings that sounded strange to the Athenians.* How would Paul defend his message to individuals who had no background in the Scriptures?

"Men of Athens, I Behold" (Acts 17:22, 23)

⁹ Recall that Paul was greatly disturbed by all the idolatry he had seen. Rather than unleash an unbridled attack on idol worship, however, he maintained his composure. With the utmost tact, he endeavored to win over his audience by establishing common ground. He began: "Men of Athens, I behold that in all things you seem to be more

---

* Located northwest of the Acropolis, the Areopagus was the traditional meeting place of the chief council of Athens. The term "Areopagus" may refer either to the council or to the actual hill. Hence, there are differences of opinion among scholars as to whether Paul was brought to or near this hill or to a meeting of the council elsewhere, perhaps in the agora.

9-11. (a) How did Paul endeavor to establish common ground with his audience? (b) How can we imitate Paul's example in our ministry?

ATHENS—CULTURAL CAPITAL OF THE ANCIENT WORLD

The Acropolis of Athens was a strongly fortified citadel well before the city's history began to be recorded in the seventh century B.C.E. Athens became the chief city of the district of Attica and dominated an area of some 1,000 square miles, bounded by mountains and sea. The city's name seems to be related to that of its patron goddess, Athena.

In the sixth century B.C.E., an Athenian legislator named Solon reformed the social, political, juridical, and economic structures of the city. He improved the lot of the poor and laid the basis for a democratic form of government. It was a democracy only for the free, however, and a large part of the city's population was made up of slaves.

Following Greek victories over the Persians in the fifth century B.C.E., Athens became the capital of a small empire that extended its maritime trade from Italy and Sicily in the west to Cyprus and Syria in the east. At the height of its splendor, Athens was the cultural center of the ancient world, excelling in art, drama, philosophy, rhetoric, and science. Many public buildings and temples adorned the city. Its skyline was dominated by the Acropolis, a commanding hill on which stood the Parthenon and its 40-foot gold and ivory statue of Athena.

Athens was conquered first by the Spartans, then by the Macedonians, and finally by the Romans, who stripped the city of its wealth. Even so, in the time of the apostle Paul, Athens still enjoyed a privileged status because of its illustrious past. In fact, the city was never incorporated into any Roman province but was granted juridical authority over its own citizens and exemption from Roman taxes. Though its greatest glories were gone, Athens remained a university city, where the sons of the wealthy were sent to study.

given to the fear of the deities than others are." (Acts 17:22) In a sense, Paul was saying, 'I see that you are very religious.' Wisely, Paul commended them for being religiously inclined. He recognized that some who are blinded by false beliefs may have receptive hearts. After all, Paul knew that he himself was once "ignorant and acted with a lack of faith."—1 Tim. 1:13.

¹⁰ Building on common ground, Paul mentioned that he had observed tangible evidence of the Athenians' religiousness—an altar dedicated "To an Unknown God." According to one source, "it was customary for Greeks and others to dedicate altars to 'unknown gods,' for fear that in their worship they had omitted some god who might otherwise be offended." By means of such an altar, the Athenians admitted the existence of a God who was unknown to them. Paul used the presence of this altar to make a transition into the good news that he was preaching. He explained: "What you are unknowingly giving godly devotion to, this I am publishing to you." (Acts 17:23) Paul's reasoning was subtle but powerful. He was not preaching a new or strange god, as some had charged. He was explaining the God that was unknown to them—the true God.

¹¹ How can we imitate Paul's example in our ministry? If we are observant, we may see evidence that a person is religiously devout, perhaps by noting some religious item that he is wearing or that is displayed on his home or in the yard. We might say: 'I see that you are a religious person. I was hoping to talk to someone who is religiously inclined.' By tactfully acknowledging the person's religious feelings, we may establish common ground on which to build. Remember that it is not our aim to prejudge others based on their religious convictions. Among our fellow worshippers are many who at one time sincerely embraced false religious beliefs.

God "Is Not Far Off From Each One of Us" (Acts 17:24-28)

¹² Paul had established common ground but could he maintain it when giving a witness? Knowing that his listeners were educated in Greek philosophy and unfamiliar with the Scriptures, he adapted his approach in several ways. First, he presented Biblical teachings without directly quoting from the Scriptures. Second, he identified himself with his listeners, at times using the words "us" and "we." Third, he quoted from Greek literature to show that certain things he was teaching were expressed in their own writings. Let us now examine Paul's powerful speech. What important truths did he convey about the God who was unknown to the Athenians?

---

12. How did Paul adapt his approach to his listeners?

The Epicureans and Stoics were followers of two separate schools of philosophy. Neither believed in a resurrection.

The Epicureans believed in the existence of gods but thought that the gods had no interest in men and would neither reward nor punish them, so prayer or sacrifice was useless. Epicureans held pleasure to be the supreme good in life. Their thinking and actions were devoid of moral principle. Moderation was urged, however, on the grounds that it prevented the negative consequences of overindulgence. Knowledge was sought only to rid a person of religious fears and superstition.

The Stoics, on the other hand, believed that all things were part of an impersonal deity and that the human soul emanated from such a source. Some Stoics held that the soul would eventually be destroyed along with the universe. Other Stoics believed that the soul would ultimately be reabsorbed by this deity. According to Stoic philosophers, happiness was to be obtained by following nature.

[13] *God created the universe.* Said Paul: "The God that made the world and all the things in it, being, as this One is, Lord of heaven and earth, does not dwell in handmade temples."* (Acts 17:24) The universe did not come about by accident. The true God is the Creator of all things. (Ps. 146:6) Unlike Athena or the other deities whose glory depended on temples, shrines, and altars, the Sovereign Lord of heaven and earth cannot be contained in temples built by human hands. (1 Ki. 8: 27) The implication of Paul's words was clear: The true God is grander than any man-made idols found in man-made temples.—Isa. 40:18-26.

[14] *God is not dependent on humans.* Idolaters were accustomed to clothing their images with lavish garments, showering them with expensive gifts, or bringing them food and drink—as if the idols needed such things! However, some of the Greek philosophers in Paul's audience may have believed that a god would need nothing from humans. If so, they no doubt agreed with Paul's statement that God is not "attended to by human hands as if he needed anything." Indeed, there is nothing material that humans can give to the Creator! Rather, he gives humans what they need —"life and breath and all things," including the sun, the rain, and fruitful soil. (Acts 17:25; Gen. 2:7) So God, the Giver, is not dependent on humans, the receivers.

[15] *God made man.* The Athenians believed that they were superior to non-Greeks. But pride of nationality or race goes against Bible truth. (Deut. 10:17) Paul addressed this delicate matter with tact and skill.

---

* The Greek word rendered "world" is *ko′smos*, which the Greeks applied to the material universe. It is possible that Paul, who was trying to maintain common ground with his Grecian audience, here used the term in that sense.

---

13. What did Paul explain about the origin of the universe, and what was the implication of his words?

14. How did Paul show that God is not dependent on humans?

15. How did Paul address the Athenians' belief that they were superior to non-Greeks, and what important lesson can we learn from his example?

When he said, "[God] made out of one man every nation of men," Paul's words no doubt gave his listeners pause. (Acts 17:26) He was referring to the Genesis account of Adam, the progenitor of the human race. (Gen. 1:26-28) Since all humans have a common ancestor, no race or nationality is superior to another. How could any of Paul's listeners miss the point? We learn an important lesson from his example. While we want to be tactful and reasonable in our witnessing work, we do not want to water down Bible truth so as to make it more acceptable to others.

[16] *God purposed that humans be close to him.* Even if the philosophers in Paul's audience had long debated the purpose of human existence, they could never have explained it satisfactorily. Paul, however, clearly revealed the Creator's purpose for humans, namely "for them to seek God, if they might grope for him and really find him, although, in fact, he is not far off from each one of us." (Acts 17:27) The God who was unknown to the Athenians is by no means unknowable. On the contrary, he is not far off from those who truly want to find him and learn about him. (Ps. 145:18) Notice that Paul used the term "us," thus including himself among those who needed "to seek" and "grope for" God.

[17] *Humans should feel drawn to God.* Because of Him, Paul said, "we have life and move and exist." Some scholars say that Paul was

---

16. What is the Creator's purpose for humans?

17, 18. Why should humans feel drawn to God, and what can we learn from the way Paul appealed to his audience?

Seek to establish common ground on which to build

alluding to the words of Epimenides, a Cretan poet of the sixth century B.C.E. and "a figure significant in Athenian religious tradition." Paul gave another reason why humans should feel drawn to God: "Certain ones of the poets among you have said, 'For we are also his progeny.'" (Acts 17:28) Humans should feel a kinship with God; he created the one man from whom all humans descend. To appeal to his audience, Paul wisely quoted directly from Greek writings that his listeners no doubt respected.* In harmony with Paul's example, we may at times make limited use of quotations from secular history, encyclopedias, or other accepted reference works. For example, an appropriate quote from a respected source might help to convince a non-Witness about the origin of certain false religious practices or observances.

[18] Up to this point in his speech, Paul conveyed key truths about God, skillfully tailoring his words to his audience. What did the apostle want his Athenian listeners to do with this vital information? Without delay, he went on to tell them as he continued his speech.

"They Should All Everywhere Repent" (Acts 17:29-31)

[19] Paul was ready to exhort his listeners to act. Referring back to the quote from Greek writings, he said: "Seeing, therefore, that we are the progeny of God, we ought not to imagine that the Divine Being is like gold or silver or stone, like something sculptured by the art and contrivance of man." (Acts 17:29) Indeed, if humans are a product of God, then how could God take the form of idols, which are a product of men? Paul's tactful reasoning exposed the folly of worshipping man-made idols. (Ps. 115:4-8; Isa. 44:9-20) By saying "we ought not to . . . ," Paul no doubt removed some of the sting from his rebuke.

[20] The apostle made it clear that action was needed: "God has overlooked the times of such ignorance [of imagining that God could be pleased with humans who worshipped idols], yet now he is telling mankind that they should all everywhere repent." (Acts 17:30) Some of Paul's listeners might have been shocked to hear this call for repentance. But his powerful speech plainly showed that they owed their life to God and were thus accountable to Him. They needed to seek God, learn the truth about him, and bring their whole way of life into harmony with that truth. For the Athenians, that meant recognizing and turning away from the sin of idolatry.

---

* Paul quoted from the astronomical poem *Phaenomena*, by the Stoic poet Aratus. Similar words are found in other Greek writings, including *Hymn to Zeus*, by the Stoic writer Cleanthes.

19, 20. (a) How did Paul tactfully expose the folly of worshipping man-made idols? (b) What action did Paul's listeners need to take?

²¹ Paul ended his speech with forceful words: "[God] has set a day in which he purposes to judge the inhabited earth in righteousness by a man whom he has appointed, and he has furnished a guarantee to all men in that he has resurrected him from the dead." (Acts 17:31) A coming Judgment Day—what a sobering reason to seek and find the true God! Paul did not name the appointed Judge. Rather, Paul said something startling about this Judge: He had lived as a man, died, and been raised from the dead by God!

²² That rousing conclusion is filled with meaning for us today. We know that the Judge appointed by God is the resurrected Jesus Christ. (John 5:22) We also know that Judgment Day will be a thousand years long and is fast approaching. (Rev. 20:4, 6) We do not fear Judgment Day, for we understand that it will bring untold blessings to those judged faithful. The fulfillment of our hope for a glorious future is guaranteed by the greatest of miracles—the resurrection of Jesus Christ!

"Some . . . Became Believers" (Acts 17:32-34)

²³ There were mixed reactions to Paul's speech. "Some began to mock" when they heard of a resurrection. Others were polite but noncommittal, saying: "We will hear you about this even another time." (Acts 17:32) A few, however, responded positively: "Some men joined themselves to him and became believers, among whom also were Dionysius, a judge of the court of the Areopagus, and a woman named Damaris, and others besides them." (Acts 17:34) We experience similar reactions in our ministry. Some people may deride us, while others respond with polite indifference. However, we are thrilled when some accept the Kingdom message and become believers.

²⁴ As we reflect on Paul's speech, we can learn much about logical development and convincing argumentation as well as how to adapt to our audience. In addition, we can learn about the need to be patient and tactful with those who are blinded by false religious beliefs. We can also learn this important lesson: We must never compromise Bible truth just to appease our listeners. Yet, by imitating the example of the apostle Paul, we can become more effective teachers in the field ministry. Furthermore, overseers can thereby become better qualified teachers in the congregation. We will thus be well-equipped to help others to "seek God . . . and really find him."—Acts 17:27.

21, 22. Paul ended his speech with what forceful words, and what meaning do his words have for us today?

23. What were the mixed reactions to Paul's speech?

24. What can we learn from the speech that Paul gave as he stood in the midst of the Areopagus?

CHAPTER 19

"Keep On Speaking and Do Not Keep Silent"

Paul supports himself yet puts his ministry first

Based on Acts 18:1-22

IT IS the latter part of 50 C.E. The apostle Paul is in Corinth, a wealthy trade center that hosts a large population of Greeks, Romans, and Jews.* Paul has not come here to buy or sell goods or to look for secular work. He has come to Corinth for a far more important reason—to bear witness about God's Kingdom. Still, Paul needs a place to stay, and he is determined not to be a financial burden on others. He does not want to give anyone the impression that he is living off the word of God. What will he do?

² Paul knows a trade—tentmaking. Making tents is not easy, but he is willing to work with his hands to support himself. Will he find employment here in this bustling city? Will he locate a suitable place to stay? Although faced with these challenges, Paul does not lose sight of his main work, the ministry.

³ As matters turned out, Paul stayed in Corinth for some time, and his ministry there bore much fruit. What can we learn from Paul's activities in Corinth that will help us to bear thorough witness about God's Kingdom in our territory?

"They Were Tentmakers by Trade" (Acts 18:1-4)

⁴ Some time after arriving in Corinth, Paul met a hospitable couple —a natural Jew named Aquila and his wife, Priscilla, or Prisca. The couple took up residence in Corinth because of a decree by Emperor Claudius ordering "all the Jews to depart from Rome." (Acts 18:1, 2) Aquila and Priscilla welcomed Paul not only into their home but also into their business. We read: "On account of being of the same trade [Paul] stayed at their home, and they worked, for they were tentmak-

---

* See the box "Corinth—Master of Two Seas," on page 149.

1-3. Why has the apostle Paul come to Corinth, and what challenges does he face?

4, 5. (a) Where did Paul stay while in Corinth, and what secular work did he do? (b) How may Paul have come to be a tentmaker?

ers by trade." (Acts 18:3) The home of this warmhearted couple remained Paul's place of dwelling during his ministry in Corinth. While he was staying with Aquila and Priscilla, Paul may have written some of the letters that later became part of the Bible canon.*

5 How is it that Paul, a man who had been educated "at the feet of Gamaliel," was also a tentmaker by trade? (Acts 22:3) The Jews of the first century apparently did not consider it beneath their dignity to teach their children a trade, even though such children may have received additional education as well. Having come from Tarsus in Cilicia, the area famous for a cloth named *cilicium* from which tents were made, Paul likely learned the trade during his youth. What did tentmaking involve? The trade could involve weaving the tent cloth or cutting and sewing the coarse, stiff material in order to make the tents. Either way, it was hard work.

6 Paul did not consider tentmaking his vocation, or career. He worked at this trade only to support himself in the ministry, declaring the good news "without cost." (2 Cor. 11:7) How did Aquila and Priscilla view their trade? As Christians, they no doubt viewed secular work as Paul did. In fact, when Paul left Corinth in 52 C.E., Aquila and Priscilla pulled up stakes and followed him to Ephesus, where their home was used as the meeting place for the local congregation. (1 Cor. 16:19) Later, they returned to

---

* See the box "Inspired Letters That Provided Encouragement," on page 150.

6, 7. (a) How did Paul view tentmaking, and what indicates that Aquila and Priscilla had a similar view? (b) How do Christians today follow the example of Paul, Aquila, and Priscilla?

Ancient Corinth lay on an isthmus between the Greek mainland and the southern peninsula, the Peloponnese. The isthmus was less than four miles wide at its narrowest point, so Corinth had two ports. On the Gulf of Corinth was Lechaeum, serving sea routes heading westward to Italy, Sicily, and Spain. On the Saronic Gulf, Cenchreae served maritime traffic to and from the Aegean region, Asia Minor, Syria, and Egypt.

Since the capes at the southern extremity of the Peloponnese were windswept and dangerous for shipping, navigators often preferred to anchor at one of Corinth's two ports, have their cargo transported overland, and reload it at the other port. Lightweight ships could even be hauled over the isthmus on a platform that ran along a grooved pavement from sea to sea. The city's position thus allowed it to dominate east-west maritime commerce and also north-south overland trade. Lively commerce brought to Corinth not only wealth but also vices common to many ports.

In the apostle Paul's day, Corinth was the capital of the Roman province of Achaia and an important administrative center. The religious diversity of the city is attested to by the presence of a temple for the imperial cult, shrines and temples dedicated to numerous Greek and Egyptian divinities, and a Jewish synagogue.—Acts 18:4.

The athletic competitions held every two years at nearby Isthmia were second in importance only to the Olympic Games. The apostle Paul would have been in Corinth during the games of 51 C.E. Hence, comments one Bible dictionary, "it can hardly be coincidental that his first use of athletic imagery appears in a letter to Corinth."—1 Cor. 9:24-27.

Rome and then went back again to Ephesus. This zealous couple put Kingdom interests first and willingly expended themselves in the service of others, thereby earning the gratitude of "all the congregations of the nations."—Rom. 16:3-5; 2 Tim. 4:19.

⁷ Present-day Christians follow the example of Paul, Aquila, and Priscilla. Zealous ministers today work hard "so as not to put an expensive burden upon" others. (1 Thess. 2:9) Commendably, many full-time Kingdom proclaimers work part-time or do seasonal work to support themselves in their vocation, the Christian ministry. Like Aquila and Priscilla, many warmhearted servants of Jehovah open their homes to traveling overseers. Those who thus "follow the course of hospitality" know how encouraging and upbuilding doing so can be. —Rom. 12:13.

INSPIRED LETTERS THAT PROVIDED ENCOURAGEMENT

During his 18-month stay in Corinth, about 50-52 C.E., the apostle Paul wrote at least two letters that became part of the Christian Greek Scriptures—First and Second Thessalonians. He wrote his letter to the Galatians either during the same period or shortly afterward.

First Thessalonians is the earliest of Paul's inspired writings. Paul visited Thessalonica in about 50 C.E., during his second preaching tour. The congregation that was formed there soon had to contend with opposition, which forced Paul and Silas to leave the city. (Acts 17:1-10, 13) Concerned about the welfare of the fledgling congregation, Paul twice attempted to return, but "Satan cut across [his] path." Paul therefore sent Timothy to comfort and strengthen the brothers. Likely late in the year 50 C.E., Timothy rejoined Paul in Corinth and brought a good report about the Thessalonian congregation. Thereafter, Paul penned this letter.—1 Thess. 2:17–3:7.

Second Thessalonians was probably written soon after the first letter, perhaps in 51 C.E. In both letters, Timothy and Silvanus (called Silas in Acts) joined Paul in sending greetings, but we have no record of these three being together again after Paul's stay in Corinth. (Acts 18:5, 18; 1 Thess. 1:1; 2 Thess. 1:1) Why did Paul write this second letter? He had apparently received more news about the congregation, perhaps via the person who had delivered his first letter. This report moved Paul not only to praise the brothers for their love and endurance but also to correct the idea of some in Thessalonica that the Lord's presence was imminent. —2 Thess. 1:3-12; 2:1, 2.

Paul's letter to the *Galatians* implies that he had visited them at least twice before writing to them. In 47-48 C.E., Paul and Barnabas visited Pisidian Antioch, Iconium, Lystra, and Derbe, all of which lay within the Roman province of Galatia. In 49 C.E., Paul returned to the same area with Silas. (Acts 13:1–14:23; 16:1-6) Paul penned this letter because Judaizers, who followed quickly on his heels, were teaching that circumcision and observance of the Law of Moses were necessary for Christians. Doubtless Paul wrote to the Galatians as soon as he heard of this false teaching. He may well have written from Corinth, but it is also possible that he wrote either from Ephesus, during a brief stopover on his journey back to Syrian Antioch, or from Antioch itself.—Acts 18:18-23.

"Many of the Corinthians . . . Began to Believe" (Acts 18:5-8)

⁸ That Paul viewed secular work as a means to an end became obvious when Silas and Timothy arrived from Macedonia with generous gifts. (2 Cor. 11:9) Immediately, Paul "began to be intensely occupied with the word ["devoted all his time to preaching," *The Jerusalem Bible*]." (Acts 18:5) However, this intense witnessing to the Jews met with considerable opposition. Disclaiming any further responsibility for their refusal to accept the lifesaving message about the Christ, Paul shook out his garments and told his Jewish opposers: "Let your blood be upon your own heads. I am clean. From now on I will go to people of the nations."—Acts 18:6; Ezek. 3:18, 19.

⁹ Where, then, would Paul now preach? A man named Titius Justus, likely a Jewish proselyte whose house was adjacent to the synagogue, opened up his home to Paul. So Paul transferred from the synagogue to the house of Justus. (Acts 18:7) The home of Aquila and Priscilla remained Paul's residence while he was in Corinth, but the house of Justus became the center from which the apostle carried on his preaching activity.

¹⁰ Did Paul's statement that he would henceforth go to people of the nations mean that he completely turned his attention away from all Jews and Jewish proselytes, even responsive ones? That could hardly have been the case. For example, "Crispus the presiding officer of the synagogue became a believer in the Lord, and so did all his household." Evidently, a number of those associated with the synagogue joined Crispus, for the Bible says: "Many of the Corinthians that heard began to believe and be baptized." (Acts 18:8) The house of Titius Justus thus became the location where the newly formed Christian congregation of Corinth met. If the Acts account is presented in Luke's characteristic style—that is, chronologically—then the conversion of those Jews or proselytes took place *after* Paul shook out his garments. The incident would then speak volumes about the apostle's flexibility.

¹¹ In many lands today, the churches of Christendom are well-established and have a strong hold on their members. In some countries and islands of the sea, the missionaries of Christendom have done a great deal of proselytizing. People claiming to be Christian are often bound by tradition, as were the Jews in first-century Corinth. Still, like Paul, we as Jehovah's Witnesses zealously reach out to such

---

8, 9. How did Paul respond when his intense witnessing to the Jews met with opposition, and where did he then go to preach?

10. What shows that Paul was not determined to preach only to people of the nations?

11. How do Jehovah's Witnesses today imitate Paul as they reach out to those in Christendom?

Acts 18:18 states that while Paul was in Cenchreae, "he had the hair of his head clipped short . . . , for he had a vow." What kind of vow was it?

Generally, a vow is a solemn promise voluntarily made to God to perform some act, make some offering, or enter some condition. Some suppose that Paul had his hair cut to fulfill a Nazirite vow. Yet, it should be noted that according to the Scriptures, on completing a period of special service to Jehovah, a Nazirite was to have his head shaved "at the entrance of the tent of meeting." It would seem that such a requirement could be carried out only in Jerusalem and thus not in Cenchreae.—Num. 6:5, 18.

The Acts account says nothing regarding when Paul made his vow. It could conceivably have been made even before he became a Christian. The account is equally silent concerning whether Paul made any specific request of Jehovah. One reference work suggests that Paul's having his hair clipped short could have been "an expression of thanksgiving to God for his protection, which had enabled [Paul] to complete his ministry at Corinth."

people, building on whatever knowledge of the Scriptures they may have. Even when they oppose us or their religious leaders persecute us, we do not lose hope. Among those who "have a zeal for God; but not according to accurate knowledge," there may be many meek ones who need to be searched for and found.—Rom. 10:2.

"I Have Many People in This City" (Acts 18:9-17)

[12] If Paul had any doubt about continuing his ministry in Corinth, it must have disappeared on the night when the Lord Jesus appeared to him in a vision and told him: "Have no fear, but keep on speaking and do not keep silent, because I am with you and no man will assault you so as to do you injury; for I have many people in this city." (Acts 18:9, 10) What an encouraging vision! The Lord himself assured Paul that he would be protected from injury and that there were many deserving ones in the city. How did Paul respond to the vision? We read: "He stayed set there a year and six months, teaching among them the word of God." —Acts 18:11.

[13] After spending about a year in Corinth, Paul received further proof of the Lord's support. "The Jews rose up with one accord against Paul and led him to the judgment seat," called the *be'ma.* (Acts 18:12) Thought by some to be a raised platform of blue and white marble full of decorative carvings, the *be'ma* may have been situated near the center of Corinth's marketplace. The open area in front of the *be'ma* was large enough for a sizable crowd to gather. Archaeological discoveries suggest that the judgment seat may have been only a few steps from the synagogue and, therefore, from Justus' house. As Paul approached the *be'ma*, he may have thought about the stoning of Stephen, who is

---

12. What assurance does Paul receive in a vision?

13. What incident might Paul have thought of as he approached the judgment seat, but what reason did he have to expect a different outcome?

sometimes referred to as the first Christian martyr. Paul, known then as Saul, had approved of "the murder of him." (Acts 8:1) Would something similar now happen to Paul? No, for he had been promised: "No one shall . . . injure you."—Acts 18:10, *An American Translation.*

[14] What happened when Paul got to the judgment seat? The magistrate occupying it was the proconsul of Achaia, named Gallio—the older brother of the Roman philosopher Seneca. The Jews launched this accusation against Paul: "Contrary to the law this person leads men to another persuasion in worshiping God." (Acts 18:13) The Jews implied that Paul had been proselytizing illegally. However, Gallio saw that Paul had committed no "wrong" and was not guilty of any "wicked act of villainy." (Acts 18:14) Gallio had no intention of getting involved in the controversies of the Jews. Why, before Paul uttered even a word in his own defense, Gallio dismissed the case! The accusers were enraged. They vented their anger on Sosthenes, who had perhaps replaced Crispus as the presiding officer of the synagogue. They seized Sosthenes "and went to beating him in front of the judgment seat."—Acts 18:17.

[15] Why did Gallio not prevent the crowd from thrashing Sosthenes? Perhaps Gallio thought that Sosthenes was the leader of the mob action against Paul and was therefore getting what he deserved. Whether that was the case or not, the incident possibly had a good outcome. In his first letter to the Corinthian congregation, written several years later, Paul referred to a certain Sosthenes as a brother. (1 Cor. 1: 1, 2) Was this the same Sosthenes who had been beaten in Corinth? If so, the painful experience may have helped Sosthenes to embrace Christianity.

[16] Recall that it was after the Jews had rejected Paul's preaching that the Lord Jesus assured Paul: "Have no fear, but keep on speaking and do not keep silent, because I am with you." (Acts 18:9, 10) We do well to keep those words in mind, especially when our message is rejected. Never forget that Jehovah reads hearts and draws honesthearted ones to himself. (1 Sam. 16:7; John 6:44) What an encouragement that is for us to keep busy in the ministry! Each year hundreds of thousands are getting baptized—hundreds every day. To those who heed the command to "make disciples of people of all the nations," Jesus offers this reassurance: "I am with you all the days until the conclusion of the system of things."—Matt. 28:19, 20.

14, 15. (a) What accusation did the Jews launch against Paul, and why did Gallio dismiss the case? (b) What happened to Sosthenes, and what might have become of him?

16. What bearing do the Lord's words, "Keep on speaking and do not keep silent, because I am with you," have on our ministry?

"If Jehovah Is Willing" (Acts 18:18-22)

¹⁷ Whether Gallio's stance toward Paul's accusers resulted in a period of peace for the fledgling Christian congregation in Corinth cannot be ascertained. However, Paul stayed "quite some days longer" before saying good-bye to his Corinthian brothers. In the spring of 52 C.E., he made plans to sail away to Syria from the port of Cenchreae, about seven miles east of Corinth. Before leaving Cenchreae, though, Paul "had the hair of his head clipped short . . . , for he had a vow."* (Acts 18:18) Afterward, he took Aquila and Priscilla with him and sailed across the Aegean Sea to Ephesus in Asia Minor.

¹⁸ As Paul sailed from Cenchreae, he likely reflected on his time in Corinth. He had many fine memories and a basis for deep satisfaction. His 18-month ministry there had borne fruit. The first congregation in Corinth had been established, with the house of Justus as its meeting place. Among those who became believers were Justus, Crispus and his household, and many others. Those new believers were dear to Paul, for he had helped them to become Christians. He would later write to them and describe them as a letter of recommendation inscribed on his heart. We too feel a closeness to those whom we have had the privilege of helping to embrace true worship. How satisfying it is to see such living "letters of recommendation"!—2 Cor. 3:1-3.

¹⁹ Upon arriving in Ephesus, Paul immediately went about his work. He "entered into the synagogue and reasoned with the Jews." (Acts 18:19) Paul stayed in Ephesus for only a short time on that occasion. Although asked to stay longer, "he would not consent." When saying good-bye, he told the Ephesians: "I will return to you again, if Jehovah is willing." (Acts 18:20, 21) Paul no doubt recognized that there was much preaching to be done in Ephesus. The apostle planned on returning, but he chose to leave matters in Jehovah's hands. Is that not a good example for us to keep in mind? In pursuing spiritual goals, we need to take the initiative. However, we must always rely on Jehovah's direction and seek to act in harmony with his will.—Jas. 4:15.

²⁰ Leaving Aquila and Priscilla in Ephesus, Paul put out to sea and came down to Caesarea. He apparently "went up" to Jerusalem and greeted the congregation there. (Acts 18:22; ftn.) Then Paul went to his home base—Syrian Antioch. His second missionary journey had come to a successful conclusion. What awaited him on his final missionary journey?

---

* See the box "Paul's Vow," on page 152.

17, 18. What might Paul have reflected on as he sailed to Ephesus?

19, 20. What did Paul do upon arriving in Ephesus, and what do we learn from him about pursuing spiritual goals?

"With that he drove them away from the judgment seat."
—Acts 18:16

"TEACHING...PUBLICLY AND FROM HOUSE TO HOUSE"
ACTS 20:20

Why do we need to be humble as well as adaptable in teaching others? What is the primary method of preaching the good news? How can we show that the doing of God's will is more important than our own personal pursuits? The thrilling record of Paul's third and final missionary journey can help us to answer these vital questions.

CHAPTER 20

"Growing and Prevailing" Despite Opposition

How Apollos and Paul contribute toward the continued victory of the good news

Based on Acts 18:23–19:41

THE streets of Ephesus resound with shouts, cries, and the thunder of crowds running. A mob has formed, and a full-blown riot is under way! Two of the apostle Paul's traveling companions are seized and dragged along. The wide, colonnaded street where the shops are located empties quickly as the rabid crowd swells and storms into the city's huge amphitheater, which could accommodate 25,000 spectators. Most of the people do not even know what has caused the uproar, but they have a faint idea that their temple and their beloved goddess Artemis are being threatened. So they begin to chant frantically: "Great is Artemis of the Ephesians!"—Acts 19:34.

[2] Once again, we see Satan trying to use mob violence to stop the spread of the good news of God's Kingdom. Of course, the threat of violence is not Satan's only tactic. In this chapter, we will discuss a number of Satan's schemes to undermine the work and unity of those first-century Christians. More important, we will see that all his tactics failed, for "in a mighty way the word of Jehovah kept growing and prevailing." (Acts 19:20) Why did those Christians prove victorious? For the same reasons that we do today. Of course, the victory is Jehovah's, not ours. However, like the first-century Christians, we must do our part. With the aid of Jehovah's spirit, we can acquire qualities that will help to ensure the success of our ministry. Let us first consider the example of Apollos.

"He Was Well Versed in the Scriptures" (Acts 18:24-28)

[3] While Paul was on his way to Ephesus during his third missionary tour, a Jew named Apollos arrived in the city. He was from the famed city of Alexandria, Egypt. Apollos had some outstanding qualities. He

---

1, 2. (a) Paul and his companions face what danger in Ephesus? (b) What will we discuss in this chapter?

3, 4. What lack did Aquila and Priscilla perceive in Apollos, and how did they address it?

"Men, you well know that from this business
we have our prosperity."
—Acts 19:25

spoke very well. In addition to his eloquence, "he was well versed in the Scriptures." Furthermore, he was "aglow with the spirit." Full of zeal, Apollos spoke boldly before Jewish audiences in the synagogue.—Acts 18:24, 25.

⁴ Aquila and Priscilla heard Apollos speak. No doubt they were thrilled to hear him teach "with correctness the things about Jesus." What he said about Jesus was accurate. However, before long that Christian couple detected an important gap in Apollos' knowledge. He was "acquainted with only the baptism of John." This humble couple, tentmakers by trade, were not intimidated by the eloquence or education of Apollos. Rather, "they took him into their company and expounded the way of God more correctly to him." (Acts 18:25, 26) And how did this well-spoken, learned man respond? Evidently, he showed one of the most important qualities that a Christian can cultivate—humility.

⁵ Because Apollos accepted the assistance of Aquila and Priscilla, he became a more effective servant of Jehovah. He traveled on to Achaia, where he "greatly helped" the believers. His preaching also proved effective against those Jews in that region who insisted that Jesus was not the foretold Messiah. Luke reports: "With intensity he thoroughly proved the Jews to be wrong publicly, while he demonstrated by the Scriptures that Jesus was the Christ." (Acts 18:27, 28) What a blessing Apollos became! In effect, he was another reason why "the word of Jehovah" went on prevailing. What can we learn from Apollos' example?

⁶ Cultivating humility is absolutely essential for Christians. Each of us is blessed with various gifts—whether these have to do with natural abilities, experience, or knowledge that we have acquired. However, our humility must exceed our gifts. Otherwise, our assets may become liabilities. We may become fertile ground for the growth of that poisonous weed haughtiness. (1 Cor. 4:7; Jas. 4:6) If we are truly humble, we will endeavor to see others as superior to us. (Phil. 2:3) We will neither resent correction nor resist being taught by others. We will certainly not cling proudly to our own ideas when we learn that these are out of harmony with the present leadings of the holy spirit. As long as we remain humble, we are useful to Jehovah and his Son.—Luke 1:51, 52.

⁷ Humility also defuses rivalry. Can you imagine how eager Satan was to create divisions among those early Christians? How delighted

---

5, 6. What enabled Apollos to become more useful to Jehovah, and what may we learn from Apollos' example?

7. How did Paul and Apollos set an example of humility?

he would have been if two such dynamic personalities as Apollos and the apostle Paul had allowed themselves to become rivals, perhaps jealously vying for influence among the congregations! It would have been easy for them to do so. In Corinth, some Christians began saying, "I belong to Paul," while others said, "But I to Apollos." Did Paul and Apollos encourage such divisive sentiments? No! And Paul humbly acknowledged Apollos' contribution to the work, granting him privileges of service. For his part, Apollos followed Paul's direction. (1 Cor. 1:10-12; 3: 6, 9; Titus 3:12, 13) What a fine example of humble cooperation for us today!

"Using Persuasion Concerning the Kingdom" (Acts 18:23; 19:1-10)

8 Paul had promised to return to Ephesus, and he kept his word.* (Acts 18:20, 21) Note, though, *how* he returned. We last saw him in Antioch, Syria. To reach Ephesus, he could have made the short trip to Seleucia, boarded a ship, and sailed directly to his destination. Instead, he traveled "through the inland parts." By one estimate, Paul's journey as traced out in Acts 18:23 and 19:1 encompassed about a thousand miles! Why did Paul choose such an arduous route? Because he had as his aim, "strengthening all the disciples." (Acts 18:23) His third missionary journey, like the previous two, would demand much of him, but he considered it all worthwhile. Traveling ministers and their wives today display a like spirit. Do we not appreciate their self-sacrificing love?

9 Upon his arrival at Ephesus, Paul found a group of about a dozen disciples of John the Baptizer. They had been baptized under an arrangement that was no longer valid. Furthermore, they seemed to know little or nothing about the holy spirit. Paul brought them up-to-date, and like Apollos, they proved to be humble and eager to learn. After being baptized in the name of Jesus, they received holy spirit and some miraculous gifts. Clearly, then, keeping up with Jehovah's advancing theocratic organization brings blessings.—Acts 19:1-7.

10 Another example of progress soon followed. Paul preached boldly in the synagogue for three months. Although he was "using persuasion concerning the kingdom of God," some hardened themselves and became real opposers. Rather than wasting time with those who

---

* See the box "Ephesus—Capital of Asia," on page 161.

---

8. By what route did Paul return to Ephesus, and why?

9. Why did a group of disciples need to be rebaptized, and what lesson may we learn from their course?

10. Why did Paul move from the synagogue to an auditorium, setting what example for us in our ministry?

were "speaking injuriously about The Way," Paul made arrangements to speak in a school auditorium. (Acts 19:8, 9) Those who wanted to make spiritual progress needed to make a move from the synagogue to the auditorium. Like Paul, we may withdraw from some conversations when we recognize that the householder is unwilling to listen or only wants to argue. There are still plenty of sheeplike people who need to hear our encouraging message!

[11] Paul may have spoken in that school auditorium daily from about 11:00 a.m. until about 4:00 p.m. (Acts 19:9, ftn.) Those were likely the quietest but hottest hours of the day when many stopped their work to eat and rest. Imagine if Paul followed that rigorous schedule for two full years, he would have spent well over 3,000 hours teaching.* Here, then, is another reason why the word of Jehovah kept growing and prevailing. Paul was industrious and adaptable. He adjusted his schedule so that his ministry met the needs of the people in that community. The result? "All those inhabiting the district of Asia heard the word of the Lord, both Jews and Greeks." (Acts 19:10) What a thorough witness he gave!

[12] Jehovah's Witnesses in modern times have likewise proved to be industrious and adaptable. We endeavor to reach people wherever and whenever they can be found. We witness on the streets, at the marketplaces, and in parking lots. We may contact people by telephone or by letter. And in the house-to-house work, we make efforts to reach people at times when we are most likely to find them at home.

---

* Paul also wrote *1 Corinthians* while in Ephesus.

11, 12. (a) How did Paul set an example in being industrious and adaptable? (b) How have Jehovah's Witnesses endeavored to be industrious and adaptable in their public ministry?

EPHESUS—CAPITAL OF ASIA

Ephesus was the largest city in western Asia Minor. In the apostle Paul's day, its population probably exceeded 250,000. As the capital of the Roman province of Asia, it proudly bore the title "First and Greatest Metropolis of Asia."

Ephesus derived great wealth from commerce and religion. Located close to the mouth of a navigable river, its seaport stood at the intersection of trade routes. Ephesus was home not only to the famous temple of Artemis but also to the shrines and temples of numerous other Greco-Roman, Egyptian, and Anatolian deities.

The temple of Artemis, lauded as one of the seven wonders of the ancient world, measured approximately 350 feet by 160 feet. It contained some 100 marble pillars, each about 6 feet in diameter at the base and almost 55 feet high. The temple was considered sacrosanct throughout the ancient Mediterranean area, and huge sums of money were entrusted to the safekeeping of Artemis; so the temple also became the most important banking center in Asia.

Other important buildings in Ephesus were a stadium for athletic contests and possibly even gladiatorial combat, a theater, civic and commercial squares, and colonnades housing shops.

The Greek geographer Strabo reports that the harbor of Ephesus suffered from silting. In time, the city therefore ceased to function as a port and was abandoned. Since no modern city stands on the same site, present-day visitors to the extensive ruins of Ephesus can, in effect, step back into the ancient world.

We endeavor to reach people wherever they can be found

"Growing and Prevailing" Despite Wicked Spirits (Acts 19:11-22)

¹³ Luke informs us that a remarkable period ensued, with Jehovah enabling Paul to perform "extraordinary works of power." Even cloths and aprons that Paul wore were taken to sick people, who were cured. Wicked spirits were driven out by these means too.* (Acts 19:11, 12) Such outstanding victories over Satan's forces drew much attention, not all of it positive.

¹⁴ Some "roving Jews who practiced the casting out of demons" sought to duplicate Paul's miracles. Certain ones of those Jews tried to expel demons by invoking the names of Jesus and Paul. Luke gives the example of the seven sons of Sceva—members of a priestly family—who sought to do this. The demon said to them: "I know Jesus and I am acquainted with Paul; but who are you?" The possessed man then attacked those charlatans, leaping upon them like a wild beast, sending them scurrying off, wounded and naked. (Acts 19:13-16) This was a resounding victory for "the word of Jehovah," as the contrast between the power given to Paul and the powerlessness of those false religionists could not have been plainer. There are millions today who wrongly assume that simply calling on the name of Jesus or labeling oneself "Christian" is enough. As Jesus indicated, though, only those actually doing the will of his Father have a real hope for the future.—Matt. 7:21-23.

¹⁵ The humiliation of the sons of Sceva led to a widespread godly fear, which influenced many to become believers and abandon spiritistic practices. Ephesian culture was steeped in the magical arts. Spells and amulets were commonplace, as were incantations, often in written form. Many Ephesians were now moved to bring out their

---

* The cloths may have been handkerchiefs worn by Paul around the forehead to keep perspiration from running into the eyes. That Paul also wore aprons at this time suggests that he may have been plying his trade of tentmaking during his free hours, perhaps in the early mornings.—Acts 20:34, 35.

13, 14. (a) Jehovah enabled Paul to do what? (b) What mistake did the sons of Sceva make, and how do many in Christendom today err in a similar way?

15. When it comes to spiritism and objects connected with spiritistic practices, how can we follow the example of the Ephesians?

books on magical arts and burn them publicly—though these were evidently worth tens of thousands of dollars by present standards.* Luke reports: "Thus in a mighty way the word of Jehovah kept growing and prevailing." (Acts 19:17-20) What a marvelous victory of truth over falsehood and demonism! Those faithful people set a good example for us today. We likewise live in a world steeped in spiritism. Should we find that we own something connected to spiritism, we would do as the Ephesians did—get rid of it promptly! Let us keep far away from such disgusting practices, whatever the cost.

"There Arose No Little Disturbance" (Acts 19:23-41)

16 We come now to the tactic of Satan described by Luke when he wrote that "there arose no little disturbance concerning The Way." He was hardly overstating matters.# (Acts 19:23) A silversmith named Demetrius started the trouble. He got the attention of his fellow craftsmen by first reminding them that their prosperity came from selling idols. He went on to suggest that the message Paul preached was bad for business, since the Christians did not worship idols. Then he appealed to the civic pride and nationalism of his audience, warning them that their goddess Artemis and their world-famous temple to her were in danger of being "brought down to nothing."—Acts 19:24-27.

17 Demetrius' speech had the desired effect. The silversmiths began chanting "Great is Artemis of the Ephesians," and the city became filled with confusion, leading to the fanatic mob scene described at the outset of this chapter.△ Paul, self-sacrificing soul that he was, wanted to go into the amphitheater to address the crowd, but the disciples insisted that he stay out of danger. A certain Alexander stood before the crowd and attempted to speak. Since he was a Jew, he may have been eager to explain the difference between Jews and these Christians. Such explanations would have been lost on that crowd.

* Luke cites a value of 50,000 silver pieces. If he meant the denarius, it would have taken a worker back then 50,000 days—about 137 years—to earn that amount of money if he worked seven days a week.

Some say that Paul referred to this incident when he told the Corinthians that "we were very uncertain even of our lives." (2 Cor. 1:8) However, he may have had in mind a more dangerous occasion. When Paul wrote that he "fought with wild beasts at Ephesus," he could have been referring to an experience with ferocious animals in an arena or to human opposition. (1 Cor. 15:32) Both the literal and the figurative interpretations are possible.

△ Such guilds, or unions, of craftsmen could be quite powerful. About a century later, for example, the bakers' guild incited a similar riot in Ephesus.

16, 17. (a) Describe how Demetrius got the riot started in Ephesus. (b) How did the Ephesians show their fanaticism?

When they recognized him as a Jew, they shouted him down, repeating the chant "Great is Artemis of the Ephesians" for about two hours. Religious fanaticism has not changed since then. It still makes people completely unreasonable.—Acts 19:28-34.

[18] Finally, the city recorder quieted the crowd. A capable man with presence of mind, this official assured the mob that their temple and goddess were in no danger from these Christians, that Paul and his companions had committed no crime against the temple of Artemis, and that there was a due process in place for raising such issues. Perhaps most tellingly, he reminded the mob that they were in danger of incurring the wrath of Rome for this unlawful and unruly gathering. With that, he dismissed the crowd. As quickly as their rage had erupted, it now subsided because of these rational and practical words. —Acts 19:35-41.

[19] This was not the first time that a levelheaded man in a position of secular authority had acted to protect Jesus' followers, nor would it be the last. In fact, the apostle John foresaw in a vision that during these last days, the stable elements of this world, pictured by the earth, would swallow up a veritable flood of satanic persecution against Jesus' followers. (Rev. 12:15, 16) That has proved true. In many cases, fair-minded judges have moved to protect the rights of Jehovah's Witnesses to meet for worship and to share the good news with others. Of course, our own conduct may play a role in such victories. Paul's conduct had apparently won him the friendly respect of some governmental officials in Ephesus, so they were eager to see him safe. (Acts 19:31) May our honest and respectful conduct make a favorable impression on those we meet as well. We never know how far-reaching the effects may be.

[20] Is it not thrilling to contemplate how "the word of Jehovah kept growing and prevailing" in the first century? It is equally thrilling to see how Jehovah has been behind similar victories in our time. Would you like to have the privilege of playing a part, however small, in such victories? Then learn from the examples we have considered. Stay humble, keep up with Jehovah's progressive organization, keep working hard, repudiate spiritism, and do your utmost to give a good witness through your honest and respectful conduct.

18, 19. (a) How did the city recorder quiet the mob in Ephesus? (b) How have Jehovah's people at times been protected by secular authorities, and what role may we play in such protection?

20. (a) How do you feel about the way Jehovah's word prevailed in the first century and is prevailing today? (b) What is your resolve regarding Jehovah's victories in our time?

CHAPTER 21

"I Am Clean From the Blood of All Men"

Paul's zeal in the ministry and his counsel to elders

Based on Acts 20:1-38

PAUL is in a crowded upper chamber in Troas. He speaks at length to the brothers, since this is the last evening he will be with them. It is now midnight. There are quite a few lamps burning in the room, adding to the heat and perhaps contributing to a smoky atmosphere. Seated at one of the windows is a young man named Eutychus. As Paul is speaking, Eutychus falls asleep and tumbles out of the third-story window!

[2] As a physician, Luke is likely among the first to rush outside and examine the young man. There is no question about his condition. Eutychus is "picked up dead." (Acts 20:9) But then a miracle occurs. Paul throws himself upon the young man and says to the crowd: "Stop raising a clamor, for his soul is in him." Paul has raised Eutychus back to life!—Acts 20:10.

[3] That incident demonstrates the power of God's holy spirit. Paul could not rightly be blamed for the death of Eutychus. Still, he did not want the young man's death to mar this important occasion or to stumble anyone spiritually. By resurrecting Eutychus, Paul left the congregation comforted and fully invigorated to carry on their ministry. Clearly, Paul took a very responsible view of the lives of others. We are reminded of his words: "I am clean from the blood of all men." (Acts 20: 26) Let us consider how Paul's example can help us in this regard.

"He Went Forth to Journey Into Macedonia" (Acts 20:1, 2)

[4] As discussed in the preceding chapter, Paul had been through a harrowing ordeal. His ministry in Ephesus had stirred up quite a commotion. Indeed, the silversmiths whose livelihood depended on the worship of Artemis had taken part in a riot! "After the uproar had subsided," Acts 20:1 relates, "Paul sent for the disciples, and when he had

---

1-3. (a) Describe the circumstances surrounding the death of Eutychus. (b) What does Paul do, and what does this incident show about Paul?

4. What harrowing ordeal had Paul been through?

encouraged them and bidden them farewell, he went forth to journey into Macedonia."

⁵ On the way to Macedonia, Paul stopped in the seaport of Troas and spent time there. Paul hoped that Titus, who had been sent to Corinth, would join him there. (2 Cor. 2:12, 13) However, when it became evident that Titus was not coming, Paul went on to Macedonia, perhaps spending a year or so "encouraging the ones there with many a word."* (Acts 20:2) Titus finally joined Paul in Macedonia, bringing good news regarding the Corinthians' response to Paul's first letter. (2 Cor. 7:5-7) This moved Paul to write another letter to them, which we now know as 2 Corinthians.

⁶ It is noteworthy that Luke uses the words "encouraged" and "encouraging" to describe Paul's visits to the brothers in Ephesus and Macedonia. How well those words express Paul's attitude toward fellow believers! In contrast with the Pharisees, who looked upon others with contempt, Paul viewed the sheep as fellow workers. (John 7:47-49;

---

* See the box "Paul's Letters From Macedonia," on this page.

5, 6. (a) How long may Paul have been in Macedonia, and what did he do for the brothers there? (b) What attitude did Paul maintain toward his fellow believers?

PAUL'S LETTERS FROM MACEDONIA

In his second letter to the *Corinthians,* Paul says that when he arrived in Macedonia, he was anxious about his brothers in Corinth. However, Titus brought him good news from Corinth, and Paul was comforted. It was then, in about 55 C.E., that Paul wrote 2 Corinthians in which he indicates that he was still in Macedonia. (2 Cor. 7:5-7; 9:2-4) One of the things on Paul's mind during this period was the completing of the collection for the holy ones in Judea. (2 Cor. 8:18-21) He was also worried about the presence in Corinth of "false apostles, deceitful workers."—2 Cor. 11:5, 13, 14.

It is possible that Paul's letter to *Titus* was written from Macedonia. Sometime during the years 61 to 64 C.E., after being released from his first Roman captivity, Paul visited the island of Crete. He left Titus there to correct certain problems and make congregation appointments. (Titus 1:5) Paul asked Titus to meet him in Nicopolis. There were a number of cities of this name in the ancient Mediterranean area, but it seems most likely that Paul was referring to the Nicopolis in northwest Greece. The apostle was probably working in that general area when he wrote to Titus.—Titus 3:12.

Paul's first letter to *Timothy* also belongs to the period between his two imprisonments in Rome, from 61 to 64 C.E. In the introduction to this letter, Paul indicates that he asked Timothy to remain in Ephesus, while he himself went to Macedonia. (1 Tim. 1:3) From there, it seems, Paul wrote this letter to give Timothy fatherly advice, encouragement, and direction on certain procedures to be followed in the congregations.

1 Cor. 3:9) Paul maintained that attitude even when he had to give them strong counsel.—2 Cor. 2:4.

⁷ Today, congregation elders and traveling overseers strive to imitate Paul's example. Even when giving reproof, they have the goal of strengthening those needing assistance. Overseers empathetically seek to encourage rather than condemn. One experienced traveling overseer put it this way: "Most of our brothers and sisters want to do what is right, but they often struggle with frustrations, fears, and the feeling that they are powerless to help themselves." Overseers can be a source of strength to such fellow believers.—Heb. 12:12, 13.

"A Plot Was Hatched Against Him" (Acts 20:3, 4)

⁸ From Macedonia, Paul went to Corinth.* After spending three months there, he was eager to move on to Cenchreae, where he planned to board a boat to Syria. From there, he would be able to go to Jerusalem and deliver the contributions to the needy brothers there.# (Acts 24:17; Rom. 15:25, 26) However, an unexpected turn of events changed Paul's plans. Acts 20:3 reports: "A plot was hatched against him by the Jews"!

⁹ It is not surprising that the Jews harbored animosity toward Paul, for they considered him to be an apostate. Earlier, his ministry had led to the conversion of Crispus—a prominent figure in the Corinthian synagogue. (Acts 18:7, 8; 1 Cor. 1:14) On another occasion, the Jews in Corinth had brought charges against Paul before Gallio, proconsul of Achaia. Yet, Gallio had dismissed those charges as baseless—a decision that infuriated Paul's enemies. (Acts 18:12-17) The Jews in Corinth may have known or assumed that Paul would soon set sail from near-by Cenchreae, so they devised a scheme to ambush him there. What would Paul do?

¹⁰ In the interests of personal safety—and to protect the funds with which he had been entrusted—Paul opted to stay away from Cenchreae and to retrace his steps through Macedonia. Granted, traveling on land would have its own dangers. Bandits often lurked along ancient roads. Even the inns could be unsafe. Still, Paul chose the risks on land over those that awaited him at Cenchreae. Thankfully, he was not traveling

---

* It was likely during this visit to Corinth that Paul wrote his letter to the *Romans*.

See the box "Paul Delivers Relief Contributions," on page 169.

---

7. How can Christian overseers today imitate Paul's example?

8, 9. (a) What interrupted Paul's plans to sail to Syria? (b) Why might the Jews have harbored animosity toward Paul?

10. Was it cowardly of Paul to avoid Cenchreae? Explain.

alone. Paul's companions for this part of his missionary tour included Aristarchus, Gaius, Secundus, Sopater, Timothy, Trophimus, and Tychicus.—Acts 20:3, 4.

[11] Like Paul, Christians today take measures to protect themselves while in the ministry. In some areas, they travel in groups—or at least in pairs—rather than alone. What about persecution? Christians realize that it is inevitable. (John 15:20; 2 Tim. 3:12) Still, they do not deliberately put themselves in harm's way. Consider the example of Jesus. On one occasion, when opposers in Jerusalem began picking up stones to hurl at him, "Jesus hid and went out of the temple." (John 8:59) Later, when the Jews were plotting to kill him, "Jesus no longer walked about publicly among the Jews, but he departed from there to the country near the wilderness." (John 11:54) Jesus took reasonable measures to protect himself when doing so did not conflict with God's will for him. Christians today do the same.—Matt. 10:16.

They Were "Comforted Beyond Measure" (Acts 20:5-12)

[12] Paul and his companions traveled through Macedonia together and then apparently split up. Evidently, the group reunited at Troas.* The account says: "We came to them in Troas within five days."# (Acts 20:6) It is here that the young man Eutychus was resurrected, as discussed at the outset of this chapter. Imagine how the brothers felt to see their companion Eutychus raised back to life! As the account reports, they were "comforted beyond measure."—Acts 20:12.

[13] Of course, miracles of that sort do not occur today. Still, those who have lost loved ones in death are "comforted beyond measure" by the Bible-based hope of the resurrection. (John 5:28, 29) Consider: Because he was imperfect, Eutychus eventually died again. (Rom. 6:23) But those who are resurrected in God's new world have the prospect of living forever! Moreover, those who are raised to rule with Jesus in heaven are clothed with immortality. (1 Cor. 15:51-53) Christians today —whether of the anointed or of the "other sheep"—have good reason to be "comforted beyond measure."—John 10:16.

---

* Luke's use of the first person at Acts 20:5, 6 seems to indicate that he rejoined Paul at Philippi after having been left there by him some time earlier.—Acts 16:10-17, 40.

The journey from Philippi to Troas took five days. There may have been adverse winds, for previously the same trip was made in just two days.—Acts 16:11.

---

11. How do Christians today take reasonable measures to protect themselves, and what example did Jesus set in this regard?

12, 13. (a) What effect did the resurrection of Eutychus have on the congregation? (b) What Bible-based hope comforts those today who have lost loved ones in death?

"Publicly and From House to House" (Acts 20:13-24)

¹⁴ Paul and his group traveled from Troas to Assos, then to Mitylene, Chios, Samos, and Miletus. Paul's goal was to reach Jerusalem in time for the Festival of Pentecost. His haste to get to Jerusalem by Pentecost explains why he selected a vessel that bypassed Ephesus on this re-turn trip. Since Paul wanted to talk to the Ephesian elders, however, he requested that they meet him at Miletus. (Acts 20:13-17) When they ar-rived, Paul said to them: "You well know how from the first day that I stepped into the district of Asia I was with you the whole time, slaving for the Lord with the greatest lowliness of mind and tears and trials that befell me by the plots of the Jews; while I did not hold back from telling you any of the things that were profitable nor from teaching you publicly and from house to house. But I thoroughly bore witness both to Jews and to Greeks about repentance toward God and faith in our Lord Jesus."—Acts 20:18-21.

¹⁵ There are many ways to reach people with the good news today. Like Paul, we strive to go where the people are, whether at bus stops,

---

14. What did Paul tell the Ephesian elders when he met with them at Miletus?

15. What are some advantages of house-to-house witnessing?

PAUL DELIVERS RELIEF CONTRIBUTIONS

In the years that followed Pentecost 33 C.E., Christians in Jerusalem suffered many hard-ships—famine, persecution, and the plundering of their belongings. As a consequence, some of them were in need. (Acts 11:27–12:1; Heb. 10:32-34) Hence, in about 49 C.E. when the el-ders in Jerusalem directed Paul to concentrate his preaching activities among the Gentiles, they urged him to "keep the poor in mind." That is just what Paul did by supervising the collection of relief funds in the congregations.—Gal. 2:10.

In 55 C.E., Paul told the Corinthians: "Just as I gave orders to the congregations of Galatia, do that way also yourselves. Every first day of the week let each of you at his own house set some-thing aside in store as he may be prospering, so that when I arrive collections will not take place then. But when I get there, whatever men you approve of by letters, these I shall send to car-ry your kind gift to Jerusalem." (1 Cor. 16:1-3) Shortly thereafter, when Paul wrote his second inspired letter to the Corinthians, he urged them to get their gift ready, and he mentioned that the Macedonians too were contributing.—2 Cor. 8:1–9:15.

Thus it was that in 56 C.E., representatives of various congregations met with Paul to deliver the proceeds of the collection. Nine men travel-ing together not only provided a certain degree of security but also shielded Paul from any pos-sible accusation of impropriety in the handling of donated funds. (2 Cor. 8:20) The delivery of these contributions was the main purpose of Paul's journey to Jerusalem. (Rom. 15:25, 26) Paul later remarked to Governor Felix: "Af-ter quite a number of years I arrived to bring gifts of mercy to my nation, and offerings."—Acts 24:17.

on busy streets, or in marketplaces. Yet, going from house to house remains the primary preaching method used by Jehovah's Witnesses. Why? For one thing, house-to-house preaching gives all an adequate opportunity to hear the Kingdom message on a regular basis, thus demonstrating God's impartiality. It also allows honesthearted ones to receive personal assistance according to their needs. In addition, the house-to-house ministry builds the faith and endurance of those who engage in it. Indeed, a trademark of true Christians today is their zeal in witnessing "publicly and from house to house."

[16] Paul explained to the Ephesian elders that he did not know what dangers would await him upon his return to Jerusalem. "Nevertheless, I do not make my soul of any account as dear to me," he told them, "if only I may finish my course and the ministry that I received of the Lord Jesus, to bear thorough witness to the good news of the undeserved kindness of God." (Acts 20:24) Fearlessly, Paul refused to let any circumstance—whether poor health or bitter opposition—prevent him from completing his assignment.

[17] Christians today likewise endure a variety of negative circumstances. Some face governmental ban and persecution. Others courageously battle debilitating physical or emotional illnesses. Christian youths deal with peer pressure at school. In whatever circumstances they find themselves, Jehovah's Witnesses display steadfastness, as did Paul. They are determined to "bear thorough witness to the good news."

"Pay Attention to Yourselves and to All the Flock" (Acts 20:25-38)

[18] Paul next gave straightforward admonition to the Ephesian elders, using his own course as an example. First he informed them that this was likely the last time they would see him. Then he stated: "I am clean from the blood of all men, for I have not held back from telling you all the counsel of God." How could the Ephesian elders imitate Paul, thus keeping themselves free from bloodguilt? He told them: "Pay attention to yourselves and to all the flock, among which the holy spirit has appointed you overseers, to shepherd the congregation of God, which he purchased with the blood of his own Son." (Acts 20:26-28) Paul warned that "oppressive wolves" would infiltrate the flock and would "speak twisted things to draw away the disciples after themselves." What should the elders do? "Keep awake," Paul warned, "and bear in

---

16, 17. How did Paul show himself to be fearless, and how do Christians today imitate his example?

18. How did Paul keep himself free from bloodguilt, and how could the Ephesian elders do the same?

"Quite a bit of weeping broke out among them all."
—Acts 20:37

mind that for three years, night and day, I did not quit admonishing each one with tears."—Acts 20:29-31.

[19] "Oppressive wolves" made their appearance by the end of the first century. About 98 C.E., the apostle John wrote: "There have come to be many antichrists; . . . They went out from us, but they were not of our sort; for if they had been of our sort, they would have remained with us." (1 John 2:18, 19) By the third century, apostasy had led to the development of the clergy class of Christendom, and in the fourth century, Emperor Constantine gave official recognition to this corrupt form of "Christianity." By adopting pagan rituals and giving them a "Christian" veneer, religious leaders did indeed "speak twisted things." The effects of that apostasy are still seen in the teachings and customs of Christendom.

[20] Paul's life course was in stark contrast to that of those who would in later times take advantage of the flock. He worked to support himself so as not to impose a burden on the congregation. His efforts in behalf of fellow believers were not for personal gain. Paul urged the Ephesian elders to display a self-sacrificing spirit. "You must assist those who are weak," he told them, "and must bear in mind the words of the Lord Jesus, when he himself said, 'There is more happiness in giving than there is in receiving.' "—Acts 20:35.

[21] Like Paul, Christian elders today are self-sacrificing. In contrast with the clergy of Christendom, who fleece their flocks, those who are entrusted with the responsibility to "shepherd the congregation of God" perform their duties unselfishly. Pride and ambition have no place in the Christian congregation, for those who "search out their own glory" will fail in the long run. (Prov. 25:27) Presumptuousness can only lead to dishonor.—Prov. 11:2.

[22] Paul's genuine love for his brothers endeared him to them. Indeed, when it was time for him to depart, "quite a bit of weeping broke out among them all, and they fell upon Paul's neck and tenderly kissed him." (Acts 20:37, 38) Christians truly appreciate and love those who, like Paul, give of themselves unselfishly in behalf of the flock. After considering Paul's sterling example, would you not agree that he was neither boasting nor exaggerating when he stated: "I am clean from the blood of all men"?—Acts 20:26.

---

19. What apostasy developed by the end of the first century, and what did this lead to in later centuries?

20, 21. How did Paul show a self-sacrificing spirit, and how can Christian elders today do the same?

22. What endeared Paul to the elders of Ephesus?

CHAPTER 22

"Let the Will of Jehovah Take Place"

Determined to do God's will, Paul goes to Jerusalem

Based on Acts 21:1-17

THE parting at Miletus is an emotional one. How difficult it is for Paul and Luke to tear themselves away from the Ephesian elders, whom they have come to love! The two missionaries stand on the deck of the boat. Their baggage is packed with supplies needed for the journey. They are also carrying the funds collected for needy Christians in Judea and are eager to see the delivery of this gift through to its completion.

2 A gentle breeze fills the sails, and the ship leaves the clamor of the quay. The two men, along with their seven traveling companions, gaze at their sad-faced brothers on the shore. (Acts 20:4, 14, 15) The travelers keep waving farewell until their friends fade into the distance.

3 For about three years, Paul has worked closely with the elders in Ephesus. But now, directed by holy spirit, he is on his way to Jerusalem. To some extent, he knows what awaits him. Earlier, he told those elders: "Bound in the spirit, I am journeying to Jerusalem, although not knowing the things that will happen to me in it, except that from city to city the holy spirit repeatedly bears witness to me as it says that bonds and tribulations are waiting for me." (Acts 20:22, 23) Despite the danger, Paul feels "bound in the spirit"—both obligated and willing to follow the spirit's direction to go to Jerusalem. He values his life, but the doing of God's will is the most important thing to him.

4 Is that how you feel? When we dedicate ourselves to Jehovah, we solemnly promise to make the doing of his will the most important thing in our life. We can benefit by considering the faithful example of the apostle Paul.

Passing "the Island of Cyprus" (Acts 21:1-3)

5 The boat that Paul and his companions boarded "ran with a straight course." That is, it sailed before the wind, without tacking, and

---

1-4. Why is Paul going to Jerusalem, and what awaits him there?

5. By what course did Paul and his companions travel to Tyre?

under fair winds until they reached Cos later that same day. (Acts 21:1) It seems that the boat anchored there overnight before sailing on to Rhodes and Patara. At Patara, on the southern coast of Asia Minor, the brothers boarded a large cargo ship, which carried them directly to Tyre, in Phoenicia. On the way, they passed "the island of Cyprus . . . on the left [port] side." (Acts 21:3) Why did Luke, the writer of Acts, mention that detail?

[6] Perhaps Paul pointed out the island and told of his experiences there. On his first missionary journey about nine years earlier, Paul, along with Barnabas and John Mark, had encountered the sorcerer Elymas, who opposed their preaching. (Acts 13:4-12) Seeing that island and reflecting on what had occurred there may have encouraged Paul and strengthened him for what lay ahead. We too can profit by reflecting on how God has blessed us and helped us to endure trials. Such reflection may help us to echo the words of David, who wrote: "Many are

6. (a) Why might the sight of Cyprus have been encouraging to Paul? (b) As you reflect on how Jehovah has blessed and helped you, what conclusion do you reach?

CAESAREA—ROMAN PROVINCIAL CAPITAL OF JUDEA

During the period covered by Acts, Caesarea was the provincial capital of the Roman province of Judea, the seat of its governor and the headquarters of its military contingent. Herod the Great built the city and named it in honor of Caesar Augustus. Caesarea contained all the elements common to pagan Hellenistic cities of the day—a temple dedicated to the "divine" Caesar, a theater, a hippodrome, and an amphitheater. The population was predominantly Gentile.

Caesarea was a fortified port city. Herod's ambition was that his new harbor complex called Sebastos (Greek for Augustus), equipped with a huge breakwater on a coast otherwise inhospitable to shipping, would rival Alexandria as the emporium of the eastern Mediterranean. Although it never surpassed Alexandria, Caesarea did achieve international importance because of its strategic position on major trade routes.

The evangelizer Philip preached the good news in Caesarea, and it seems that he raised his family there. (Acts 8:40; 21:8, 9) It was the city where the Roman centurion Cornelius was stationed and was the scene of his conversion. —Acts 10:1.

The apostle Paul visited Caesarea a number of times. Shortly after his conversion, when enemies plotted to kill him, the disciples hurried their new brother the 55 miles from Jerusalem to Caesarea in order to send him off by boat to Tarsus. Paul passed through Caesarea's port when heading for Jerusalem at the end of his second and his third missionary journeys. (Acts 9:28-30; 18:21, 22; 21:7, 8) He was held for two years in Herod's palace in Caesarea. Paul there conversed with Felix, Festus, and Agrippa, and from there he finally sailed to Rome.—Acts 23:33-35; 24:27–25:4; 27:1.

the calamities of the righteous one, but out of them all Jehovah delivers him."—Ps. 34:19.

"We Found the Disciples" (Acts 21:4-9)

[7] Paul appreciated the value of Christian association and was eager to be with those of like faith. Upon arriving at Tyre, Luke writes, "by a search we found the disciples." (Acts 21:4) Knowing there were fellow Christians in Tyre, the travelers sought them out and probably stayed with them. One of the great blessings of having the truth is that no matter where we go, we can find like-minded believers who will welcome us. Those who love God and who practice true worship have friends all over the world.

[8] In describing the seven days they stayed in Tyre, Luke records something that may at first seem puzzling: "Through the spirit [the brothers in Tyre] repeatedly told Paul not to set foot in Jerusalem." (Acts 21:4) Had Jehovah changed his mind? Was he now directing Paul not to go to Jerusalem? No. The spirit had indicated that Paul would be mistreated in Jerusalem, not that he should avoid the city. It seems that by means of holy spirit, the brothers in Tyre correctly concluded that Paul would have trouble in Jerusalem. Therefore, out of concern for Paul, they urged him not to go up to the city. Their desire to protect Paul from impending danger was understandable. Nevertheless, determined to do Jehovah's will, Paul continued on his way to Jerusalem. —Acts 21:12.

[9] Upon hearing the concerns of the brothers, perhaps Paul recalled that Jesus had met a similar objection after telling his disciples that he would go to Jerusalem, suffer many things, and be killed. Moved by sentimentality, Peter had said to Jesus: "Be kind to yourself, Lord; you will not have this destiny at all." Jesus replied: "Get behind me, Satan! You are a stumbling block to me, because you think, not God's thoughts, but those of men." (Matt. 16:21-23) Jesus was determined to accept the self-sacrificing course that God had assigned to him. Paul felt the same way. The brothers in Tyre, like the apostle Peter, undoubtedly had good intentions, but they did not discern God's will.

[10] The idea of being kind to yourself or following the course of least resistance appeals to many today. People in general tend to seek a religion that is comfortable and requires little of its members. In contrast,

---

7. What did the travelers do upon arriving at Tyre?

8. How are we to understand Acts 21:4?

9, 10. (a) Upon hearing the concerns of the brothers in Tyre, Paul might have recalled what similar situation? (b) What idea is common in the world today, and how does it contrast with the words of Jesus?

Following Jesus requires
a self-sacrificing spirit

Jesus urged a far different mental attitude. He told his disciples: "If anyone wants to come after me, let him disown himself and pick up his torture stake and continually follow me." (Matt. 16:24) To follow Jesus is the wise course, the right course, but it is not the easy course.

¹¹ Soon it was time for Paul, Luke, and the others who were with them to continue on their way. The description of their departure is touching. It shows the affection the Tyrian brothers had for Paul as well as their strong support for his ministry. The men, women, and children accompanied Paul and those with him to the beach. As a group, they kneeled and prayed together and then said farewell. Afterward, Paul, Luke, and their traveling companions boarded another boat and continued on to Ptolemais, where they met the brothers and stayed with them for one day.—Acts 21:5-7.

¹² Next, Luke reports, Paul and those traveling with him set out for Caesarea. Once there, they "entered into the house of Philip the evangelizer."* (Acts 21:8) They must have rejoiced to see Philip. Some 20 years earlier in Jerusalem, he had been appointed by the apostles to help care for the distribution of food in the infant Christian congregation. Philip had a long record of zealous preaching. Remember that when persecution scattered the disciples, Philip went to Samaria and began to preach. Later, he preached to and baptized the Ethiopian eunuch. (Acts 6:2-6; 8:4-13, 26-38) What a record of faithful service!

¹³ Philip had not lost his zeal for the ministry. Based now in Caesarea, he was still busy in the preaching work, as Luke shows by calling him "the evangelizer." We also learn that he now had four daughters who prophesied, which suggests that they followed in their father's footsteps.# (Acts 21:9) Philip, then, must have done much to build up

---

* See the box "Caesarea—Roman Provincial Capital of Judea," on page 174.

See the box "Could Women Be Christian Ministers?" on page 177.

---

11. How did the disciples in Tyre show their affection and support for Paul?

12, 13. (a) What record of faithful service did Philip have? (b) How is Philip a good example for Christian fathers today?

the spirituality of his household. Christian fathers today do well to follow his example, taking the lead in the ministry and helping their children to develop a love for the evangelizing work.

[14] In one place after another, Paul sought out fellow believers and spent time with them. Surely the local brothers were eager to extend hospitality to this traveling missionary and his companions. Such visits no doubt resulted in "an interchange of encouragement." (Rom. 1:11, 12) Similar opportunities exist today. Great benefits result from opening your home, however humble, to a traveling overseer and his wife. —Rom. 12:13.

"I Am Ready . . . to Die" (Acts 21:10-14)

[15] During Paul's stay with Philip, another respected visitor arrived—Agabus. Those gathered at Philip's home knew Agabus to be a prophet; he had foretold a great famine during the reign of Claudius. (Acts 11:27, 28) Perhaps they wondered: 'Why has Agabus come? What message does he bring?' As they watched intently, he took Paul's girdle—a long beltlike strip of cloth that could hold money and other items and was worn around the waist. With it, Agabus bound his own feet and hands. Then he spoke. The message was sobering: "Thus says the holy spirit, 'The man to whom this girdle belongs the Jews will bind in this manner in Jerusalem and deliver into the hands of people of the nations.'"—Acts 21:11.

[16] The prophecy confirmed that Paul would go to Jerusalem. It also indicated that his dealings with the Jews there would result in his being delivered "into the hands of people of the nations." The prophecy had a profound effect on those who were present. Luke writes: "Now

---

14. What no doubt resulted from Paul's visits with fellow believers, and what similar opportunities exist today?

15, 16. What message did Agabus bring, and what effect did it have on those who heard it?

COULD WOMEN BE CHRISTIAN MINISTERS?

What was the role of women in the first-century Christian congregation? Could women be ministers?

Jesus instructed his followers to preach the good news of the Kingdom and to make disciples. (Matt. 28:19, 20; Acts 1:8) This commission to be ministers of the good news applies to all Christians, whether men, women, boys, or girls. That this is so can be seen from the prophecy found at Joel 2:28, 29, which the apostle Peter showed had a fulfillment at Pentecost 33 C.E.: "'In the last days,' God says, 'I shall pour out some of my spirit upon every sort of flesh, and your sons and your *daughters* will prophesy . . . and even upon my men slaves and upon my *women* slaves I will pour out some of my spirit in those days, and they will prophesy.'" (Acts 2:17, 18) As we have noted, the evangelizer Philip had four daughters who prophesied.—Acts 21:8, 9.

When it came to teaching within the congregation, however, God's Word limited the appointment of Christian overseers and ministerial servants to men. (1 Tim. 3:1-13; Titus 1:5-9) Paul, in fact, stated: "I do not permit a woman to teach, or to exercise authority over a man, but to be in silence." —1 Tim. 2:12.

when we heard this, both we and those of that place began entreating him not to go up to Jerusalem. Then Paul answered: 'What are you doing by weeping and making me weak at heart? Rest assured, I am ready not only to be bound but also to die at Jerusalem for the name of the Lord Jesus.'"—Acts 21:12, 13.

¹⁷ Imagine the scene. The brothers, including Luke, entreat Paul not to proceed. Some are weeping. Moved by the loving concern they show for him, Paul tenderly says that they are making him "weak at heart," or as some translations render the Greek, they are "breaking [his] heart." Still, his resolve is firm, and as was the case when he met with the brothers in Tyre, he will not allow entreaties or tears to cause him to waver. Instead, he explains to them why he must proceed. What courage and determination he showed! Like Jesus before him, Paul set his face steadfastly to go to Jerusalem. (Heb. 12:2) Paul was not seeking to be a martyr, but if that happened, he would consider it an honor to die as a follower of Christ Jesus.

¹⁸ How did the brothers react? In a word, respectfully. We read: "When he would not be dissuaded, we acquiesced with the words: 'Let the will of Jehovah take place.'" (Acts 21:14) Those who tried to convince Paul to avoid going to Jerusalem did not insist on having their way. They listened to Paul and yielded, recognizing and accepting the will of Jehovah, even though doing so was difficult for them. Paul had embarked on a course that would eventually lead to his death. It would be easier for Paul if those who loved him did not try to dissuade him.

¹⁹ We learn a valuable lesson from what happened to Paul: We never want to try to dissuade others from pursuing a self-sacrificing course in serving God. We can apply this lesson to many situations, not just those that involve life and death. For example, while many Christian parents have found it difficult to see their children leave home to serve Jehovah in distant assignments, they are determined not to discourage them. Phyllis, who lives in England, recalls how she felt when her only daughter took up missionary service in Africa. "It was an emotional time," said Phyllis. "It was hard for me to know that she would be so far away. I felt sad and proud at the same time. I prayed a lot about it. But it was her decision, and I never tried to alter that. After all, I had always taught her to put Kingdom interests first! She has served in foreign assignments for the past 30 years, and I thank Jehovah every day for her faithfulness." How fine it is when we encourage self-sacrificing fellow believers!

17, 18. How did Paul demonstrate his firm resolve, and how did the brothers react?

19. What valuable lesson do we learn from what happened to Paul?

It is good to encourage self-sacrificing fellow believers

"The Brothers Received Us Gladly" (Acts 21:15-17)

[20] Preparations were made, and Paul continued on his way, accompanied by brothers who thus gave evidence of their wholehearted support. At every stage of the journey to Jerusalem, Paul and those accompanying him sought the companionship of their Christian brothers and sisters. At Tyre, they had found disciples and had remained with them seven days. In Ptolemais, they had greeted their sisters and brothers and had spent one day with them. At Caesarea, they had stayed for a number of days at the home of Philip. Next, some of the disciples from Caesarea escorted Paul and his companions to Jerusalem, where they were entertained by Mnason, an early disciple. Finally, upon the travelers' arrival in Jerusalem, Luke reports that "the brothers received us gladly."—Acts 21:17.

[21] Clearly, Paul wanted to be with those of like faith. The apostle drew encouragement from his brothers and sisters, just as we do today. Doubtless, that encouragement strengthened Paul to face the angry opposers who would seek to put him to death.

20, 21. What illustrates Paul's desire to be with the brothers, and why did he want to be with those of like faith?

"PREACHING THE KINGDOM OF GOD...WITHOUT HINDRANCE"
ACTS 28:31

In this section, we will follow Paul as he faces angry mobs, endures imprisonments, and appears before the court of one Roman official after another. Through it all, the apostle continues bearing witness about God's Kingdom. As you consider the exciting conclusion to the book of Acts, ask yourself, 'How can I imitate this bold and zealous evangelizer?'

CHAPTER 23

"Hear My Defense"

Paul defends the truth before angry mobs and the Sanhedrin

Based on Acts 21:18–23:10

JERUSALEM! Once again, Paul is walking along its narrow, bustling streets. No city on earth is so steeped in the history of Jehovah's dealings with his people. By and large, its inhabitants revel in that glorious past. Paul knows that many Christians here are putting too much stock in the past, failing to progress with Jehovah's advancing purposes. Paul thus sees a case of spiritual need in addition to the material need that moved him—back when he was still in Ephesus—to decide to revisit this great city. (Acts 19:21) Despite the prospect of danger, he has held fast to his purpose.

² What, now, will Paul face in Jerusalem? One challenge will come from Christ's followers, some of whom are troubled by rumors about Paul. Greater challenges will come from Christ's enemies. They will launch false accusations against Paul, beat him, and threaten to kill him. These tumultuous events will also give Paul an opportunity to make a defense. His humility, courage, and faith in handling such challenges provide a sterling example for Christians today. Let us see how.

"They Began to Glorify God" (Acts 21:18-20a)

³ The day after their arrival in Jerusalem, Paul and his companions went to see the responsible older men of the congregation. None of the surviving apostles are mentioned in the account; perhaps by then they had all left to serve in other parts of the world. However, James the brother of Jesus was still there. (Gal. 2:9) Likely, James presided at the meeting when "all the older men were present" with Paul.—Acts 21:18.

⁴ Paul greeted the older men "and began giving in detail an account of the things God did among the nations through his ministry." (Acts 21:19) We can only imagine how encouraging that was. We today are likewise thrilled to hear of the progress of the work in other lands. —Prov. 25:25.

1, 2. What brings the apostle Paul to Jerusalem, and what challenges will he face there?

3-5. (a) What meeting did Paul attend in Jerusalem, and what was discussed? (b) What lessons may we draw from Paul's meeting with the elders in Jerusalem?

⁵ At some point, Paul likely mentioned the contributions he had brought from Europe. The concern manifested by the brothers in far-flung places must have warmed the hearts of Paul's listeners. Why, in response to Paul's report, the record says: "They [the older men] began to glorify God"! (Acts 21:20a) Similarly, the hearts of many today who endure disasters or grievous sicknesses are deeply moved when fellow believers offer timely help and words of encouragement.

Many Still "Zealous for the Law" (Acts 21:20b, 21)

⁶ The elders then revealed to Paul that there was a problem in Judea that involved him personally. They said: "You behold, brother, how many thousands of believers there are among the Jews; and they are all zealous for the Law. But they have heard it rumored about you that you have been teaching all the Jews among the nations an apostasy from Moses, telling them neither to circumcise their children nor to walk in the solemn customs."*—Acts 21:20b, 21.

⁷ Why were so many Christians still zealous for the Mosaic Law, well over 20 years after it had been abolished? (Col. 2:14) In 49 C.E. the apostles and older men meeting in Jerusalem had sent a letter to the congregations explaining that believers from among the nations did not need to submit to circumcision and come under the Mosaic Law. (Acts 15:23-29) However, that letter had not mentioned *Jewish* believ-

---

* There must have been many congregations meeting in private homes in order to care for the spiritual needs of such a large number of Jewish Christians.

---

6. What problem did Paul learn about?

7, 8. (a) What mistaken view did many Christians in Judea have? (b) Why did the mistaken thinking of some Jewish Christians not amount to apostasy?

When no Scriptural principles were violated, Paul yielded. Do you?

ers, many of whom did not understand that the Mosaic Law no longer applied.

⁸ Did that mistaken thinking disqualify such Jewish believers from being Christians? No. It was not as if they had once been worshippers of pagan gods and were now continuing to follow the religious customs of their former faith. The Law that was so important to those Jewish believers had originally been given by Jehovah. Nothing in it was demonic or wrong in itself. But that Law had to do with the old covenant, whereas Christians were now under the new covenant. The observances of the Law covenant were now obsolete as far as pure worship was concerned. Hebrew Christians who were zealous for the Law lacked understanding and confidence in the Christian congregation. They needed to bring their thinking into line with the progressive revelation of truth.*—Jer. 31:31-34; Luke 22:20.

"There Is Nothing to the Rumors" (Acts 21:22-26)

⁹ What about the rumors stating that Paul was teaching Jews among the nations "neither to circumcise their children nor to walk in the solemn customs"? Paul was an apostle to the Gentiles, and to them he upheld the decision that Gentiles did not have to submit to the Law. He also exposed the error of any who tried to persuade Gentile believers

---

* A few years later, the apostle Paul wrote his letter to the Hebrews, in which he proved the superiority of the new covenant. In that letter, he clearly demonstrated that the new covenant made the old covenant obsolete. In addition to providing convincing arguments that Jewish Christians could use to answer their Jewish detractors, Paul's powerful reasoning doubtless strengthened the faith of some Christians who were putting too much emphasis on the Mosaic Law.—Heb. 8:7-13.

---

9. What did Paul teach regarding the Mosaic Law?

Roman authorities usually interfered little in local government. Generally speaking, Jewish law governed Jewish affairs. The Romans got involved in Paul's case only because the riot that erupted upon his appearing in the temple was a threat to public order.

The Roman authorities had considerable power over ordinary provincial subjects. Things were different, however, when the authorities dealt with Roman citizens.* Citizenship afforded a person certain privileges that were recognized and honored throughout the empire. It was illegal, for example, to bind or beat an uncondemned Roman, since such treatment was considered fit for slaves only. Roman citizens also had the right to appeal the decisions of a provincial governor to the emperor, in Rome.

Roman citizenship could be obtained in a number of ways. The first was by inheritance. Emperors occasionally awarded citizenship to individuals or to the free populations of whole cities or districts for services rendered. A slave who bought his freedom from a Roman citizen, a slave who was set free by a Roman, or a veteran of the auxiliary forces who was discharged from the Roman army would himself become a Roman. Apparently, under certain circumstances it was also possible to purchase citizenship. The military commander Claudius Lysias thus told Paul: "I purchased these rights as a citizen for a large sum of money." Paul responded: "I was even born in them." (Acts 22:28) Hence, one of Paul's male ancestors must somehow have acquired Roman citizenship, although the circumstances remain unknown.

---

* In the first century C.E., not many Roman citizens would have lived in Judea. Only in the third century were all provincial subjects given Roman citizenship.

to undergo circumcision as a sign of submission to the Mosaic Law. (Gal. 5:1-7) Paul also preached the good news to Jews in the cities he visited. He certainly would have explained to responsive ones that Jesus' death had made the Law obsolete and that righteousness was attained by faith, not by works of Law. —Rom. 2:28, 29; 3:21-26.

[10] Nevertheless, Paul showed understanding toward those who felt comfortable observing some Jewish customs, such as abstaining from work on the Sabbath or avoiding certain foods. (Rom. 14:1-6) And he did not set down rules about circumcision. Indeed, Paul had Timothy circumcised so that the Jews would not be suspicious of Timothy, whose father was a Greek. (Acts 16:3) Circumcision was a matter for personal decision. Paul told the Galatians: "Neither circumcision is of any value nor is uncircumcision, but faith operating through love is." (Gal. 5:6) However, to get circumcised so as to come under the Law or to present the practice as being necessary in order to obtain Jehovah's approval would betray a lack of faith.

[11] Hence, although the rumors were gross distortions, Jewish believers were still disturbed by them. For that reason, the older men offered Paul this direction: "We have four men with a vow upon themselves. Take these men along and cleanse yourself ceremonially with them and take care of their expenses, that they may have their heads shaved. And so everybody will know that there is nothing to the rumors they were told about

---

10. What balanced attitude did Paul have in matters pertaining to the Law and circumcision?

11. What counsel did the elders give Paul, and what would have been involved in carrying it out? (See also footnote.)

you, but that you are walking orderly, you yourself also keeping the Law."*—Acts 21:23, 24.

¹² Paul could have objected that the real problem was, not the rumors about him, but the zeal of those Jewish believers for the Mosaic Law. But he was willing to be flexible, as long as he did not have to compromise godly principles. Earlier he had written: "To those under law I became as under law, though I myself am not under law, that I might gain those under law." (1 Cor. 9:20) On this occasion, Paul cooperated with the Jerusalem elders and became "as under law." In so doing, he set a fine example for us today to cooperate with the elders and not insist on doing things our own way.—Heb. 13:17.

"He Was Not Fit to Live!" (Acts 21:27–22:30)

¹³ Things did not go well at the temple. As the days for the completion of the vows drew to a close, Jews from Asia caught sight of Paul, falsely accused him of bringing Gentiles into the temple, and incited a riot. If the Roman military commander had not intervened, Paul would have been beaten to death. As it was, the Roman commander took him into custody. From that day, it would take more than four years for Paul to regain his freedom. And the immediate danger to Paul was not yet over. When the commander asked the Jews why they were attacking Paul, they shouted different accusations. In the tumult, the commander could understand nothing. Eventually, Paul had to be physically carried away from the scene. When Paul and the Roman soldiers were about to enter the soldiers' quarters, Paul said to the commander: "I beg you, permit me to speak to the people." (Acts 21:39) The commander consented, and Paul went on to defend his faith courageously.

¹⁴ "Hear my defense," Paul began. (Acts 22:1) Paul addressed the crowd in Hebrew, which quieted them down. He gave a forthright

---

* Scholars suggest that the men had made a Nazirite vow. (Num. 6:1-21) True, the Mosaic Law, under which such a vow would have been made, was now obsolete. Still, Paul might have reasoned that it would not be wrong for the men to fulfill a vow made to Jehovah. Therefore, it would not be wrong for him to pay their expenses and accompany them. We do not know exactly what type of vow was involved, but whatever it was, it is unlikely that Paul would have supported the offering of an animal sacrifice (as Nazirites did), believing that it would cleanse the men of sin. The perfect sacrifice of Christ had stripped such sacrifices of any sin-atoning value. Whatever he did, we can be sure that Paul would not have agreed to anything that would have violated his conscience.

---

12. How did Paul show a flexible and cooperative spirit in his response to the counsel of the Jerusalem elders?

13. (a) Why did some Jews cause a tumult in the temple? (b) How was Paul's life saved?

14, 15. (a) What did Paul explain to the Jews? (b) What steps did the Roman commander take to learn the reason for the Jews' anger?

explanation of why he was now a follower of Christ. In doing so, Paul skillfully mentioned points that the Jews could verify if they wished. Paul had studied at the feet of the famous Gamaliel and had persecuted the followers of Christ, as some present likely knew. However, on his way to Damascus, he had a vision of the resurrected Christ, who spoke to him. Paul's traveling companions saw a bright light and heard a voice, but they did not "hear understandingly" the words. (Acts 9:7; 22:9, ftn.) Afterward, the companions had to lead Paul, who was blinded by the vision, into Damascus. There Ananias, a man known to the Jews of that region, miraculously restored Paul's sight.

15 Paul went on to relate that after his return to Jerusalem, Jesus appeared to him in the temple. At this point, the Jews became very disturbed, and they clamored: "Take such a man away from the earth, for he was not fit to live!" (Acts 22:22) To save Paul, the commander had him taken into the soldiers' quarters. Determined to discover the reason for the Jews' anger at Paul, the commander ordered him to be prepared for interrogation under scourging. Paul, though, took advantage of a legal protection at his disposal and revealed that he was a Roman citizen. Jehovah's worshippers today have similarly used legal protections available to them to defend the faith. (See the boxes "Roman Law and Roman Citizens," on page 184, and "Modern-Day Legal Battles," below.) On hearing of Paul's Roman citizenship, the commander realized

MODERN-DAY LEGAL BATTLES

Like the apostle Paul, Jehovah's modern-day Witnesses have sought every legal recourse open to them to combat restrictions imposed on their preaching work. They have been zealous in "the defending and legally establishing of the good news."—Phil. 1:7.

During the 1920's and 1930's, hundreds were arrested for distributing Bible literature. For instance, by 1926, there were 897 cases pending in German courts. So much litigation was involved that it became necessary to establish a Legal Department at the Germany branch. During the 1930's, arrests for house-to-house preaching in the United States alone ran into the hundreds every year. In 1936, that number rose to 1,149. To provide needed counsel, a Legal Department was also established in the United States. From 1933 to 1939, Witnesses in Romania faced 530 lawsuits. However, appeals to the Romanian High Court won many favorable decisions. Similar situations have developed in many other lands.

Legal challenges have arisen when Christians could not conscientiously agree to take part in activities that would violate their neutrality. (Isa. 2:2-4; John 17:14) Opposers have falsely accused them of sedition, which has sometimes resulted in a complete ban on their activities. Over the years, however, many governments have acknowledged that Jehovah's Witnesses present no threat to them.*

* For a discussion of the legal victories of Jehovah's Witnesses in various lands, see chapter 30 of the book Jehovah's Witnesses—Proclaimers of God's Kingdom.

that he would have to find another way to get more information. The next day, he brought Paul before a specially convened meeting of the Sanhedrin, the supreme court of the Jews.

"I Am a Pharisee" (Acts 23:1-10)

[16] Beginning his defense before the Sanhedrin, Paul said: "Men, brothers, I have behaved before God with a perfectly clear conscience down to this day." (Acts 23:1) He got no further. The record says: "At this the high priest Ananias ordered those standing by him to strike him on the mouth." (Acts 23:2) What an insult! And what a revelation of prejudice, to brand Paul a liar before any evidence was heard! No wonder Paul responded: "God is going to strike you, you whitewashed wall. Do you at one and the same time sit to judge me in accord with the Law and, transgressing the Law, command me to be struck?"—Acts 23:3.

Like Paul, we seek common ground when speaking to those of a different religious background

[17] Some standing by professed shock —not at the one who struck Paul but at Paul's reaction! They demanded: "Are you reviling the high priest of God?" In answer, Paul gave them a lesson in humility and in respect for the Law. He said: "Brothers, I did not know he was high priest. For it is written, 'You must not speak injuriously of a ruler of your people.' "* (Acts 23:4, 5; Ex. 22:28) Paul now adopted a different strategy. Taking note that the Sanhedrin was made up of Pharisees and Sadducees, he said: "Men, brothers, I am a Pharisee, a son of Pharisees. Over the hope of the resurrection of the dead I am being judged."—Acts 23:6.

[18] Why did Paul call himself a Pharisee? Because he was "a son of Pharisees" from a family belonging to that sect. Hence, many would

---

* Some have suggested that Paul had weak eyesight that prevented him from recognizing the high priest. Or perhaps he had been absent from Jerusalem for so long that he could not identify the current high priest. Or maybe Paul just could not see through the crowd who it was that gave the order to strike him.

16, 17. (a) Describe what happened when Paul addressed the Sanhedrin. (b) When he was struck, how did Paul set an example of humility?

18. Why did Paul call himself a Pharisee, and how might we use similar reasoning in certain circumstances?

still view him as such.* How, though, could Paul associate himself with the Pharisees' belief in a resurrection? Reportedly, the Pharisees believed that a conscious soul survived death and that the souls of the righteous would live again in human bodies. Paul did not believe such notions. He believed in the resurrection as taught by Jesus. (John 5:25-29) Still, Paul did agree with the Pharisees that there was a hope of life beyond death—as opposed to the Sadducees, who did not believe in a future life. We might use similar reasoning when discussing matters with Catholics or Protestants. We could say that like them, we believe in God. Granted, they may believe in the Trinity while we believe in the God of the Bible. Still, we do share the belief that there is a God.

[19] Paul's statement split the Sanhedrin. The record says: "There broke out a loud screaming, and some of the scribes of the party of the Pharisees rose and began contending fiercely, saying: 'We find nothing wrong in this man; but if a spirit or an angel spoke to him,—.'" (Acts 23:9) The very suggestion that an angel might have spoken to Paul was anathema to the Sadducees, who did not believe in angels! (See the box "The Sadducees and the Pharisees," below.) The tumult became so great that the Roman military commander once again rescued the apostle. (Acts 23:10) Still, Paul was hardly out of danger. What would happen to the apostle now? We will learn more in the following chapter.

---

* In 49 C.E., when the apostles and older men were discussing whether Gentiles had to submit to the Mosaic Law, some among the Christians present were identified as "those of the sect of the Pharisees that had believed." (Acts 15:5) Evidently, those believers were still identified in some sense with their Pharisaic background.

---

19. Why did the meeting of the Sanhedrin break up in disorder?

THE SADDUCEES AND THE PHARISEES

The Sanhedrin, the national administrative council and high court of the Jews, was dominated by two rival sects—the Sadducees and the Pharisees. According to first-century historian Flavius Josephus, the main difference between these parties was that the Pharisees sought to impose a great number of traditional observances on the people, whereas the Sadducees considered obligatory only what was found in the Law of Moses. Both schools of thought were united in their opposition to Jesus.

It appears that the Sadducees, who were basically conservative, had close ties to the priesthood and that Annas and Caiaphas, both of whom had served as the high priest, belonged to this powerful sect. (Acts 5:17) Josephus says, however, that its teachings could "persuade none but the rich."

The Pharisees, on the other hand, had great influence over the masses. Yet, their views, which included insistence on extreme ceremonial purity, made observing the Law burdensome for the people. In contrast with the Sadducees, the Pharisees attributed great importance to fate and believed that a soul survived death, after which it received a just reward or punishment for its virtues or its vices.

CHAPTER 24

"Be of Good Courage!"

Paul escapes a plot on his life and makes his defense before Felix

Based on Acts 23:11–24:27

SNATCHED from an angry mob in Jerusalem, Paul is in custody once again. The zealous apostle is not surprised by the persecution he is facing here in Jerusalem. He was told to expect "bonds and tribulations" in this city. (Acts 20:22, 23) And while not exactly certain of what may lie ahead, Paul knows that he will continue to suffer for Jesus' name. —Acts 9:16.

[2] Even Christian prophets warned Paul that he would be bound and delivered "into the hands of people of the nations." (Acts 21:4, 10, 11) Recently, a Jewish crowd sought to kill him, and shortly thereafter, it seemed as if he "would be pulled to pieces" by the members of the Sanhedrin as they argued over him. Now the apostle is a prisoner in the custody of Roman soldiers and facing more trials and accusations. (Acts 21:31; 23:10) Indeed, the apostle Paul needs encouragement!

[3] In this time of the end, we know that "all those desiring to live with godly devotion in association with Christ Jesus will also be persecuted." (2 Tim. 3:12) From time to time, we too need encouragement to press on in our preaching work. How grateful we are for the timely, heartening words we receive through the publications and the meetings arranged by "the faithful and discreet slave"! (Matt. 24:45) Jehovah has assured us that no enemies of the good news will succeed. They will neither destroy his servants as a group nor stop their preaching work. (Isa. 54:17; Jer. 1:19) What, though, about the apostle Paul? Did he receive encouragement to continue bearing thorough witness despite opposition? If so, what was it, and how did he respond?

Foiling an "Oath-Bound Conspiracy" (Acts 23:11-34)

[4] The apostle Paul received much-needed encouragement on the night following his rescue from the Sanhedrin. The inspired account tells us: "The Lord stood by him and said: 'Be of good courage! For as

---

1, 2. Why is Paul not surprised by the persecution he is facing in Jerusalem?

3. From where do we receive encouragement to press on in our preaching work?

4, 5. What encouragement did Paul receive, and why was it timely?

"More than forty men of theirs are lying in wait."
—Acts 23:21

you have been giving a thorough witness on the things about me in Jerusalem, so you must also bear witness in Rome.'" (Acts 23:11) With those encouraging words from Jesus, Paul was assured of deliverance. He knew that he would survive to reach Rome and have the privilege of bearing witness to Jesus there.

[5] The encouragement given Paul was timely. The very next day, over 40 Jewish men "formed a conspiracy and bound themselves with a curse, saying they would neither eat nor drink until they had killed Paul." This "oath-bound conspiracy" showed just how determined those Jews were to murder the apostle. If they did not succeed in carrying out their plot, the end result, they believed, would be a curse, or an evil, to them. (Acts 23:12-15) Their plan, sanctioned by the chief priests and older men, was to have Paul brought back to the Sanhedrin for further questioning, as if to ascertain matters concerning him more accurately. But en route, the conspirators would be lying in wait to pounce on Paul and kill him.

[6] Paul's nephew, however, heard of this plot and reported it to Paul. In turn, Paul had the young man report it to the Roman military commander Claudius Lysias. (Acts 23:16-22) Surely Jehovah loves young ones who, like this unnamed nephew of Paul, courageously put the welfare of God's people ahead of their own and faithfully do whatever they can to promote Kingdom interests.

[7] Immediately upon being informed about the plot against Paul, Claudius Lysias, who commanded 1,000 men, ordered that a military guard of 470—soldiers, spearmen, and horsemen—be formed to leave Jerusalem that night and safely conduct Paul to Caesarea. Once there, he was to be turned over to Governor Felix.* Although Caesarea, the Roman administrative capital of Judea, had a substantial number of Jewish residents, it was populated mainly by Gentiles. The orderly conditions existing there contrasted with the situation that prevailed in Jerusalem, where many displayed emotional religious prejudice and were involved in riots. Caesarea was also the main headquarters of the Roman military forces in Judea.

[8] Complying with Roman law, Lysias sent a letter to Felix outlining the case. Lysias mentioned that upon learning that Paul was a Roman citizen, he had rescued Paul from being "done away with" by the Jews. Lysias stated that he did not find Paul guilty of anything "deserving of

---

* See the box "Felix—Procurator of Judea," on page 193.

---

6. How was the plot to kill Paul uncovered, and what example may young people today find in this account?

7, 8. What arrangements did Claudius Lysias make for Paul's safety?

death or bonds," but because of a plot against Paul, he was turning him over to Felix so that the governor could hear the accusers and render judgment on the matter.—Acts 23:25-30.

⁹ Was Lysias truthful in what he wrote? Not entirely. It seems that he was trying to present himself in the most favorable light. He really had not come to Paul's rescue because he found out that the apostle was a Roman citizen. Additionally, Lysias failed to mention that he had had Paul "bound with two chains" and had later given the order that he "be examined under scourging." (Acts 21:30-34; 22:24-29) Lysias had thereby violated Paul's rights as a Roman citizen. Today, Satan uses the religious fanaticism of opposers to fan the flames of persecution, and we may find our civil liberties violated. But like Paul, God's people can often take advantage of the rights accorded them as citizens of a country and seek protection under the law.

"I Readily Speak in My Defense" (Acts 23:35–24:21)

¹⁰ In Caesarea, Paul was "kept under guard in the praetorian palace of Herod" to await the arrival of the accusers from Jerusalem. (Acts 23: 35) Five days later, they came—High Priest Ananias, a public speaker named Tertullus, and a group of older men. Tertullus first praised Felix for what he was doing for the Jews, evidently to flatter him and gain his favor.* Then, getting to the matter at hand, Tertullus referred to Paul as "a pestilent fellow and stirring up seditions among all the Jews throughout the inhabited earth and a spearhead of the sect of the Nazarenes, one who also tried to profane the temple and whom we seized." The other Jews "joined in the attack, asserting that these things were so." (Acts 24:5, 6, 9) Stirring up sedition, spearheading a dangerous sect, and profaning the temple—these were serious charges that could result in a sentence of death.

¹¹ Paul was then allowed to speak. "I readily speak in my defense," he began. He flatly denied the accusations. The apostle had not profaned the temple, nor had he tried to stir up sedition. He pointed out that

---

* Tertullus thanked Felix for the "great peace" he brought to the nation. However, the truth was that less peace prevailed in Judea during the time that Felix was governor than during any other administration up until the revolt against Rome. Also far from the truth was the mention of "the greatest thankfulness" of the Jews for reforms that Felix had made. In reality, Felix was despised by most Jews for making their lives miserable and for his brutality in crushing their insurrections.—Acts 24:2, 3.

---

9. (a) How were Paul's rights as a Roman citizen violated? (b) Why might we take advantage of our rights as citizens of a country?

10. What serious accusations were leveled against Paul?

11, 12. How did Paul refute the charges against him?

In about 52 C.E., Roman Emperor Claudius appointed one of his favorites, Antonius Felix, as procurator, or governor, of Judea. Like his brother Pallas, Felix was a freed slave of the emperor's family. The appointment of a freedman to the post of procurator with a military command was unprecedented.

Because of his brother's influence with the emperor, Felix "believed that he could commit all kinds of enormities with impunity," states Roman historian Tacitus. As procurator, Felix "practised every kind of cruelty and lust, wielding the power of king with all the instincts of a slave." During his tenure as procurator, Felix married Drusilla, daughter of Herod Agrippa I, after seducing her away from her husband. Felix treated the apostle Paul in a corrupt and illegal manner, considering him a likely source of a bribe.

Felix's administration was so corrupt and oppressive that Emperor Nero recalled him in 58 C.E. A deputation of Jews followed Felix to Rome to accuse him of misgovernment, but Pallas reportedly saved his brother from punishment.

---

he had actually been absent from Jerusalem for "quite a number of years" and had come with "gifts of mercy"—contributions for Christians whose poverty may have resulted from famine and persecution. Paul insisted that before he entered the temple, he had been "ceremonially cleansed" and that he had conscientiously striven to commit "no offense against God and men."—Acts 24:10-13, 16-18.

[12] Paul did admit, however, that he rendered sacred service to the God of his forefathers "according to the way that they call a 'sect.'" But he insisted that he believed "all the things set forth in the Law and written in the Prophets." And as did his accusers, he held to the hope of "a resurrection of both the righteous and the unrighteous." Paul then challenged his accusers: "Let the men here say for themselves what wrong they found as I stood before the Sanhedrin, except with respect to this one utterance which I cried out while standing among them, 'Over the resurrection of the dead I am today being judged before you!'"—Acts 24:14, 15, 20, 21.

[13] Paul set a good example for us to follow if we are ever brought before secular authorities because of our worship and are falsely accused of such things as being rabble-rousers, seditionists, or members of a "dangerous sect." Paul did not fawn over the governor, uttering words of flattery as did Tertullus. Paul stayed calm and respectful. Tactfully, he gave clear and truthful testimony. Paul mentioned that the "Jews from

---

13-15. Why can we look to Paul as a good example of giving a bold witness before secular authorities?

the district of Asia" who had accused him of defiling the temple were not present and that legally, he should be able to face them and hear their accusations.—Acts 24:18, 19.

[14] Most strikingly, Paul did not hold back from giving testimony regarding his beliefs. Boldly, the apostle reiterated his belief in the resurrection, the issue that had created such turmoil when he was before the Sanhedrin. (Acts 23:6-10) In his defense, Paul emphasized the resurrection hope. Why? Because Paul was bearing witness to Jesus and to His resurrection from the dead—something those opposers would not accept. (Acts 26:6-8, 22, 23) Yes, it was the issue of the resurrection —and more precisely, belief in Jesus and in his resurrection—on which the controversy was centered.

[15] Like Paul, we can give a bold witness and can draw strength from what Jesus told his disciples: "You will be objects of hatred by all people on account of my name. But he that has endured to the end is the one that will be saved." Must we worry about what we should say? No, for Jesus gave this assurance: "When they are leading you along to deliver you up, do not be anxious beforehand about what to speak; but whatever is given you in that hour, speak this, for you are not the ones speaking, but the holy spirit is."—Mark 13:9-13.

"Felix Became Frightened" (Acts 24:22-27)

[16] This was not the first time that Governor Felix had heard about Christian beliefs. The account states: "Felix, knowing quite accurately the matters concerning this Way [the term used to describe early Christianity], began to put the men off and said: 'Whenever Lysias the military commander comes down, I shall decide upon these matters involving you.' And he ordered the army officer that the man be kept and have some relaxation of custody, and that he forbid no one of his people to wait upon him."—Acts 24:22, 23.

[17] Some days later, Felix, with his wife Drusilla, a Jewess, sent for Paul and "listened to him on the belief in Christ Jesus." (Acts 24:24) However, when Paul spoke about "righteousness and self-control and the judgment to come, Felix became frightened," possibly because such things troubled his conscience on account of the wicked course he had pursued in his own life. So he dismissed Paul, saying: "For the present go your way, but when I get an opportune time I shall send for you again." Felix did see Paul many times after that, not because he wanted to learn the truth, but because he hoped that Paul would give him a bribe.—Acts 24:25, 26.

16, 17. (a) How did Felix handle Paul's trial? (b) Why may Felix have become frightened, yet for what reason did he continue to see Paul?

¹⁸ Why did Paul speak to Felix and his wife about "righteousness and self-control and the judgment to come"? Remember, they wanted to know what "belief in Christ Jesus" entailed. Paul, who knew their background of immorality, cruelty, and injustice, was making plain what was required of all who would become Jesus' followers. What Paul said showed the stark contrast between God's standards of righteousness and the life course that Felix and his wife pursued. This should have helped them to see that all humans are accountable to God for what they think, say, and do and that more important than the judgment to be rendered with respect to Paul was the judgment that they faced before God. No wonder Felix "became frightened"!

¹⁹ In our ministry, we may find people who are like Felix. At first they might appear to show interest in the truth, but they are really seeking their own selfish course. We rightfully remain wary of such ones. Yet, like Paul, we can tactfully tell them of God's righteous standards. Perhaps the truth will touch their hearts. However, if it becomes evident that they have no intention of abandoning a sinful course, we leave them alone and search out those who really are seeking the truth.

²⁰ In the case of Felix, his true heart condition was revealed in these words: "When two years had elapsed, Felix was succeeded by Porcius Festus; and because Felix desired to gain favor with the Jews, he left Paul bound." (Acts 24:27) Felix was no real friend to Paul. Felix knew that followers of "The Way" were neither seditionists nor revolutionaries. (Acts 19:23) He also knew that Paul had not violated any Roman law. Yet, Felix kept the apostle in custody in order to "gain favor with the Jews."

²¹ As shown in the last verse of Acts chapter 24, Paul was still a prisoner when Porcius Festus succeeded Felix as governor. Thus began a series of hearings, and Paul was handed over from one official to another. Truly, this courageous apostle was "haled before kings and governors." (Luke 21:12) As we will see, he would later give a witness to the most powerful ruler of his day. Through it all, Paul never wavered in his faith. No doubt he continued to draw strength from Jesus' words: "Be of good courage!"

---

18. Why did Paul speak to Felix and his wife about "righteousness and self-control and the judgment to come"?

19, 20. (a) In our ministry, how should we deal with people who appear to be interested but who are really seeking their own selfish course? (b) How do we know that Felix was no friend to Paul?

21. What happened to Paul after Porcius Festus became governor, and from what did Paul no doubt continue to draw strength?

CHAPTER 25

"I Appeal to Caesar!"

Paul sets an example in defending the good news

Based on Acts 25:1–26:32

PAUL remains under heavy guard in Caesarea. Two years earlier when he had returned to Judea, within days the Jews had tried to kill him at least three times. (Acts 21:27-36; 23:10, 12-15, 27) Till now, his enemies have been unsuccessful, but they do not give up. When Paul sees that he may yet fall into their hands, he tells Roman Governor Festus: "I appeal to Caesar!"—Acts 25:11.

² Did Jehovah support Paul's decision to appeal to the emperor of Rome? The answer is important to us, who are bearing thorough witness about God's Kingdom in this time of the end. We need to know whether Paul set a pattern for us to follow "in the defending and legally establishing of the good news."—Phil. 1:7.

"Standing Before the Judgment Seat" (Acts 25:1-12)

³ Three days after taking office, Festus, the new Roman governor of Judea, went to Jerusalem.* There he listened as the chief priests and the principal men of the Jews accused Paul of serious crimes. They knew that the new governor was under pressure to keep peace with them and all the Jews. So they asked a favor of Festus: Bring Paul to Jerusalem, and try him there. However, there was a dark plan behind this request. Those enemies were scheming to kill Paul on the road from Caesarea to Jerusalem. Festus turned them down, saying: "Let those who are in power among you . . . come down with me [to Caesarea] and accuse him, if there is anything out of the way about the man." (Acts 25:5) Therefore, Paul escaped death yet another time.

⁴ During all of Paul's trials, Jehovah through the Lord Jesus Christ sustained him. Recall that in a vision, Jesus told his apostle: "Be of good courage!" (Acts 23:11) Today, God's servants also face obstacles

---

*See the box "Roman Procurator Porcius Festus," on page 199.

1, 2. (a) In what circumstances does Paul find himself? (b) What question arises regarding Paul's appeal to Caesar?

3, 4. (a) What was behind the Jews' request to have Paul brought to Jerusalem, and how did he escape death? (b) How does Jehovah sustain his modern-day servants, as he did Paul?

and threats. Jehovah does not shield us from every difficulty, but he gives us the wisdom and strength to endure. We can always count on "the power beyond what is normal" that our loving God provides. —2 Cor. 4:7.

5 Some days later, Festus "sat down on the judgment seat" in Caesarea.* Before him stood Paul and Paul's accusers. In answer to their baseless charges, Paul countered: "Neither against the Law of the Jews nor against the temple nor against Caesar have I committed any sin." The apostle was innocent and deserved to be freed. How would Festus decide? Wanting to gain favor with the Jews, he asked Paul: "Do you wish to go up to Jerusalem and be judged there before me concerning these things?" (Acts 25:6-9) What an absurd proposal! If Paul were remanded to Jerusalem, his accusers would become his judges and he would face certain death. In this instance, Festus was choosing political expediency over true justice. An earlier governor, Pontius Pilate, had acted similarly in a case involving an even more important prisoner. (John 19:12-16) Modern-day judges may also give in to political pressure. Therefore, we should not be surprised when courts decide contrary to evidence in cases involving God's people.

---

* "The judgment seat" was a chair placed on a dais. The elevated position was viewed as giving weight and finality to the judge's rulings. Pilate sat on a judgment seat when he weighed the charges against Jesus.

---

5. How did Festus deal with Paul?

We appeal unfavorable legal decisions

⁶ Festus' desire to indulge the Jews could have put Paul in mortal danger. Therefore, Paul used a right he possessed as a Roman citizen. He told Festus: "I am standing before the judgment seat of Caesar, where I ought to be judged. I have done no wrong to the Jews, as you also are finding out quite well. . . . I appeal to Caesar!" Once made, such an appeal was usually irrevocable. Festus emphasized this, saying: "To Caesar you have appealed; to Caesar you shall go." (Acts 25:10-12) By appealing to a higher legal authority, Paul set a precedent for true Christians today. When opposers try to frame "trouble by decree," Jehovah's Witnesses avail themselves of legal provisions to defend the good news.*—Ps. 94:20.

⁷ Thus, after over two years of incarceration for crimes he did not commit, Paul was granted the opportunity to present his case in Rome. Before his departure, however, another ruler wanted to see him.

"I Did Not Become Disobedient" (Acts 25:13–26:23)

⁸ Some days after Festus heard Paul's appeal to Caesar, King Agrippa and his sister Bernice paid "a visit of courtesy" to the new governor.# In Roman times, it was customary for officials to make such visits to newly appointed governors. By congratulating Festus on his appointment, Agrippa was undoubtedly trying to cement political and personal ties that could be useful in the future.—Acts 25:13.

⁹ Festus told the king about Paul, and Agrippa was intrigued. The next day, the two rulers sat down on the judgment seat. But their power and pomp were by no means more impressive than the words that the prisoner before them was about to speak.—Acts 25:22-27.

¹⁰ Paul respectfully thanked King Agrippa for the opportunity to present a defense to him, acknowledging that the king was an expert on all the customs as well as the controversies among Jews. Paul then described his past life: "According to the strictest sect of our form of worship I lived a Pharisee." (Acts 26:5) As a Pharisee, Paul had hoped in the coming of the Messiah. Now, as a Christian, he boldly identified Jesus Christ as that long-awaited one. A belief that he and his accusers had in common—that is, the hope of the fulfillment of God's promise

---

* See the box "Appealing on Behalf of True Worship in Modern Times," on page 200.

See the box "King Herod Agrippa II," on page 201.

6, 7. Why did Paul appeal to Caesar, and what precedent did he thereby set for true Christians today?

8, 9. Why did King Agrippa visit Caesarea?

10, 11. How did Paul accord Agrippa respect, and what details about Paul's own past did the apostle reveal to the king?

Our only firsthand information about Porcius Festus comes from Acts of Apostles and the writings of Flavius Josephus. Festus succeeded Felix as procurator of Judea in about 58 C.E. and evidently died in office after governing just two or three years.

For the most part, Festus appears to have been a prudent and capable procurator, in contrast with his predecessor, Felix, and his successor, Albinus. At the beginning of Festus' time in office, Judea was plagued by bandits. According to Josephus, "Festus . . . made it his business to correct those that made disturbances in the country. So he caught the greatest part of the robbers, and destroyed a great many of them." During his tenure, the Jews built a wall to prevent King Agrippa from observing what took place in the temple area. Festus initially ordered them to dismantle it. At the Jews' request, however, he later allowed them to present the matter to the Roman Emperor Nero.

Festus appears to have taken a firm stand against criminals and insurgents. But in his desire to maintain good relations with the Jews, he was willing to set aside justice—at least in his dealings with the apostle Paul.

to their forefathers—was the reason that Paul was on trial that day. This situation left Agrippa even more interested in what Paul had to say.*

¹¹ Recalling his past outrageous treatment of Christians, Paul said: "I, for one, really thought within myself I ought to commit many acts of opposition against the name of Jesus the Nazarene . . . Since I was extremely mad against them [the followers of Christ], I went so far as to persecuting them even in outside cities." (Acts 26:9-11) Paul was not exaggerating. Many people knew of the violence he had done to the Christians. (Gal. 1:13, 23) 'What could have changed such a man?' Agrippa may have wondered.

¹² Paul's next words provided the answer: "As I was journeying to Damascus with authority and a commission from the chief priests, I saw at midday on the road, O king, a light beyond the brilliance of the sun flash from heaven about me and about those journeying with me. And when we had all fallen to the ground I heard a voice say to me in the Hebrew language, 'Saul, Saul, why are you persecuting me? To keep kicking against the goads makes it hard for you.' But I said, 'Who are

---

* As a Christian, Paul accepted Jesus as the Messiah. The Jews, who rejected Jesus, viewed Paul as an apostate.—Acts 21:21, 27, 28.

12, 13. (a) How did Paul describe his conversion? (b) How had Paul been "kicking against the goads"?

Jehovah's Witnesses have at times appealed to high courts in hopes of removing obstacles to the preaching of the good news of God's Kingdom. Here are two examples.

On March 28, 1938, the U.S. Supreme Court overturned state court decisions and exonerated a group of Witnesses who had been arrested for distributing Bible literature in Griffin, Georgia, U.S.A. This was the first of many appeals made to that high court regarding the right of the Witnesses to preach the good news.*

Another case involved a Witness in Greece named Minos Kokkinakis. Over a period of 48 years, he was arrested more than 60 times for "proselytism." On 18 occasions, he faced prosecution in court. He spent years in prison and in exile on remote islands in the Aegean Sea. After his last conviction in 1986, Brother Kokkinakis lost his appeals to the higher courts of Greece. He then sought relief through the European Court of Human Rights (ECHR). On May 25, 1993, that Court ruled that Greece had violated Brother Kokkinakis' freedom of religion.

Jehovah's Witnesses have appealed to the ECHR for relief in dozens of cases, prevailing in most of them. No other organization, religious or otherwise, has had such success in defending basic human rights before the ECHR.

Do others benefit from the legal victories of Jehovah's Witnesses? Scholar Charles C. Haynes wrote: "We all owe the Jehovah's Witnesses a debt of gratitude. No matter how many times they're insulted, run out of town or even physically attacked, they keep on fighting for their (and thus our) freedom of religion. And when they win, we all win."

---

* For a more recent example, see the account of the U.S. Supreme Court's decision regarding free speech, which was published in *Awake!* January 8, 2003, pages 3-11.

you, Lord?' And the Lord said, 'I am Jesus, whom you are persecuting.'"*—Acts 26:12-15.

[13] Before this supernatural event, Paul had figuratively been "kicking against the goads." Just as a beast of burden would injure itself unnecessarily by kicking against the sharp end of an oxgoad, Paul had hurt himself spiritually by resisting the will of God. By appearing to Paul on the road to Damascus, the resurrected Jesus caused this sincere but clearly misguided man to change his thinking. —John 16:1, 2.

[14] Paul did indeed make drastic changes in his life. Addressing Agrippa, he said: "I did not become disobedient to the heavenly sight, but both to those in Damascus first and to those in Jerusalem, and over all the country of Judea, and to the nations I went bringing the message that they should repent and turn to God by doing works that befit repentance." (Acts 26:19, 20) For years, Paul had been fulfilling the commission that Jesus Christ had given him in that midday vision. With what results? Those who responded to the good news that Paul preached repented of their immoral, dishonest conduct and turned to God. Such ones became good citizens, contributing to and showing respect for law and order.

[15] Those benefits, however, meant nothing to Paul's Jewish opposers. Paul said: "On account of these things Jews seized

---

* Regarding Paul's words that he was journeying "at midday," one Bible scholar noted: "Unless a traveller was in a really desperate hurry he rested during the midday heat. So we see how Paul was driving himself on this mission of persecution."

14, 15. What did Paul say regarding the changes that he had made in his life?

me in the temple and attempted to slay me. However, because I have obtained the help that is from God I continue to this day bearing witness to both small and great."—Acts 26:21, 22.

[16] As true Christians, we must be "always ready to make a defense" of our faith. (1 Pet. 3:15) When speaking to judges and rulers about our beliefs, we may find it helpful to imitate the method Paul used in speaking to Agrippa and Festus. By respectfully telling them how Bible truths have changed lives for the better—our own life as well as the lives of those who respond to our message—we may touch the hearts of these high officials.

"You Would Persuade Me to Become a Christian" (Acts 26:24-32)

[17] As they listened to Paul's persuasive testimony, the two rulers could not remain detached. Note what took place: "Now as [Paul] was

16. How may we imitate Paul when speaking to judges and rulers about our beliefs?
17. How did Festus react to Paul's defense, and what similar attitude is seen today?

KING HEROD AGRIPPA II

The Agrippa referred to in Acts chapter 25 was King Herod Agrippa II, great-grandson of Herod the Great and son of the Herod who had attacked the Jerusalem congregation 14 years earlier. (Acts 12:1) Agrippa was the last of the Herodian princes.

At the death of his father in 44 C.E., 17-year-old Agrippa was in Rome, where he was being educated at the court of Roman Emperor Claudius. The emperor's advisers considered Agrippa too young to inherit his father's domain; thus, a Roman governor was appointed instead. Even so, according to Flavius Josephus, while Agrippa was still in Rome, he intervened for the Jews and represented their interests.

In about 50 C.E., Claudius assigned Agrippa kingship over Chalcis and in 53 C.E., over Ituraea, Trachonitis, and Abilene. Agrippa was also given oversight of Jerusalem's temple, with authority to appoint the Jewish high priests. Claudius' successor Nero extended Agrippa's realm to include parts of Galilee and Perea. At the time of his meeting Paul, Agrippa was in Caesarea with his sister Bernice, who had left her husband, the king of Cilicia.—Acts 25:13.

In 66 C.E., when Agrippa's efforts failed to calm the Jewish rebellion against Rome, he himself became a target of the rebels, and he was left no choice but to join the Romans. After the Jewish revolt was crushed, a new emperor, Vespasian, gave Agrippa further territories as a reward.

saying these things in his defense, Festus said in a loud voice: 'You are going mad, Paul! Great learning is driving you into madness!'" (Acts 26: 24) Festus' outburst may have betrayed an attitude seen even today. To many people, those who teach what the Bible really says are fanatics. Worldly-wise ones often find it hard to accept the Bible teaching of the resurrection of the dead.

[18] But Paul had a reply for the governor: "I am not going mad, Your Excellency Festus, but I am uttering sayings of truth and of soundness of mind. In reality, the king to whom I am speaking with freeness of speech well knows about these things . . . Do you, King Agrippa, believe the Prophets? I know you believe." Agrippa responded: "In a short time you would persuade me to become a Christian." (Acts 26:25-28) These words, sincere or not, show that Paul's witness had a profound effect on the king.

[19] Then Agrippa and Festus stood, signaling an end to the audience. "As they withdrew they began talking with one another, saying: 'This man practices nothing deserving death or bonds.' Moreover, Agrippa said to Festus: 'This man could have been released if he had not appealed to Caesar.'" (Acts 26:31, 32) They knew that an innocent man had stood before them. Perhaps they would now look with greater favor on Christians.

[20] Neither of the powerful rulers in this account seems to have accepted the good news of God's Kingdom. Was there wisdom in the apostle Paul's appearing before those men? The answer is yes. Paul's "being haled before kings and governors" in Judea resulted in a witness reaching areas of the Roman government that might then have been inaccessible. (Luke 21:12, 13) Also, his experiences and faithfulness under trial encouraged his brothers and sisters in the faith.—Phil. 1: 12-14.

[21] The same is true today. By pressing on with the Kingdom work despite trials and opposition, we may see a number of positive results. We may give a witness to officials who might otherwise be difficult to reach. Our faithful endurance may be a source of encouragement to our Christian brothers and sisters, moving them to show even greater boldness in the work of bearing thorough witness about God's Kingdom.

---

18. How did Paul respond to Festus, leading to what response from Agrippa?

19. What decision did Festus and Agrippa make regarding Paul?

20. What results did Paul's witness to high officials produce?

21. By pressing on with the Kingdom work, what positive results may we see?

CHAPTER 26

"Not a Soul of You Will Be Lost"

Paul faces shipwreck, showing great faith and love for people

Based on Acts 27:1–28:10

PAUL turns the words over in his mind, for they will have a great bearing on his future. "To Caesar you shall go," Governor Festus had said. Paul has spent two years cooped up in prison, so the long trip to Rome will, at the least, bring a change of scenery. (Acts 25:12) However, Paul's many vivid memories of sea voyages involve far more than refreshing breezes and open horizons. The prospect of this voyage to appear before Caesar may also raise a number of grave questions in Paul's mind.

² Paul has been "in dangers at sea" many times, having survived three shipwrecks, even spending a night and a day in the open sea. (2 Cor. 11:25, 26) Furthermore, this trip will be quite unlike the missionary journeys he has taken as a free man. Paul will be traveling as a prisoner and over a tremendous distance—some 2,000 miles from Caesarea to Rome. Can he survive such a voyage unscathed? Even if he can, is he sailing toward his own doom? Remember, he faces the judgment of the mightiest secular power in Satan's world at that time.

³ After all that you have read about Paul, do you think that he gave in to hopelessness and despair over the prospect before him? Hardly! He knew that hardships lay ahead, but he did not know what form his troubles would take. Why should he bury the joy of his ministry under a load of anxiety about things he could not control? (Matt. 6:27, 34) Paul knew that Jehovah's will for him was that he use every occasion to preach the good news of God's Kingdom, even to secular rulers. (Acts 9:15) Paul was determined to live up to his commission, come what may. Is that not our determination as well? So let us follow Paul on this historic voyage as we weigh the practical value of his example.

"The Winds Were Contrary" (Acts 27:1-7a)

⁴ Paul and some other prisoners were entrusted to the care of a Roman officer named Julius, who chose to board a merchant ship that had arrived at Caesarea. The ship had come from Adramyttium, a port

---

1, 2. What kind of voyage is Paul facing, and what might be some of his concerns?

3. What was Paul's determination, and what will we discuss in this chapter?

4. On what kind of vessel did Paul begin his voyage, and who were his companions?

on the west coast of Asia Minor, across from the city of Mitylene on the island of Lesbos. This ship would sail north and then westward, making stops to unload and take on cargo. Such vessels were not outfitted for passenger comfort, especially not for prisoners. (See the box "Sea Travel and Trade Routes.") Thankfully, Paul would not be the only Christian among a group of criminals. At least two fellow believers accompanied him—Aristarchus and Luke. It was Luke, of course, who penned the account. We do not know whether these two loyal companions paid for their passage or acted as servants to Paul.—Acts 27:1, 2.

⁵ After spending one day at sea and traveling about 70 miles north, the ship docked at Sidon, on the Syrian coast. Apparently Julius did not treat Paul as an ordinary criminal, possibly because Paul was a Roman citizen who had not been proved guilty. (Acts 22:27, 28; 26:31, 32) Julius let Paul go ashore to see fellow Christians. How the brothers and sisters must have enjoyed caring for the apostle after his long imprisonment! Can you think of occasions when you might be able to provide similar loving hospitality and be upbuilt in return?—Acts 27:3.

⁶ Putting out to sea from Sidon, the ship then continued up the coast and past Cilicia, near Paul's hometown, Tarsus. Luke does not mention other stops, although he includes the ominous detail that "the winds were contrary." (Acts 27:4, 5) Still, we can envision Paul seizing every opportunity to share the good news. Surely he witnessed to fellow prisoners and others on board, including the crew and the soldiers, as well as to people at any of the ports where the ship docked. Do we today likewise make good use of the opportunities to preach that are open to us?

---

5. What fellowship was Paul able to enjoy at Sidon, and what may we learn from this?

6-8. How did Paul's journey progress from Sidon to Cnidus, and what opportunities did Paul likely seize with regard to preaching?

SEA TRAVEL AND TRADE ROUTES

In the ancient world, ships were principally used to transport cargo, not to accommodate passengers. Travelers who wanted to make a voyage had to look for a merchant vessel that was about to sail in the desired direction, haggle over the price of passage, and then wait until the ship sailed.

Thousands of vessels crisscrossed the Mediterranean to transport foodstuffs and other merchandise. Many who secured passage on such ships would have to sleep on deck, perhaps under a tentlike shelter that they themselves erected at night and dismantled each morning. They would also have to take with them all that they needed for the journey, including food and bedding.

The duration of voyages depended entirely on the winds. Because of inclement weather during the winter, navigation was generally considered closed from mid-November to mid-March.

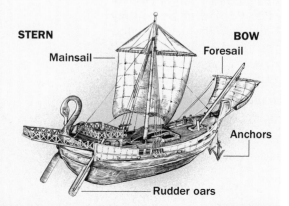

STERN

Mainsail

BOW

Foresail

Anchors

Rudder oars

⁷ In time, the ship reached Myra, a port on the southern coast of Asia Minor. There Paul and others had to change to another vessel, which would take them to Rome, their final destination. (Acts 27:6) In those days, Egypt was a granary for Rome, and Egyptian grain ships docked at Myra. Julius located such a ship and had the soldiers and prisoners board. This vessel must have been much larger than the first ship. It carried a valuable cargo of wheat as well as 276 people—the crew, the soldiers, the prisoners, and likely others heading to Rome. Clearly, with this change of ships, Paul's witnessing territory expanded, and he undoubtedly took advantage of that situation.

⁸ The next stop was Cnidus, on the southwest corner of Asia Minor. With favorable winds, a ship could cover that distance in about a day. Yet, Luke reports that they were "sailing on slowly quite a number of days and coming to Cnidus with difficulty." (Acts 27:7a) Sailing conditions had deteriorated. (See the box "The Contrary Winds of the Mediterranean," on page 208.) Think of the people on board as the ship bucked the strong winds and rough waters.

"Violently Tossed With the Tempest" (Acts 27:7b-26)

⁹ The ship's captain planned to continue westward from Cnidus, but eyewitness Luke says that "the wind did not let us." (Acts 27:7b) As the ship moved away from the mainland, it lost the shore current, and then a powerful adverse wind from the northwest pushed it southward, perhaps at great speed. Just as the island of Cyprus had earlier sheltered the coastal vessel from contrary winds, this time, the island of Crete did so. Once the ship passed the promontory of Salmone at the east end of Crete, things improved a bit. Why? The ship came to be on the lee, or southern, side of the island, so there was some protection from the powerful winds. Imagine the relief that those on board must have felt—at first! But as long as the ship was at sea, the crew could not ignore the approach of winter. They had cause for concern.

¹⁰ Luke states with precision: "Coasting along [Crete] *with difficulty* we came to a certain place called Fair Havens." Even in the shelter of the landmass, it was hard to control the ship. At last, though, they found an anchorage in a small bay that is thought to lie in the region just before the coast turns northward. How long did they remain there? Luke says a "considerable time," but time was not in their favor. In September/October, navigation was more hazardous.—Acts 27:8, 9.

¹¹ Some passengers may have sought Paul's advice because of his experience in traveling the Mediterranean. He recommended that the

---

9, 10. What difficulties arose in the vicinity of Crete?
11. Paul gave his shipmates what advice, yet what decision was made?

"He . . . gave thanks to God before them all."
—Acts 27:35

ship not sail on. If it did, there would be "damage and great loss," maybe even loss of life. However, the pilot and the shipowner wanted to keep going, possibly feeling it urgent to find a safer location. They convinced Julius, and the majority felt that they should try to reach Phoenix, a port farther along the coast. It may have had a larger and better harbor in which to spend the winter. So when a deceptively soft breeze from the south blew, the ship departed.—Acts 27:10-13.

[12] Then came more trouble: a "tempestuous wind" from the northeast. For a time, they found shelter behind a "small island called Cauda" some 40 miles from Fair Havens. Still, the ship was in danger of being driven southward until it would crash on the sandbanks off the coast of Africa. Frantic to avoid that end, the sailors pulled in the small boat that the ship was towing. They struggled to perform the task, for the skiff was likely full of water. Then they labored to undergird the large ship, passing ropes or chains under it to hold its planks together. And they lowered its gear, the mainsail or rigging, and strained to keep the ship headed into the wind to weather the storm. Imagine how terrifying this experience must have been! Even these measures were not enough, as the ship continued to be "violently tossed with the tempest." On the third day, they heaved the tackling overboard, probably to recover buoyancy.—Acts 27:14-19.

[13] Terror must have reigned. But Paul and his companions were of good courage. The Lord had previously assured Paul that the apostle would bear witness in Rome, and an angel later confirmed this promise. (Acts 19:21; 23:11) Nevertheless, night and day for two weeks, the driving storm kept on. Because of unrelenting rain and a thick cloud cover that blocked out the sun and stars, the pilot could not make sightings to determine the ship's location or heading. Even a normal meal would have been out of the question. How could anyone think of eating, given the cold, rain, seasickness, and fear?

[14] Paul stood up. He mentioned his earlier warning but not as if to say, 'I told you so.' Rather, the unfolding of events was proof that his words were well worth heeding. Then he said: "Now I recommend to you to be of good cheer, for not a soul of you will be lost, only the boat will." (Acts 27:21, 22) How those words must have warmed the hearts of his listeners! Paul would have been intensely pleased, too, that Jehovah had given him such a hopeful message to share. It is vital that we remember that Jehovah cares about every human life. Each person mat-

---

12. After leaving Crete, the ship faced what dangers, and how did the crew attempt to stave off disaster?

13. What must life have been like aboard Paul's ship during the storm?

14, 15. (a) In speaking to his shipmates, why did Paul mention his earlier warning? (b) What may we learn from the hopeful message that Paul delivered?

ters to him. The apostle Peter wrote: "Jehovah . . . does not desire any to be destroyed but desires all to attain to repentance." (2 Pet. 3:9) How urgent it is, then, that we endeavor to share Jehovah's message of hope with as many people as possible! Precious lives are at stake.

¹⁵ Likely Paul had been witnessing to many on the ship about "the hope of the promise that was made by God." (Acts 26:6; Col. 1:5) Now, with shipwreck probable, Paul could offer a powerful basis for a more immediate hope. He said: "This night there stood near me an angel . . . , saying, 'Have no fear, Paul. You must stand before Caesar, and, look! God has freely given you all those sailing with you.'" Paul urged them: "Therefore be of good cheer, men; for I believe God that it will be exactly as it has been told me. However, we must be cast ashore on a certain island."—Acts 27:23-26.

"All Were Brought Safely to Land" (Acts 27:27-44)

¹⁶ After two frightful weeks, during which the ship was driven some 540 miles, the sailors sensed a change, maybe hearing breakers. They

---

16, 17. (a) Paul took what occasion to pray, and with what effect? (b) How did Paul's warning come to be fulfilled?

THE CONTRARY WINDS OF THE MEDITERRANEAN

The wind and the season greatly affected where and when ancient merchant ships sailed the Mediterranean, or the Great Sea. On the sea's eastern end, the wind usually blew from west to east during midyear. This made sailing eastward easier, as Paul experienced while returning from his third missionary tour. He and his companions were on a ship that left Miletus, passed Rhodes, and docked at Patara. It was almost a straight run from there to Tyre, on the coast of Phoenicia. Luke writes that they passed Cyprus on their left, meaning that they sailed to the south of Cyprus.—Acts 21:1-3.

What about sailing in the opposite direction, going westward? Ships might move westward along a similar route if the wind permitted. But sometimes that was virtually impossible. "In winter," states *The International Standard Bible Encyclopedia,* "the atmosphere is much less stable and powerful cyclones move eastward across the Mediterranean bringing with them strong winds, sometimes of gale force, and often torrential rain or even snow." Under such conditions, the hazards were great.

In almost any season, vessels close to shore could move northward up the coast of Palestine and continue westward by Pamphylia. On the latter stretch, breezes from the mainland and west-flowing currents could help ships. That was the case with the vessel on which prisoner Paul made the first leg of his trip to Rome. Yet, the winds could turn "contrary." (Acts 27:4) The grain ship that figured prominently in Luke's account may have sailed north from Egypt and then around into the protected waters between Cyprus and Asia Minor. From Myra, the captain intended to keep going westward—around the tip of Greece and up the west coast of Italy. (Acts 27:5, 6) However, the wind and the season held something else in store for that voyage!

let out anchors from the stern to prevent drift and to direct the bow toward land in case they could beach the ship. At that point, they attempted to leave the ship but were prevented from doing so by the soldiers. Paul told the army officer and the soldiers: "Unless these men remain in the boat, you cannot be saved." With the ship now a bit steadier, Paul urged all to take a meal, assuring them again that they would survive. Paul then "gave thanks to God before them all." (Acts 27:31, 35) In offering this appreciative prayer, he set an example for Luke, Aristarchus, and Christians today. Are your public prayers a source of encouragement and comfort to others?

[17] Following Paul's prayer, "they all became cheerful and themselves began taking some food." (Acts 27:36) They further lightened the ship by jettisoning the cargo of wheat, thus giving the ship a shallower draft for its approach to the shore. When day arrived, the crew cut away the anchors, unlashed the rudder oars at the stern, and hoisted a small foresail so that they would have some maneuverability as they ran the ship aground. Then the front of the ship got stuck, perhaps on a sandbar or in mud, and the stern started to break apart under the crashing waves. Some soldiers wanted to kill the prisoners so that none would escape, but Julius intervened to prevent this. He urged all to swim or float to shore. What Paul had foretold came true—all 276 survived. Yes, "all were brought safely to land." But where were they?—Acts 27:44.

MALTA—WHERE?

Various islands have at times been suggested as the "Malta" where Paul was shipwrecked. One theory singled out an island near Corfu, off the western coast of Greece. Another suggestion is based on the word for "Malta" used in Acts. That Greek word is Me·li′te. Therefore, some have pointed to Melite Illyrica, now known as Mljet, located off the coast of Croatia, in the Adriatic Sea.

Granted, Acts 27:27 does mention "the sea of Adria," but in Paul's day "Adria" applied to an area larger than the present Adriatic Sea. It included the Ionian Sea and waters east of Sicily and west of Crete, thus encompassing the sea near modern-day Malta.

The ship on which Paul traveled was forced southward from Cnidus to below Crete. In view of the prevailing winds in that storm, it is hardly likely that the ship then turned and sailed as far northward as Mljet or an island near Corfu. So a more likely location for Malta would be farther to the west. That makes the island of Malta, south of Sicily, the probable location where the shipwreck occurred.

"Extraordinary Human Kindness" (Acts 28:1-10)

[18] It turned out that the survivors were on the island of Malta, south of Sicily. (See the box "Malta—Where?") The foreign-speaking people of the island showed them "extraordinary human kindness." (Acts 28:2) They made a fire for these strangers who had reached their shore

---

18-20. How did the people of Malta show "extraordinary human kindness," and what miracle did God perform through Paul?

drenched and shivering. The fire helped them to get warm despite the cold and rain. It also gave rise to a miracle.

¹⁹ Paul lent a hand for the general good. He collected some sticks, which he put on the fire. As he did so, a poisonous viper emerged and bit him, fastening onto his hand. The Maltese people thought this was some sort of divine punishment.*

²⁰ The local people who saw that Paul had been bitten thought that he would "swell up with inflammation." The original-language word found here is "a medical term," according to one reference work. It is not surprising that such an expression might readily come to the mind of "Luke the beloved physician." (Acts 28:6; Col. 4:14) At any rate, Paul shook off the venomous serpent and was unharmed.

²¹ The wealthy landowner Publius lived in the area. He may have been the leading Roman officer on Malta. Luke described him as "the *principal man* of the island," employing the exact title that has been found on two Maltese inscriptions. He hospitably entertained Paul and his companions for three days. However, Publius' father was ill. Again Luke described a condition with accuracy. He wrote that the man "was lying down distressed with fever and dysentery," citing the precise medical nature of the illness. Paul prayed and laid his hands on the man, and he was healed. Deeply impressed by this miracle, the local people brought other sick ones to be healed, and they brought gifts to fill the needs of Paul and his companions.—Acts 28:7-10.

²² The portion of Paul's voyage that we have considered so far resounds with accuracy and truth. One professor said: "Luke's account . . . stands out as one of the most vivid pieces of descriptive writing in the whole Bible. Its details regarding first-century seamanship are so precise and its portrayal of conditions on the eastern Mediterranean so accurate" that it must have been based on a written journal. Luke may well have made such notes as he traveled with the apostle. If so, the next leg of the trip gave him plenty to write about as well. What would happen to Paul when they finally arrived in Rome? Let us see.

---

* That the people knew of such snakes indicates that vipers existed on the island back then. In modern times, vipers are not found on Malta. That difference might well be the result of changes in the habitat over the centuries. Or the increase in human population on the island may have eradicated vipers.

---

21. (a) What are some examples of exactness, or accuracy, that we find in this portion of Luke's account? (b) What miracles did Paul perform, and with what effect on the Maltese people?

22. (a) How has one professor praised Luke's account of the voyage to Rome? (b) What will we consider in the next chapter?

CHAPTER 27

"Bearing Thorough Witness"

Imprisoned in Rome, Paul continues to preach

Based on Acts 28:11-31

A VESSEL bearing the figurehead "Sons of Zeus," likely a large grain carrier, is sailing from the Mediterranean island of Malta to Italy. The year is about 59 C.E. On board are the apostle Paul—a prisoner under escort—and fellow Christians Luke and Aristarchus. (Acts 27:2) Unlike the ship's crew, these evangelizers seek no protection from the sons of the Greek god Zeus—the twin brothers Castor and Pollux. (Acts 28: 11, ftn.) Rather, Paul and his companions serve Jehovah, who made known that Paul would bear witness to the truth in Rome and stand before Caesar.—Acts 23:11; 27:24.

² Three days after docking at Syracuse, a beautiful Sicilian city rivaling Athens and Rome, the ship sails to Rhegium on the toe of the Italian peninsula. Then, aided by a south wind, the vessel makes the 175-nautical-mile trip to the Italian port of Puteoli (near modern-day Naples) in optimum time, arriving on the second day.—Acts 28:12, 13.

³ Paul is now on the final leg of his trip to Rome, where he will appear before Emperor Nero. From start to finish, "the God of all comfort" has been with Paul. (2 Cor. 1:3) As we shall see, that support does not diminish; nor does Paul lose his zeal as a missionary.

"Paul Thanked God and Took Courage" (Acts 28:14, 15)

⁴ At Puteoli, Paul and his companions "found brothers and were entreated to remain with them seven days." (Acts 28:14) What a wonderful example of Christian hospitality! No doubt those hospitable brothers were repaid many times over by the spiritual encouragement they received from Paul and his companions. Why, though, would a prisoner under watch be granted so much liberty? Possibly because the apostle had won the full trust of his Roman guards.

---

1. What confidence do Paul and his companions have, and why?

2, 3. What route does Paul's ship take, and what support has Paul enjoyed from the start?

4, 5. (a) What hospitality did Paul and his companions receive at Puteoli, and why may he have been granted so much liberty? (b) Even when in prison, how may Christians benefit from their good conduct?

⁵ Likewise today, Jehovah's servants, while in prisons and concentration camps, have often been granted special freedoms and privileges because of their Christian conduct. In Romania, for example, a man serving 75 years for robbery began to study God's Word and underwent a remarkable change in personality. In response, the prison authorities assigned him to go into town—unescorted—to purchase items for the prison! Above all, of course, our good conduct glorifies Jehovah.—1 Pet. 2:12.

⁶ From Puteoli, Paul and his companions likely walked some 30 miles to Capua on the Appian Way, which led to Rome. Paved with large, flat blocks of lava, this famous road offered splendid views of the Italian countryside and, at certain points along its course, of the Mediterranean Sea. The road also took travelers through the Pontine Marshes, a swampy area some 40 miles from Rome and the location of the Marketplace of Appius. When the brothers in Rome "heard the news about us," wrote Luke, some came as far as the Marketplace, while others waited at Three Taverns, a rest stop about 30 miles from Rome. What extraordinary love!—Acts 28:15.

⁷ The Marketplace of Appius provided little comfort for the traveler needing a respite from the rigors of his journey. Roman poet and satirist Horace describes the Marketplace as "crowded with sailors and surly inn-keepers." He wrote that "the water was most execrable," or foul. And he even refused to dine there! Despite all the discomforts, however, the delegation from Rome happily waited for Paul and his companions in order to escort them safely along the final leg of their journey.

6, 7. How did the Roman brothers show extraordinary love?

THE FIVE LETTERS OF PAUL'S FIRST ROMAN CAPTIVITY

Five of the apostle Paul's letters were written about 60-61 C.E., during his first captivity in Rome. In the letter to *Philemon,* a fellow believer, Paul explains that Philemon's runaway slave Onesimus had become a Christian. Paul was Onesimus' spiritual father and was sending the "formerly useless" slave back to his owner as a Christian brother.—Philem. 10-12, 16.

In his letter to the *Colossians,* Paul indicates that Onesimus was "from among" them. (Col. 4:9) Onesimus and fellow Christian Tychicus had the privilege of delivering both of the aforementioned letters as well as the one that Paul wrote to the *Ephesians.* —Eph. 6:21.

When writing to the *Philippians,* Paul mentions his "prison bonds" and again speaks of the situation of the letter carrier—this time, Epaphroditus. The Philippians had sent Epaphroditus to assist Paul. But Epaphroditus had become ill almost to the point of death. He had also become depressed because the Philippians "heard he had fallen sick." Hence, Paul told them to treasure "men of that sort."—Phil. 1:7; 2:25-30.

The letter to the *Hebrews* was addressed to the Hebrew Christians in Judea. Although the letter does not specifically identify the writer, evidence suggests that it was Paul. The writing is in his style. Paul sends greetings from Italy, and he mentions Timothy, who was with him in Rome.—Phil. 1:1; Col. 1:1; Philem. 1; Heb. 13:23, 24.

8 "Upon catching sight of" his brothers, the account says, "Paul thanked God and took courage." (Acts 28:15) Yes, at the mere sight of these dear ones, some of whom the apostle may have known personally, he felt strengthened and comforted. Why did Paul thank God? He knew that unselfish love is an aspect of the spirit's fruitage. (Gal. 5:22) Today, too, holy spirit moves Christians to put themselves out for one another and to comfort those in need.—1 Thess. 5:11, 14.

9 For example, holy spirit impels responsive ones to extend hospitality to traveling overseers, visiting missionaries, and other full-time servants, many of whom have made great sacrifices in order to serve Jehovah more fully. Ask yourself: 'Can I do more to support the visit of the circuit overseer, perhaps showing hospitality to him and his wife if he is married? Can I arrange to work along with them in the ministry?' In return, you may receive a rich blessing. For example, imagine the joy the Roman brothers felt as they listened to Paul and his companions relate some of their many upbuilding experiences.—Acts 15:3, 4.

"Everywhere It Is Spoken Against" (Acts 28:16-22)

10 When the band of travelers finally entered into Rome, "Paul was permitted to stay by himself with the soldier guarding him." (Acts 28: 16) For those in light custody, security against escape usually called for a chain that bound the prisoner to his guard. Even so, Paul was a Kingdom proclaimer, and a chain certainly could not silence him. Hence, after giving himself just three days to recover from the journey, he called together the principal men of the Jews in Rome in order to introduce himself and give a witness.

11 "Men, brothers," said Paul, "although I had done nothing contrary to the people or the customs of our forefathers, I was delivered over as a prisoner from Jerusalem into the hands of the Romans. And these, after making an examination, were desirous of releasing me, as there was no cause for death in me. But when the Jews kept speaking against it, I was compelled to appeal to Caesar, but not as though I had anything of which to accuse my nation."—Acts 28:17-19.

12 By addressing his Jewish listeners as "brothers," Paul tried to establish common ground with them and break down any prejudice they may have had. (1 Cor. 9:20) Also, he made it clear that he was there, not

8. Why did Paul thank God "upon catching sight of" his brothers?
9. How can we reflect the spirit that was shown by the brothers who met Paul?
10. What were Paul's circumstances in Rome, and what did the apostle do soon after his arrival?
11, 12. When speaking to his fellow Jews, how did Paul attempt to break down any prejudice they may have had?

to point an accusing finger at his fellow Jews, but to appeal to Caesar. Paul's appeal, however, was news to the local Jewish community. (Acts 28:21) Why this apparent lapse in communication on the part of the Jews in Judea? One reference work states: "Paul's ship must have been among the first that arrived in Italy after the winter, and representatives of the Jewish authorities in Jerusalem could not have arrived, nor could a letter about the case."

[13] Paul now introduced the Kingdom theme by way of a statement that was sure to arouse the curiosity of his Jewish guests. He said: "Really on this account I entreated to see and speak to you, for because of the hope of Israel this chain I have around me." (Acts 28:20) That hope, of course, was bound up in the Messiah and his Kingdom, as proclaimed by the Christian congregation. "We think it proper to hear from you what your thoughts are," replied the Jewish elders, "for truly as regards this sect it is known to us that everywhere it is spoken against."—Acts 28:22.

[14] When we have the opportunity to share the good news, we can imitate Paul by using thought-provoking statements or questions to arouse the interest of our listeners. Excellent suggestions can be found in such publications as *Reasoning From the Scriptures* and *Benefit*

13, 14. How did Paul introduce the Kingdom theme, and how can we imitate his example?

PAUL'S LIFE AFTER 61 C.E.

Likely in about 61 C.E., Paul appeared before Emperor Nero, who apparently pronounced him innocent. We do not know much about the apostle's activities thereafter. If he made his planned trip to Spain, it would have been during this time. (Rom. 15:28) Paul traveled "to the extreme limit of the W[est]," wrote Clement of Rome in about 95 C.E.

From Paul's three letters dated to the period after his release—1 and 2 Timothy and Titus—we learn that Paul visited Crete, Macedonia, Nicopolis, and Troas. (1 Tim. 1:3; 2 Tim. 4:13; Titus 1: 5; 3:12) Perhaps it was in Nicopolis, Greece, that he was again arrested. Whatever the case, in approximately 65 C.E., he was back in prison in Rome. This time, however, Nero would show no

mercy. Indeed, when a fire devastated the city in 64 C.E., Nero—according to Roman historian Tacitus—had falsely blamed the Christians and initiated a brutal campaign of persecution.

In his second letter to Timothy, Paul, expecting imminent death, asked him and Mark to come quickly. Noteworthy is the courage of Luke and Onesiphorus, who risked their lives to comfort Paul. (2 Tim. 1:16, 17; 4:6-9, 11) Indeed, to profess Christianity publicly was to risk arrest and death by torture. Paul likely suffered martyrdom soon after writing his final letter to Timothy in about 65 C.E. Nero himself reportedly came to a violent end about three years after Paul's martyrdom.

From Theocratic Ministry School Education. Are you making good use of these Bible study aids?

"Bearing Thorough Witness"—A Model for Us (Acts 28:23-29)

¹⁵ On the chosen day, the local Jews "came in greater numbers" to Paul's lodging place. Paul explained matters to them "by bearing thorough witness concerning the kingdom of God and by using persuasion with them concerning Jesus from both the law of Moses and the Prophets, from morning till evening." (Acts 28:23) Four things stand out in regard to Paul's witness. First, he focused on God's Kingdom. Second, he tried to appeal to his listeners "by using persuasion." Third, he reasoned from the Scriptures. Fourth, he showed a selfless attitude, witnessing "from morning till evening." What a fine example for us! The result? "Some began to believe," while others would not. Dissension ensued, and the people "began to depart," reports Luke.—Acts 28:24, 25a.

¹⁶ This response was no surprise to Paul, for it harmonized with Bible prophecy and followed a pattern with which he was familiar. (Acts 13:42-47; 18:5, 6; 19:8, 9) Hence, to his unreceptive departing guests, Paul said: "The holy spirit aptly spoke through Isaiah the prophet to your forefathers, saying, 'Go to this people and say: "By hearing, you will hear but by no means understand; and, looking, you will look but by no means see. For the heart of this people has grown unreceptive."'" (Acts 28:25b-27) The original-language term rendered "unreceptive" indicates a heart that was "thickened," or "fattened," thus preventing the Kingdom message from penetrating it. (Acts 28:27, ftn.) What a tragic situation!

¹⁷ Unlike his Jewish listeners, "the nations . . . will certainly listen," said Paul in closing. (Acts 28:28; Ps. 67:2; Isa. 11:10) Indeed, the apostle could speak with authority on that subject, for he had personally seen many Gentiles respond to the Kingdom message!—Acts 13:48; 14:27.

¹⁸ Like Paul, let us not take it personally when people reject the good news. After all, we know that comparatively few will find the road to life. (Matt. 7:13, 14) Moreover, when rightly disposed ones do take a stand for true worship, let us rejoice and welcome them with an open heart. —Luke 15:7.

"Preaching the Kingdom of God" (Acts 28:30, 31)

¹⁹ Luke concludes his narrative on a truly positive and warm note, saying: "[Paul] remained for an entire two years in his own hired house,

---

15. What four things stand out concerning Paul's witness?

16-18. Why was the negative response of the Roman Jews no surprise to Paul, and how should we feel when our message is rejected?

19. How did Paul make the most of his circumstances?

and he would kindly receive all those who came in to him, preaching the kingdom of God to them and teaching the things concerning the Lord Jesus Christ with the greatest freeness of speech, without hindrance." (Acts 28:30, 31) What an outstanding example of hospitality, faith, and zeal!

20 One of those whom Paul kindly received was a man named Onesimus, a runaway slave from Colossae. Paul helped Onesimus to become a Christian, and Onesimus, in turn, became a "faithful and beloved brother" to Paul. In fact, Paul described him as "my child, to whom I became a father." (Col. 4:9; Philem. 10-12) How Onesimus must have lifted Paul's spirits!*

21 Others too benefited from Paul's fine example. To the Philippians, he wrote: "My affairs have turned out for the advancement of the good news rather than otherwise, so that my bonds have become public knowledge in association with Christ among all the Praetorian Guard and all the rest; and most of the brothers in the Lord, feeling confidence by reason of my prison bonds, are showing all the more courage to speak the word of God fearlessly."—Phil. 1:12-14.

22 Paul took advantage of his confinement in Rome to write important letters that are now part of the Christian Greek Scriptures.# Interestingly, in his letter to the Ephesians, Paul used Roman armor to illustrate a Christian's spiritual armor. (Eph. 6:11-17) Perhaps the idea came to him while he was looking at his soldier guard. (Acts 28:16) What is the lesson for us? If we are observant, we can often find good illustrations in our surroundings.

23 By the time of his release, which is not mentioned in Acts, Paul had been in custody for some four years—two in Caesarea and two in Rome.△ (Acts 23:35; 24:27) But he maintained a positive outlook, doing all that he could in God's service. Likewise, many of Jehovah's servants today, though unjustly imprisoned because of their faith, have re-

---

* Paul wanted to keep Onesimus there with him, but this would have violated Roman law and infringed on the rights of Onesimus' master, the Christian Philemon. Hence, Onesimus returned to Philemon, taking along a letter from Paul that encouraged Philemon to receive his slave kindly, as a spiritual brother.—Philem. 13-19.

See the box "The Five Letters of Paul's First Roman Captivity," on page 212.

△ See the box "Paul's Life After 61 C.E.," on page 214.

20, 21. Mention some examples of those who benefited from Paul's ministry in Rome.

22. How did Paul take advantage of his confinement in Rome?

23, 24. Like Paul, how have many modern-day Christians demonstrated a positive attitude despite being unjustly confined?

tained their joy and kept preaching. Consider the example of Adolfo, who was imprisoned in Spain because of his Christian neutrality. "We are amazed at you," said one officer. "We have been making life impossible for you, and the worse we made it, the more you smiled and had a kind word."

²⁴ In time, Adolfo was trusted to the point that his cell door was left open. Soldiers would visit to ask about the Bible. One of the guards would even go into Adolfo's cell to read the Bible, while Adolfo would keep a lookout. So the prisoner "guarded" the sentry! May the fine example of such faithful Witnesses move us to show "all the more courage to speak the word of God fearlessly," even under difficult circumstances.

²⁵ An apostle of Christ under house arrest "preaching the kingdom of God" to all who visited him—what a heartwarming conclusion to the dynamic book of Acts! In the first chapter, we read the commission that Jesus gave his followers when he said: "You will receive power when the holy spirit arrives upon you, and you will be witnesses of me both in Jerusalem and in all Judea and Samaria and to the most distant part of the earth." (Acts 1:8) Now, less than 30 years later, the Kingdom message had been "preached in all creation that is under heaven."* (Col. 1:23) What a testimony to the power of God's spirit!—Zech. 4:6.

²⁶ Today, that same spirit has empowered the remaining ones of Christ's brothers, along with their companions of the "other sheep," to continue "bearing thorough witness concerning the kingdom of God" in more than 230 lands! (John 10:16; Acts 28:23) Are you having a full share in that work?

---

* See the box "The Good News 'Preached in All Creation.'"

25, 26. In a little less than 30 years, what amazing prophecy had Paul seen fulfilled, and how does this compare with our time?

THE GOOD NEWS "PREACHED IN ALL CREATION"

In about 61 C.E., while the apostle Paul was a prisoner in Rome, he wrote that the "good news" had been "preached in all creation that is under heaven." (Col. 1:23) How should we understand that statement?

It appears that Paul was describing in broad terms how far the "good news" had reached. For example, Alexander the Great had penetrated Asia to the borders of India in the fourth century B.C.E. Julius Caesar had invaded Britain in 55 B.C.E., and Claudius had subjugated the southern part of that island, making it part of the Roman Empire in 43 C.E. The Far East was also known, for it was a source of fine silk.

Had the good news been preached in Britain, China, and the Far East? That seems unlikely. Indeed, when Paul wrote to the Colossians, he still had not realized his own goal, stated in about 56 C.E., of preaching in the then "untouched territory" of Spain. (Rom. 15:20, 23, 24) Still, by about 61 C.E., the Kingdom message was widely known. At the very least, it had spread as far as to the homelands of the Jews and proselytes who were baptized at Pentecost 33 C.E. as well as to the lands visited by Jesus' apostles.—Acts 2:1, 8-11, 41, 42.

CHAPTER 28

"To the Most Distant Part of the Earth"

Jehovah's Witnesses continue a work that had its start with the followers of Jesus Christ in the first century of our Common Era

THEY zealously bore witness. Their hearts impelled them to accept the help and guidance of the holy spirit. Persecution did not still their lips. And the rich blessing of God was upon them. All of this was true of the early Christians, just as it is true of Jehovah's Witnesses today.

[2] Surely you have been encouraged by the faith-strengthening accounts found in the action-packed Bible book Acts of Apostles! It is unique, for it is the only divinely inspired history of early Christianity.

[3] The book of Acts names 95 individuals from 32 lands, 54 cities, and 9 islands. It is a thrilling story about people—common folk, haughty religionists, vain politicians, rabid persecutors. But most of all, it is about your first-century brothers and sisters, who not only met the usual challenges of life but also preached the good news with zeal.

[4] Almost 2,000 years now separate us from the activities of the zealous apostles Peter and Paul, the beloved physician Luke, generous Barnabas, courageous Stephen, kindhearted Dorcas, hospitable Lydia, and so many other faithful witnesses. Yet, we enjoy a special bond with them. Why? Because we have the same disciple-making commission. (Matt. 28:19, 20) How blessed we are to share in it!

[5] Reflect on the commission Jesus gave his followers. "You will receive power when the holy spirit arrives upon you," he said, "and you will be witnesses of me both in Jerusalem and in all Judea and Samaria and to the most distant part of the earth." (Acts 1:8) First, the holy spirit empowered the disciples to be witnesses *"in Jerusalem."* (Acts 1:1–8:3) Next, under the spirit's direction, they witnessed *"in all Judea and Samaria."*

---

1. What parallels are there between the early Christians and Jehovah's Witnesses today?

2, 3. What is especially noteworthy about the book of Acts?

4. Why do we enjoy a special bond with such individuals as the apostle Paul, Dorcas, and other faithful witnesses of old?

5. Where did Jesus' early followers begin to carry out their commission?

(Acts 8:4–13:3) Then they began to take the good news *"to the most distant part of the earth."*—Acts 13:4–28:31.

[6] Your fellow believers of the first century did not have the entire Bible for use in their work of bearing witness. Matthew's Gospel was not available until at least 41 C.E. Some of Paul's letters were written before Acts was completed, in about 61 C.E. But the early Christians had neither personal copies of the complete Holy Scriptures nor a variety of publications to leave with interested people. Before becoming Jesus' disciples, Jewish Christians had heard the Hebrew Scriptures read in the synagogue. (2 Cor. 3:14-16) But even they needed to be diligent students, since they probably had to quote texts from memory.

[7] Today, most of us have a personal copy of the Bible and an abundance of Bible literature. We are making disciples by declaring the good news in more than 230 lands and in many languages.

Empowered by Holy Spirit

[8] When Jesus commissioned his disciples to be witnesses, he told them: "You will receive power when the holy spirit arrives upon you." Under the direction of God's spirit, or active force, Jesus' followers would ultimately serve as witnesses in all the earth. By holy spirit, Peter and Paul effected cures, expelled demons, even raised the dead! However, the power received through holy spirit had a more important purpose. It enabled the apostles and other disciples to impart accurate knowledge that means everlasting life.—John 17:3.

[9] On the day of Pentecost 33 C.E., Jesus' disciples spoke "with different tongues, just as the *spirit* was granting them to make utterance." They thus bore witness regarding "the magnificent things of God." (Acts 2:1-4, 11) We do not miraculously speak in tongues today. With the help of God's spirit, however, the faithful slave class is producing Bible literature in many languages. For example, millions of copies of *The Watchtower* and *Awake!* are printed every month. All of this enables us to declare "the magnificent things of God" to people of all nations, tribes, and tongues.—Rev. 7:9.

[10] Since 1989 the slave class has placed emphasis on making the *New World Translation of the Holy Scriptures* available in many languages. This Bible has already been translated into scores of tongues, and tens of millions of copies have been printed—with many more to come. Only God and his spirit could have made these efforts successful.

6, 7. In performing our ministry, what advantage do we have over our first-century fellow believers?

8, 9. (a) The holy spirit enabled Jesus' disciples to do what? (b) What is the faithful slave class producing with the help of God's spirit?

10. Since 1989, what has been done with regard to Bible translation?

¹¹ Publications of Jehovah's Witnesses have been translated into more than 470 languages. Translation work is being done by hundreds of Christian volunteers in over 130 countries. This should not surprise us, for no other organization on earth is led by holy spirit in "bearing thorough witness" worldwide regarding Jehovah God, his Messianic King, and the established heavenly Kingdom!—Acts 28:23.

¹² When Paul bore witness to Jews and Gentiles at Antioch in Pisidia, "those who were rightly disposed for everlasting life became believers." (Acts 13:48) As Luke concludes the book of Acts, Paul is "preaching the kingdom of God . . . with the greatest freeness of speech, without hindrance." (Acts 28:31) Where is the apostle witnessing? Why, in Rome —the capital of a world power! Whether through discourses or by other means, Jesus' early followers did all their witnessing work with the help and guidance of holy spirit.

Persevering Despite Persecution

¹³ When Jesus' early disciples experienced persecution, they petitioned Jehovah for boldness. The result? They were filled with holy spirit and empowered to speak God's word with boldness. (Acts 4:18-31) We too pray for wisdom and strength to keep on witnessing despite persecution. (Jas. 1:2-8) Because we are blessed by God and helped by his spirit, we press on in Kingdom service. Nothing stops the work of bearing witness—neither intense opposition nor brutal persecution. When we are being persecuted, we certainly need to pray for holy spirit and for wisdom and courage to declare the good news.—Luke 11:13.

¹⁴ Stephen gave a bold witness before he met his death at enemy hands. (Acts 6:5; 7:54-60) In the "great persecution" that arose at that time, all the disciples except the apostles were scattered throughout Judea and Samaria. But that did not stop the work of bearing witness. Philip went to Samaria "to preach the Christ" and did so with excellent results. (Acts 8:1-8, 14, 15, 25) Moreover, we are told: "Those who had been scattered by the tribulation that arose over Stephen went through as far as Phoenicia and Cyprus and Antioch, but speaking the word to no one except to Jews only. However, out of them there were some men of Cyprus and Cyrene that came to Antioch and began talking to the Greek-speaking people, declaring the good news of the Lord Jesus." (Acts 11:19, 20) At that time, persecution spread the Kingdom message.

11. What has been done with respect to the translation of Witness publications?

12. How were Paul and other Christians able to do the work of bearing witness?

13. Why should we pray when we experience persecution?

14, 15. (a) What happened as a result of "the tribulation that arose over Stephen"? (b) In our time, how did many people in Siberia come to learn the truth?

15 In our time, something similar occurred in the former Soviet Union. Especially in the 1950's, thousands of Jehovah's Witnesses were exiled to Siberia. Because they were scattered in various settlements, the good news was constantly spreading in that vast land. In no way could so many Witnesses have found the money needed to travel perhaps as much as 6,000 miles to proclaim the good news! However, the government itself sent them across the country. "As it turned out," said one brother, "the authorities themselves enabled thousands of sincere people in Siberia to come to know the truth."

Richly Blessed by Jehovah

16 Jehovah's blessing was unquestionably upon the early Christians. Paul and others planted and watered, "but God kept making it grow." (1 Cor. 3:5, 6) Reports in the book of Acts provide evidence of such growth because of Jehovah's blessing on the work of bearing witness. For instance, "the word of God went on growing, and the number of the disciples kept multiplying in Jerusalem very much." (Acts 6:7) As the witness work spread, "the congregation throughout the whole of Judea and Galilee and Samaria entered into a period of peace, being built up; and as it walked in the [reverential] fear of Jehovah and in the comfort of the holy spirit it kept on multiplying."—Acts 9:31.

17 In Syrian Antioch, both Jews and Greek-speaking people heard the truth from courageous witnesses. "Furthermore," says the account, "the hand of Jehovah was with them, and a great number that became believers turned to the Lord." (Acts 11:21) Regarding further progress in that city, we read: "The word of Jehovah went on growing and spreading." (Acts 12:24) And with the witnessing work of Paul and others in full swing among Gentiles, "in a mighty way the word of Jehovah kept growing and prevailing."—Acts 19:20.

18 "The hand of Jehovah" is unquestionably with us today too. That is why so many are becoming believers and are symbolizing their dedication to God by being baptized. Moreover, it is only with God's help and blessing that we are able to endure stiff opposition—at times, intense persecution—and successfully carry out our ministry, even as Paul and other early Christians did. (Acts 14:19-21) Jehovah God is always there for us. His "indefinitely lasting arms" unfailingly support us in all our trials. (Deut. 33:27) Let us also remember that for the sake of his great name, Jehovah never deserts his people.—1 Sam. 12:22; Ps. 94:14.

16, 17. The book of Acts gives us what evidence of Jehovah's blessing on the work of bearing witness?

18, 19. (a) Why do we know that "the hand of Jehovah" is with us? (b) Give an example showing that Jehovah supports his people.

"...to the most distant part of the earth."
—Acts 1:8

[19] To illustrate: Because Brother Harald Abt kept on bearing witness, the Nazis sent him to Sachsenhausen concentration camp during World War II. In May 1942 the Gestapo went to the home of his wife, Elsa, took away their little girl, and arrested Elsa. She was sent to various camps. "My years in German concentration camps taught me an outstanding lesson," said Sister Abt. "It is, how greatly Jehovah's spirit can strengthen you when you are under extreme trial! Before I was arrested, I had read a sister's letter that said that under severe trial Jehovah's spirit causes a calmness to come over you. I thought that she must have been exaggerating a bit. But when I went through trials myself, I knew that what she had said was true. It really happens that way. It's hard to imagine it, if you have not experienced it. Yet it really happened to me."

Keep On Bearing Thorough Witness!

[20] The book of Acts ends with Paul zealously "preaching the kingdom of God." (Acts 28:31) Because he was under house arrest, he was not free to witness from house to house in Rome. Nevertheless, he kept on witnessing to all who came to him. Today, some of our dear brothers and sisters are housebound, perhaps bedfast, or are living in nursing homes because of advanced age, illness, or infirmity. Yet, their love for God and their desire to bear witness are as strong as ever. We pray for them and can well ask that our heavenly Father bring them in touch with those yearning to learn about him and his wonderful purposes.

[21] Most of us can engage in the house-to-house ministry and other features of the disciple-making work. So let each of us do everything possible to fulfill our role as Kingdom proclaimers, sharing in bearing witness "to the most distant part of the earth." This work must be done with a sense of urgency, for "the sign" of Christ's presence is clearly in evidence. (Matt. 24:3-14) There is no time to lose. Right now, we have "plenty to do in the work of the Lord."—1 Cor. 15:58.

[22] As we await "the coming of the great and fear-inspiring day of Jehovah," let us be determined to continue giving a bold and faithful witness. (Joel 2:31) We will yet find many people like the Beroeans who "received the word with the greatest eagerness of mind." (Acts 17:10, 11) May we therefore bear witness until, in effect, we hear the words: "Well done, good and faithful slave!" (Matt. 25:23) If we zealously do our part in the disciple-making work today and are ever faithful to Jehovah, we will surely rejoice throughout eternity that we had a blessed share in "bearing thorough witness" about God's Kingdom!

---

20. What did Paul do while under house arrest, and of what encouragement can this be to some of our brothers and sisters?

21. Why should we bear witness with a sense of urgency?

22. What should we be determined to do as we await Jehovah's day?

IMAGE INDEX

 Covers Paul, Dorcas, Gallio, Luke, a temple officer with the apostles, a Sadducee, Paul being escorted to Caesarea, and modern-day witnessing with a sound car and a phonograph.

 1 Paul, in chains, and Luke aboard a cargo ship on its way to Rome.

 2, 3 Brothers J. E. Barr and T. Jaracz of the Governing Body at a world map.

 11 Jesus commissions the 11 faithful apostles and other followers on a mountain in Galilee.

 14 Jesus ascends into the sky. The apostles gaze after him.

 20 At Pentecost, the disciples begin speaking to visitors in their own languages.

 36 The apostles stand before a raging Caiaphas. The temple officers are at the disposal of the Sanhedrin to make arrests.

 44 Bottom: After World War II, an East German court wrongfully convicted Jehovah's Witnesses as American spies.—Periodical *Neue Berliner Illustrierte*, October 3, 1950.

 46 Stephen stands accused before the Sanhedrin. Wealthy Sadducees are in the background, and ultraorthodox Pharisees, in the foreground.

 54 Peter lays his hands on a new disciple; Simon is shown with a coin purse.

 75 Peter and his traveling companions enter Cornelius' home. Cornelius wears a special cloak draped over his left shoulder to mark his rank as a centurion.

 83 Peter is led by an angel; the Tower of Antonia is the possible location of Peter's imprisonment.

 84 Bottom: Mob violence near Montreal, Quebec, in 1945.—Periodical *Weekend Magazine*, July 1956.

 91 Paul and Barnabas are thrown out of Pisidian Antioch. The city's new aqueduct is shown in the background, likely built during the early first century C.E.

 94 Paul and Barnabas resist adulation in Lystra. Public sacrifices were usually colorful and noisy occasions with lots of music.

 100 Top: Silas and Judas encourage the congregation in Syrian Antioch. (Acts 15:30-32) Bottom: A circuit overseer speaks to a congregation in Uganda.

 107 The Jerusalem congregation meets in a private home.

 110 Front row, left to right: Gerrit Lösch, David Splane, John Barr, Theodore Jaracz; back row, left to right: Stephen Lett, Anthony Morris, Guy Pierce, Samuel Herd, Geoffrey Jackson.

 124 Paul and Timothy are portrayed traveling aboard a Roman merchant ship. A lighthouse can be seen in the distance.

 139 Paul and Silas are depicted in a gated courtyard, escaping an angry mob.

 155 Gallio chastises Paul's accusers. He wears clothing befitting his position: a white imperial toga with a broad purple stripe and *calcei*, a type of shoe.

 158 Demetrius addresses workers in a silversmith's shop in Ephesus. The silver shrines of Artemis are sold as souvenirs.

 171 Paul and his companions board a ship. The Great Harbor Monument, built in the first century B.C.E., is shown in the background.

 180 Bottom: During the 1940's literature ban in Canada, a young Witness smuggles Bible literature. (Reenactment.)

 182 Paul yields to the elders' request. Luke and Timothy are sitting in the background, assisting with the delivery of the contributions.

 190 Paul's nephew speaks to Claudius Lysias in the Tower of Antonia, possible location of Paul's custody. Herod's temple shown in the background.

 206 Paul prays for weary travelers in the hold of a cargo ship.

 222 The prisoner Paul, chained to a Roman soldier, viewing part of the city of Rome.

AUSTRALIA: PO Box 280, Ingleburn, NSW 1890. **BAHAMAS:** PO Box N-1247, Nassau, NP. **BRITAIN:** The Ridgeway, London NW7 1RN. **CANADA:** PO Box 4100, Georgetown, ON L7G 4Y4. **CURAÇAO, NETHERLANDS ANTILLES:** PO Box 4708, Willemstad. **GHANA:** PO Box GP 760, Accra. **GUYANA:** 352-360 Tyrell St, Republic Park Phase 2 EBD. **HAWAII:** 2055 Kamehameha IV Road, Honolulu, HI 96819-2619. **JAMAICA:** PO Box 103, Old Harbour, St. Catherine. **MEXICO:** Apartado Postal 896, 06002 Mexico, DF. **NETHERLANDS:** Noordbargerstraat 77, NL-7812 AA Emmen. **NIGERIA:** PMB 1090, Benin City 300001, Edo State. **PUERTO RICO:** PO Box 3980, Guaynabo, PR 00970. **SOUTH AFRICA:** Private Bag X2067, Krugersdorp, 1740. **TRINIDAD AND TOBAGO:** Lower Rapsey Street & Laxmi Lane, Curepe. **UNITED STATES OF AMERICA:** 25 Columbia Heights, Brooklyn, NY 11201-2483.